AN UNLIKELY COUNTESS

AN UNLIKELY COUNTESS

COUNTESS

*Lily Budge
and the 13th Earl of Galloway*

LOUISE CARPENTER

HarperCollins*Publishers*

HarperCollins*Publishers*
77–85 Fulham Palace Road
Hammersmith, London, w6 8jb

www.harpercollins.co.uk

Published by HarperCollins*Publishers* 2004
1 3 5 7 9 8 6 4 2

'Small Town' Words and Music by Lou Reed and John Cale
© 1989, Screen Gems–EMI Music Inc/Metal Machine
Music/John Cale Music Inc, USA
Reproduced by permission of Screen Gems–EMI Music Ltd,
London wc2h 0qy

The publisher and the author gratefully acknowledge
Randolph Galloway, the Estate of Lily Budge, The Stewart
Society, Joseph Bonnar, William Mowat Thomson, Michael
Thornton, and Roddy Martine for permission to reproduce
photographs and press clippings from private collections.

A catalogue record for this book
is available from the British Library

ISBN 0-00-710880-X

Set in PostScript Linotype New Baskerville with
Bauer Bodoni display by
Rowland Phototypesetting Ltd,
Bury St Edmunds, Suffolk

Printed and bound in Great Britain by
Clays Ltd, St Ives plc

For Tom
and
Randolph Galloway

CONTENTS

I am very fond of the good soldier Schweik . . . I am convinced that you will sympathise with this modest, unrecognised hero. He did not set fire to the temple of the Goddess at Ephesus, like that fool of a Herostratus, merely in order to get his name into the newspapers and the school reading books.

And that, in itself, is enough.

JAROSLAV HAŠEK, *The Good Soldier Schweik*

PART ONE

When you're growing up in a small town
You know you'll grow down in a small town
There is only one good use for a small town
You hate it and you'll know you have to leave.

Lou Reed, 'Small Town'

Lily and Randolph in the *Edinburgh Tatler* following their wedding reception
at the Caledonian Hotel, Edinburgh, in November 1975.

I

The Most Caring Place in the World

On 15 May 1979, on a draughty platform at Waverley Station, Edinburgh, Lord and Lady Galloway, fresh to their titles and in a muddle with their luggage, were preparing to board a train headed for London. 'If I can have this opportunity of going to the House of Lords, I shall take it,' Lily Galloway had told their French lodger, Marie-Laurence Maître, in their tenement flat as she packed.

Lily, dressed in a bottle-green velvet suit, which was a touch thin at the elbows and cuffs, but brushed up on the lapels, struggled as usual with their trunks while Randolph Galloway walked ahead, hands clasped stiffly behind his back. If anybody had cared to study their expressions, in him they would have observed a vagueness, as if he inhabited another world, one he did not much care for but from which he could not escape, and in her the opposite, the alertness of a proficient nurse in constant anticipation of a crisis. Randolph was easily unsettled by noise and commotion – as a child he would become quite hysterical if a train blew its steam – and he was prone to wandering off. Lily would have to maintain vigilance.

Their brief wedding announcement had been published in the court and social pages of the *Daily Telegraph* on 1 November 1975. Lord Garlies, then heir to the Earldom of Galloway, had married Mrs Lily Budge, youngest daughter of the late Mr and Mrs Andrew Miller, of Duns, Berwickshire. In February 1976, following their church blessing, a large photograph of them appeared over a page of the *Edinburgh Tatler* with a brief caption outlining how the reception had taken place at the Caledonian Hotel in Edinburgh. The picture alone revealed that Lily was some years older than her husband and would not by any stretch of the imagination be capable of providing an heir. And while blessed with a mop of thick black hair and two rows of straight, pearly white teeth, she could not be described as a beauty. To those in Scotland who followed the births, deaths, and marriages of the aristocracy, the announcement that the 12th Earl of Galloway's son and heir had married came as a shock. The reception had not taken place at the family seat of Cumloden, Newton Stewart, and the 12th Earl of Galloway and his daughter, Lady Antonia, did not attend the party.

Randolph Galloway, recognised by the Stewart Society as head of the Stewart clan, noted in *Burke's Peerage, Baronetage and Knightage* as the 13th Earl of Galloway, Lord Garlies, Baron Stewart of Garlies and a Baronet (Sir Randolph Keith Reginald Stewart, 12th Bart. of Corsewell, and 10th Bart. of Burray) was now about to take his seat in the upper house. He stood at over six feet and possessed a broad, athletic build. He had thick black wavy hair, parted and combed back from his high forehead, a strong square jaw and light, piercing blue eyes, sometimes hidden behind heavy black-rimmed spectacles. He was slim and handsome in the new three-piece suit, picked and paid for by Lily.

On arriving in London unscathed by drama, Lily and Randolph checked into a tatty bed and breakfast at 20 Great Peter Street, sw1. (Shortly afterwards, they would move to temporary accommodation in sw5 and thereafter use a series of cheap tourist hotels such as The Hansel and Gretel, £12.65 a night including VAT and breakfast.) The following day, 16 May, Randolph took his seat and Lily settled herself on the red leather pews of the Peeresses' gallery, front row, first in. She watched over him proudly as he sat mute on the Conservative benches in front of her. He did not deliver a maiden speech, which was for the best.

Outside the gates of Parliament, she posed for a photograph. 'The Lords is the most caring place in the world!' she later told a newspaper reporter. 'If I had my way we would live in London permanently.'

When Lily was not guiding Randolph about the wood-panelled corridors or sitting in the chamber, with her eyes attentively trained on him in the manner of a dog to its master, she could be found in one of three places: in the House of Lords' stationery cupboard, availing herself of as many complimentary cards and envelopes as would fit into her handbag; on the telephone to family in Scotland, a service which was also complimentary; or in the tearoom, knitting needles in hand, eating tea and toast with the Scottish peeresses who befriended her.

There was nothing in Lily's outward appearance to distinguish her from the other peers' wives except perhaps a little weariness. She was set apart principally because she had no interest in behaving as expected. Her occasional guests from Scotland saw that she liked to congratulate the other wives on their appearance – 'My, Lady so and so, what a dear little hat you are wearing today' – and every morning, on entering the House, she made a point of inquiring after everyone's health – 'Good morning Mr Skelton [then a junior doorkeeper], how are you? And how is your mother? Oh, will you send her my regards?'

Lily and Randolph considered themselves to have an important patron. The 17th Earl of Lauderdale, Patrick Maitland, a well-respected Scottish hereditary peer, former MP for Lanark, former reporter for *The Times,* and one of the last men in Britain to make use of a large ear trumpet, had come to know them through the ecumenical pilgrimages he organised to St Mary's Kirk, his private chapel in the parish of Haddington, not far from Edinburgh. They were, he had long ago concluded, a very curious couple, at times exasperating, but of the sort that he found himself drawn to helping, often against his better judgement. When Lily had asked for his help in completing the necessary paperwork to propel Randolph to the House of Lords, however, he had had few misgivings. He had lent a hand, confident, as was she, that the act of elevating Randolph to the role for which he had been born might be the making of their marriage. Now that they had succeeded, within days of their arrival Lord Lauderdale found to his dismay that his good deed had returned to torment him. Lily sought him out whenever she could, falling into step beside him as he puffed his way down the corridors, or crying out to him across the tearoom. Soon, Lord Lauderdale found himself darting behind pillars to avoid her, not easy for a man of his girth. On the rare occasions that he escaped Lily's notice, he would watch with bemused fascination as Lily and Randolph huddled together with furrowed brows, poring over the weekly whip, 'more out of excitement than understanding'.

Word quickly spread about Lily and Randolph's circumstances. While the Scottish peers and peeresses might return weekly to imposing seats scattered throughout the lowlands and highlands, they were not inclined towards the high life. But even by their standards of frugality, they saw that the new recruit was unusually strapped. Lady Saltoun, chief of the Fraser clan, a cross-bencher and another addition to the upper chamber that year, recognised Randolph's limitations immediately. She remembered him as a teenager, when he was Lord Garlies, and it made her shudder. As an eighteen-year-old girl, she had been forced by her parents to dance with him at a masonic ball in Glasgow. It had been an awkward experience and one she was keen to forget. But despite faint memories of whispered talk of the boy's disappearance from Scottish society, his sudden and unexpected reappearance in the House of Lords thirty years later met no interrogation or indiscretion.

During those early exhilarating days, Lily experienced a feeling of true belonging. It was a feeling of power and privilege by proxy. But it was to become apparent that Randolph could not fulfil his role. Some time before they left, Lily had an encounter that reminded her of how far she had come from *her* world, one to which she could not now return and to which she felt she had never spiritually belonged.

The reminder came in the stately if unlikely figure of Lord Home of the Hersel, who had succeeded Harold Macmillan as Prime Minister in 1963, but who had now returned to the upper chamber as a life peer. Lily did not hesitate when she saw him walking towards her in a corridor. She stopped him in his tracks. Speaking without pause in her thick Borders accent, as was her way, she reminded him of that time when they had met quite by chance more than forty years ago. The encounter had been at the Caledonian Hotel, Edinburgh, at the wedding reception of one Bunty Johnston, the daughter of R. J. Johnston, a lawyer and the County Clerk of Berwickshire. Lily would not normally have attended such a function but her older sister, Etta, was the Johnstons' servant girl and Lily had been invited too, as she helped Etta with the Johnstons' spring cleaning. 'Oh Etta, I must come, I must!' she had said. 'It's the only time I will ever have the chance of seeing the inside of the Caledonian Hotel.'

'How nice to see you again,' the former Prime Minister replied, either out of impeccable memory or, more likely, impeccable manners. 'It has been a very, very long time.'

2

The Beginnings

Soon after Lily May Miller entered the world on 28 October 1916, she began to understand that the single benefit of being born into small-town life was that it could eventually be left behind. Her mother, nicknamed Sis and known for being fierce and cross, had spent her life bringing up her siblings and then her children, weaving blankets at Cumledge Mill, hunched, scowling, over two looms at once. Her father, a local groom, had run away from a tenement in Glasgow, desperate for country air, and when not at home and being subjected to his wife's wrath, could usually be found in the stables, content among the horses.

The Borders town of Duns, which sits close to the Berwickshire coastline, was until 1975, the county town of Berwickshire, the administrative commercial and agricultural hub of neighbouring border towns such as Selkirk and Galashiels. As well as the cattle market every other week, set up for the buying and selling of farm equipment, once a year there were the Hirings in the Town Square, where employers traded farm hands and children skipped and played in the accompanying fair.

Duns had none of the excitements or department stores of Edinburgh and Glasgow, but it was well served. Everything of significance was conducted in or close to the town square, dominated by the town hall, where ladies in hats and gloves stopped to exchange gossip. Sometimes the news was of the latest young girl who had got herself pregnant out of wedlock, reliable information put about by two of the three Miss Smalls, large spinster sisters in brown fur coats who ran the baby linen shop and sold sanitary towels in brown paper parcels tied up with string. (It is a measure of how little there was to do that the Miss Smalls had the time and inclination to track the menstrual cycles of their customers.) The women in the town square, or those propped on brooms on their doorsteps, would nod and tut and predict the girl's demise. These women preferred their husbands to travel to outlying areas to buy their birth control, the thick, ghastly condoms that were washed after use and dried with a sprinkling of talcum powder. Sex: pity the person who muttered the mere word, let alone the woman who admitted enjoying it.

As Lily grew up, there was none of the gossip that had followed the birth of her sister, Agnes, two years before. Plump and blonde, Agnes, affectionately called Etta, was as physically different from her father as a child could possibly be. Lily, by contrast, had been declared Andrew Miller's from the start. She possessed his wiry frame, the same long nose, strong jaw, and cloudy, bulbous blue eyes. When her mother scraped her black hair back from her wide pale face, knotting it in two coiled snakes by her ears, the resemblance was indeed remarkable.

John Andrew Miller liked to say he had blue blood in his veins, or bluish at least. His mother had been a Scottish servant girl called Mary Jane Bryden and she had conceived him while in service. His father, she had told him vaguely, was a man connected with the household. Once her condition had begun to show, she had been dismissed. She kept her son for eight years, but when she met a new lover she promptly gave him away to the Miller family in Glasgow, from whom he took his name.

Andrew Miller was a clever boy, the brightest in the school, he claimed, but at fourteen his education came to an abrupt halt when he discovered he now had to earn his keep. He arrived in Duns some time before 1910, probably around 1905, an unusual step, for one brother was a coal miner, the other a baker, and it would have been more natural, expected even, for him, too, to have stayed in Glasgow at the centre of the pre-war Scottish economic boom. But he wanted to work in open fields, and there were not many of those in Glasgow. The Borders made sense. After agricultural labour, domestic service provided the chief source of employment. There were many grand houses and estates dotted along the River Tweed, such as Manderston, famous for its intricate staircase, which required many servants.

Andrew Miller quickly found a job. He was taken on as a trainee groom in a large house called Anton Hills, eight miles from Duns town, where he slept on a narrow bed in a cramped grooms' dormitory with panelled walls and a basin in the corner. From Anton Hills, he moved on to the much bigger and grander estate of Duns Castle, owned by the Hay family, local gentry, patrons of the poor, and dispensers of pennies at Christmas time. By now, Andrew Miller possessed all the characteristics of an adolescent boy – a scrawny overgrown body, gangling limbs, and a ghostly teenage pallor highlighted by his black hair and light, serious eyes. To relax he boxed in matches against other grooms using his bare fists. He liked to drink, too, although rarely to excess. Add in the smell of the stables and a girl might have had reason to look beyond him for a husband. Sis, however, knew a good thing when she saw it.

Her real name was Annie Colvin, after her mother, but her brothers called her Sis and, because one was notorious in the town (for drinking and poaching), she became Sis to everybody else. Sis came from a family of drunks. Her father had dementia, her mother drank, and then there were those brothers of hers, who possessed barely a social skill between them. To begin with the Colvins were a family of nine – death would claim the sickliest, one by one – crammed into a shack-like house with an earthen floor and two windows. When Sis left school at nine to look after her mother's new baby, it was by unspoken agreement that she took over the housework too. Thereafter she cooked, cleaned, and looked after all her siblings. This upbringing was to have consequences for her own daughters. She had no notion of what it meant to be a child; her thoughts ran solely on making ends meet. She bore a hatred of alcohol; she deeply distrusted education (which she considered something to be tolerated and on no account to be pursued further than necessary); and she had a contradictory attitude towards children. She viewed them both as good – a woman's role in life – and bad – an economic drain, especially when born into poverty, which in itself she considered an act of supreme irresponsibility.

When Andrew Miller met Sis she was a well-established presence at the mill. Day after day, in the early morning darkness, she joined the gang of women who made the long walk along the road that led out from Duns. Sis was pleasant looking in the way that the plain often are: petite with wavy, mousy hair, a reasonable figure and small, round unsmiling brown eyes. (Her younger sister was the real beauty, but she was to die giving birth to her illegitimate child.) Heaven knows exactly how her path crossed with Andrew, since Sis rarely indulged in dancing and never in drinking, but in 1910, when she was twenty, she gave birth to the girl who became known as Etta. Papa, as Sis began to call Andrew, always explained his initial hesitance in marrying her as a result of his 'bachelor' job at the castle. This cannot have angered Sis too much, despite having to spend another three years under her mother's roof, for on 25 September 1913, she married him at 1 Duke Street, Glasgow, by common declaration, with Papa's brothers, William the coal miner and James the baker, as witnesses.

Papa recognised in his new wife the courage and spirit he lacked himself. She had a fighting, steely nature and offered him the prospect of a secure family environment (he had been old enough to remember his mother abandoning him). Sis saw that Papa was free of all the vices of her own family. In his knee-high boots, riding hat, and voluminous breeches, as he proudly drove his horses through town, with their polished saddles on glossy black flanks, he was considered a splendid sight and quite a gentleman. But while each filled the other's needs, they were ill-suited at heart. Aside from a skill for mimicry, Papa was quiet and self-contained, dour even, certainly not prone to the great surges of emotions that erupted from his wife. He had always regretted his thwarted education and as an adult, became a determined autodidact, spending hours poring over Scottish literature. At one stage he even attempted to compile a history of the Scots language, which Sis would throw on the bonfire after his death. Sis hated books and frippery, and found it hard to control her feelings, particularly if she suspected he had been drinking at the bar of the Swan Hotel.

They had been married one year when the First World War broke out. Papa did not have the resolve to become a conscientious objector, but the idea of war horrified him nevertheless. He could not hide in the stables for long. In January 1915, for example, *Country Life* ran an editorial posing five questions:

1. Have you a Butler, Groom, Chauffeur, Gardener, or Gamekeeper serving you who, at this moment should be serving your King and Country?
2. Have you a man serving at your table who should be serving a gun?
3. Have you a man digging your garden who should be digging trenches?
4. Have you a man driving your car who should be driving a transport wagon?
5. Have you a man preserving your game who should be helping to preserve your Country?

As Pamela Horn points out in *Life Below Stairs in the 20th Century*, in all the great houses in Scotland and England, building projects and improvements stopped, freeing up the men to fight. Gardens once lovingly tended were given over to potato growing, and much of the work on the estates, both indoors and outdoors, was carried out by women – those who did not go into munitions factories – be they former housekeepers and maids, or members of the Women's Land Army. In the various gentlemen's clubs, such as the Athenaeum in London, waitresses replaced the all-male staff. Mrs Cornwallis-West, the former Lady Randolph Churchill, readily embraced the change, and one hostess replaced her footmen with a set of 'foot girls', handsome, strapping young women in blue livery jackets, stripped waistcoats, stiff shirts, short blue skirts, black silk stockings, and patent leather shoes with three-inch heels. Most employers were less brazen. In the big hotels in Edinburgh, such as the Caledonian, staff quickly became depleted. In January 1916, conscription was introduced and Papa had no choice. He joined the Scots Greys, was wounded in the battle of the Somme in 1916, and returned home immediately. From that day on, he refused to talk of his war experiences, so his family never really knew what had happened to him – only that he came back pensioned off.

By the time Lily was born, Papa was working in the stables of the Swan Hotel in the town square, and the family was living in a cramped house in North Street, which stood directly opposite Sis's parents' house in South Street. The first few years of Lily's life were spent in the shadow of a series of Colvin crises, which taxed Sis

Papa, Etta and Sis, holding Lily, wearing Sunday best for Lily's christening at Christ Church, Duns.

face with exhaustion and despair. Sis's
...reasingly demented (he would report Papa
...out the inspectors always found them healthy
... as round as barrels). Sis's youngest brother,
...r's favourite, had not survived the war. (12 per
...o fought on the western front were killed, rising
...of officers; Duns alone lost seventy-five men to the
...her, engulfed by grief, had taken to guzzling pitchers
o... ...numb the pain. She had also contracted dropsy and
swolle... ...gargantuan proportions. She rarely rose from her bed.
Those brothers still living at home, Jock and Jim, were indolent
and disinclined to help. And then, in March 1918, Sis's younger
sister died in childbirth. Her daughter was also named Lily, but
when it became apparent that nobody could or would care for her
but Sis, the child was deposited at North Street and renamed Rose
to avoid confusion.

If these burdens took their toll on Sis, she took them out on her
own family. As a result Papa spent more time at the bar of the
Swan, which angered Sis further, and the children learned never
to approach their mother when she was in a rage or to contradict
her even when they knew her to be wrong. Later Lily would write
in the patchy beginnings of her memoirs, which she called *No Silver
Spoon*, 'Mother had a strong character . . . life had been hard for
her as a child. Her environment hadn't broken her as it might
have done but had given her determination and a strong will, so
it was she who set the rules, we were taught the difference between
right and wrong, and if we broke the rules we were punished.'

The Miller girls, always impeccably dressed and groomed, with
laundered smocks and over-combed hair, were as temperamentally
different as their parents. In personality Lily was closer to Rose, a
fiery, hot-headed girl quick to lose her temper. Rose would be the
first to challenge Sis and the first to escape Duns, running off to
Edinburgh at the age of sixteen. It was Rose with whom Lily clashed.
Each night Etta would look on, dismayed, as her sisters tugged
crossly at the oil lamp Sis had placed between them. Etta was far
more bovine, round and plump and compliant, the prettiest of the
three; a simple and uncomplicated child with no inclination to
gaze to the horizon. Lily, with her odd, bony little face, bulging

Lily, centre, with oversized ribbon and necklace, looking glum at the idea of a family portrait. She is flanked by her parents and Etta.

eyes, and pale knobbly legs protruding from her skirt like match-sticks, was the bridge between Rose and Etta. She possessed Etta's gentleness and Rose's bravado and courage. She was quixotic in attitude and agile in her movements – quite the opposite of the stolid Etta – and liked to dance and spin around, tossing her head so that her bunches twirled and bobbed about her ears. It was a show put on for anybody who would look, but the best audience was always Papa. Really, though, despite her love of dancing – 'what rubbish,' Sis would mutter – Lily learned early on that the most effective way of winning affection and love was by saying what people wanted to hear, and in this her acting skills came in useful.

Just before Lily's fifth birthday, Papa was offered a position on a private estate in Ayrshire looking after hunters and racehorses, accommodation included. If ever there was a chance for Sis to slip the Colvin leash, it was now. The family packed up their possessions, piled them onto Papa's horse and cart and set off for a new, independent life. Lily was devastated. It meant leaving behind her best friend, a wiry haired old woman called Hannah who lived in the bottom half of their council house. Hannah was an Irish immigrant, an agricultural labourer of the sort known in the lowlands as a bondager, and every night she was to be found in her bonnet and flounce sleeves, drunk in the town square, lashing out with her wizened legs at the local constable. She was, Lily later recalled, 'very special. I have never met anyone like her since.' It was life without Hannah, rather than leaving Duns, that Lily found intolerable. The old woman had fed her stories of taking to the road in a gypsy caravan, 'with a horse to drive like a pedlarrman [*sic*], just the two of us,' and one day went a step further, rasping hotly in the child's ear 'take care of those hands – one day you will become a great lady'.

Hannah might have been filling Lily's head with bunkum, but it was to have one effect: it confirmed what Lily had already begun to feel, that she was different and wanted to escape. But climbing on Papa's cart, squashed in next to Sis and her sisters, did not have the same appeal as bumping along in Hannah's imaginary caravan.

Lily need not have worried. Within eighteen months the Millers were back. Annie Colvin's health had taken a turn for the worst and, when duty called, Sis could not help but come running. Annie

Colvin died on 19 December 1922, when Lily was eight years old. When the undertakers arrived, they found the corpse so heavy and large that it could not be carried down the staircase. Eventually the body was placed in a secure box and lowered to the pavement using a rope pulley. Given the location of the two houses and the fact that the horrible business must have attracted a crowd, it is likely that Lily witnessed her grandmother's final indignity, lying on the pavement in her makeshift coffin.

The first time Lily felt what life might be like free of the Millers *en masse*, was at Duns Primary School, an unprepossessing low stone building close to North Street. The school was hardly a hotbed of self-expression. Once a week, for instance, the older girls were herded into line and marched over to Berwickshire High School so they could learn to cook for their future husbands and employers. There were also lessons in laundry and needlework, washing and ironing, hemming and patching, all practised on squares of white cotton and flannel. (At the end of the nineteenth century a series of codes was passed – by a government of men – that made it clear to schools that their grants would be adversely affected if such subjects were not included. Too many men had been rejected from fighting in the Boer War on medical grounds, and if the British male was puny and unhealthy, it seemed his wife's cooking was to blame.) But compared to the atmosphere of chaos control and pleasure policing at North Street, school promised much. Lily did not warm to many of the spinster teachers – they were starchy and sharp-tongued and made her cry by thwacking maps with pointers and asking her questions she could not answer – but Mr Thomson, the headmaster, was heaven itself.

Danny Thomson was a strict, sprightly man who wore orange tweed plus-fours and liked to show the children clippings of the hybrid plants he grew in his garden. He taught academic subjects, but was especially keen on encouraging the dramatic arts. Although tone deaf, he was keen to involve his charges in the Borders Festival, a competition of performing arts in which many of the region's schools took part. By 1928, after a string of victories that saw him banging on the school piano more fiercely than ever, in the interests of fairness, Duns Primary was asked not to enter. It was under

Lily, third from right in the front row, at the age of ten, with her class-
mates at Duns Primary. She later annotated the image with: 'When
all was young!!!'

Mr Thomson's nurturing eye that Lily learned to tap dance. 'I had
been blessed with a good singing voice,' she declared in later life,
'a pair of light dancing feet and a certain ability to act.' She became
so good that Mr Thomson soon suggested she dance in shoes made
for the job. Perhaps her mother would buy her some? Sis would
no more pay for such frippery than she would prop up the bar at
the Swan. Lily could go straight back to Mr Thomson and tell him
what to do with such a ridiculous suggestion. Mr Thomson, keener
than ever to ensure his star continued to sparkle, was not easily
dissuaded. Shortly afterwards, he presented Lily with a pair of shoes
he had found himself, cast-offs but tap shoes nonetheless. Lily
ran home to North Street suffused with joy. The tap shoes entered
through the front door and left through the window.

Lily was a bright child, but she had no encouragement at home,
not even from Papa. Sis only valued instruction of the domestic
kind. Her dream for her daughters extended to them gaining good
positions in domestic service, which would, in turn, bring adequate
and fair reward. 'Mother thought it right and proper that training
for anything should come from the landed gentry,' Lily later

Lily on the same day.

lamented. Any attempts at studying at home were met with out-and-out resistance, which meant that Lily often left North Street in her immaculate pinafore with red eyes and half-finished homework. Given Papa's regrets about his own undeveloped intellect, his inertia when it came to the minds of his daughters is less easy to explain. But he was a weak man and his position – or lack of it – is probably more a sign of how much he feared to contradict his wife than a belief that girls did not deserve the benefits of book work.

Aside from the wonderful Hannah, who, Lily later wrote, 'From the day I crawled into her house as an infant . . . had taken me to her heart', Lily (by now on the verge of adolescence) had one best friend. She was a bold, straight-talking girl called Alice Brockie, who arrived at Duns Primary tinged with the smell of the barnyard on account of living on a smallholding in the outlying reaches of

Duns. Alice came from a good home. The family had once been
successful farmers from Selkirk and her mother had employed a
maid, but the post-war depression had forced her grandfather into
bankruptcy and he had eventually sold the family business. Moving
to Duns as a qualified specialist in Border Leicester sheep was a
step down, to be sure, and it was said that Mrs Brockie was having
trouble adapting. She was known as the Duchess, for her airs and
graces, and it had also been noted that Alice's sister, Bunty, walked
about with a pet piglet under her armpit.

When Alice first arrived at the school, aged eleven, it was Lily
who had offered friendship. It was typical of her, even then, to
be drawn to someone down on her luck and apparently in need
of help. Alice Brockie would never forget this first act of kindness. Lily's friendship with her, which was to last a lifetime, was
cemented by a shared dream of the future. The two girls, in their
blue pinafores and bunches, would sit in the girls' playground and
plot their escape. 'I am not going to end up a poor servant girl
skivvying after other people! I will not! I will not!' Alice would cry
passionately.

They fantasised endlessly about leaving Duns. Mr Brockie might
have been suffering the legacy of his father's financial ruin, but
he knew the work of Dickens, and every morning he would test
Alice's arithmetic as she sat on the side of the bath watching him
shave his whiskers. He had stimulated Alice's ambition and Lily
found it to be contagious. Alice wanted to leave Duns, to leave
Scotland, travel the world, and perhaps even become a doctor. Lily
could not be so precise – it was thrilling to even think of a life
beyond the town square, let alone decide what to do with it. All
she knew for certain was that she wanted more than what Sis had
in mind.

In 1928, when Lily was twelve, she began part-time work in a
baker's shop. Lily's days now began at 7 a.m. with the collection
of morning rolls to be delivered in a large wicker basket before
school. The weekends were the busiest. Orders doubled and the
Saturday bread run started at 6.30 a.m. The bakery paid Lily three
shillings and sixpence a week, as well as a large bag of cakes and
a bag of sweets, all of which she handed over to Sis, who then
handed back nine pence, three of which she called 'pocket money'.

Lily, schooled in her mother's impressive housekeeping, saved the sixpence 'pay'. After returning home to North Street for breakfast, on Saturdays Sis would put Lily and Rose to work. The bedroom was turned out and the stairs and lobby scrubbed. When 'the chores in the house were done to my Mother's satisfaction', the girls were given a wheelbarrow and sent to the sawmill over a mile away to collect wood. They made the journey twice, first for thin logs, and then for the fat ones Sis used for cooking mutton stew in her cauldron.

All chores, including cooking Sunday lunch (always stew, usually mutton but sometimes rabbit if Sis was feeling generous) had to be finished by Saturday evening. Sis refused to work on the Sabbath. She was, in Lily's words, 'a keen church goer and she set the pattern'. Setting the pattern included herding her girls to Bible class and then afternoon Sunday school, where Lily became a teacher, and badgering Papa to convert from the Church of Scotland to the Church of England. He complied, for a quiet life, but even the children noticed their father was not quite as ardent in his beliefs as one might expect of a church warden. 'He went along with it all the same,' Lily later wrote, a succinct epitaph for Papa's general attitude to life.

The Millers worshipped at Christ Church, an Episcopalian church dating back to 1857. It is still there today, sitting high on Teindhill Green, which snakes across the top of Duns. It is surrounded on all sides by its graveyard and inside are the usual memorials to those singled out for special attention. Lily, in her best dress, became familiar with these as she sat in the third pew from the back where she was squashed in next to Papa, Sis, Etta, and Rose. The front pews were filled by the Berwickshire gentry, the descendants of those remembered on the walls: Mr and Mrs Hay of Duns Castle, Papa's old employers; Captain Tippins; Lady Miller from Manderston and the incumbents of Charterhall. The congregation encompassed the very rich and the very poor, so Sunday service gave Lily her first taste of the class divide. 'They have such loud voices,' she would whisper to Papa. 'Why do they shout at each other like that?'

For the other six days of the week, the gentry, apart from the Hays, remained hidden on their estates or in London. Their

children were educated either at boarding school or at home.
Errands were run by staff. Occasionally a car would purr through
the town and the men would tip their hats if a lady were inside,
but these sightings were akin to spotting a rare bird. No sooner
had they come into view than they were gone. Their homes ran
along banks of the River Tweed, known locally as 'Millionaire's
Row'. Lily, like all the other ordinary girls in Duns, was not destined
to breathe such air. The closest she would come to this life of
privilege was waiting at the tables, clearing the hearths, and making
the guest beds, and that, according to Sis, would do quite nicely.

If Lily had dodged thinking about the grim reality of her destiny,
preferring instead to dream with Alice, in 1930 she was given no
choice. Turning fourteen marked the official end of her education.
Sis's project was to send her into service as soon as possible and
she enlisted Etta to keep an ear to the ground for a suitable position
– nothing too grand, but enough to put Lily on the first rung of
the domestic service ladder (the last rung being a position with a
titled family). When the day came for her to leave school, her
sadness at waving goodbye to Alice and Mr Thomson was made
bearable only by the fact that Sis had not yet found her a position
and that she would not be leaving North Street. It was never Sis's
plan to have Lily moping about at home, so when the baker for
whom Lily worked offered her a job minding his children, three-
year-old Olive and five-month-old Moira, Sis was happy to let
her do it. This was a temporary measure until something 'proper'
came up.

Caring for the baker's small children brought Lily much pleasure.
She took them for long walks around town, Olive toddling along
by her side and Moira peering inquisitively from the pram. Lily
loved tidying and rearranging the nursery. This routine continued
for a few months and Lily was 'thrilled' at the way things had turned
out. 'However,' she was to recall years later, 'mother had different
ideas.'

Sis spoke endlessly about the benefits of learning from the aristocracy. In a good family Lily would be looked after and would
learn to distinguish what was good taste and what was bad. Being
surrounded by pictures, silverware, and fine china would cultivate
her. It would be impossible to live among such beauty, Sis argued,

without some of it rubbing off. On a more profound level, Sis believed the upper classes were morally 'better': it was as simple as that.

These ideas were backed up by a series of contemporary manuals. One, for example, *A Few Rules for the Manners of Servants in Good Families*, published by the Ladies' Sanitary Association in 1895, had been in wide use during Sis's childhood. The book makes the self-will and discipline required for a future of servitude all too clear. It is a bible of dos and don'ts, and could easily have engulfed an independent-minded young woman like Lily in a fog of inferiority. Don't walk on the grass unless permitted or unless the family is out, and walk quietly; never sing or whistle; when you meet the mistress or master on the stairs, stand back or move aside for them to pass; when carrying letters or parcels, use a small salver or hand tray; never hand over a letter directly, risking skin contact, but place it instead on a nearby table. Another, *A Servant's Practical Guide: A Handbook of Duties and Rules for the Use of Masters and Mistresses*, carries the same message. Its advice for coffee time leaves a mistress in no doubt of the kind of climate to cultivate:

> The women servants stand behind the buffet, and pour out the tea and coffee. The only remark offered by servants in attendance is: 'Tea or coffee, ma'am?' Not 'Will you take tea or coffee, ma'am?' or 'Shall I give you some tea ma'am?' A well-mannered servant merely says in a respectful tone of voice 'Tea or coffee, ma'am?'

Following the war, many former male and female servants had been reluctant to return to their old positions; war work had given them the taste for a more independent life. But in spite of this, post-war industrial depression and high unemployment led to a steady rise in domestic staff during the inter-war years. In the Borders, where there were large estates still operating on comparatively large incomes, domestic service never stopped being regarded as the principal source of employment for young girls.

Sis quite rightly viewed Lily's Borders upbringing as an advantage. The Fairbairn Agency on the Edgware Road in London, for example, specialised in supplying simple Scottish maids to good English families, 'mostly titled'. Glasgow girls were always rejected 'as they are too rough', as were 'stockingless or made-up girls'. Country girls were ideal because they were so sensible, unsophisticated, and lacked the wisdom of the world, the three virtues Lily desired to be rid of. But she was given no choice. 'So my days with the children were short-lived, and I was sent to "proper service".'

3

Virescit vulnere virtus: *Valour grows strong from a wound*

On 14 October 1928 at 2.45 a.m., in a large, elegant bedroom on an upper floor of 34 Bryanston Square, London W1, the 12th Countess of Galloway, gave birth to a son and heir. The boy was christened Randolph Keith Reginald Stewart, names chosen in honour of his father, grandfather, and uncle. There was also the courtesy title of Lord Garlies, which the child would keep until his father's death, whereupon he would succeed to the title of 13th Earl of Galloway. When Randolph arrived into the world that morning there was no indication of the troubles that lay ahead. Physically, he was perfect. Lord Galloway, the 12th Earl, could rest easy. Three years before Lady Galloway had delivered a daughter, Lady Antonia Marian Amy Isabel Stewart. Now that there was a boy the line would live on, for another generation at least.

Lord Galloway was an accomplished historian, particularly when it came to how the Earls of Galloway, one of Scotland's oldest noble families, fitted into Britain's history. They remain one of the main lowland branches of the Stewarts, and, in the absence of a chief, are considered by the Stewart Society, founded in Edinburgh in 1899 to collect and preserve the history and tradition of the name, to be senior representatives of the clan. If a lineage dating back to the twelfth century seemed irrelevant to a small boy born after the First World War, then it was not considered to be so by that boy's father. Documents and articles held in the Stewart Society library bear many of Lord Galloway's annotations and corrections. His heritage brought him great pride. He did not care for family members who chose to forget it.

The Galloway earldom has its roots in the Lord High Stewards of Scotland, whose line also produced the Stuart monarchs. When David I gave the 1st High Steward, Walter, his position, he effectively made him Scotland's equivalent of Chancellor of the Exchequer and occasional army general. It was the third High Steward – also called Walter – who turned the title into his family name, which continues to this day. An unbroken male line descends from Sir John Stewart of Bonkyl, who died at the battle of Falkirk in 1298. Two of his sons fought alongside Robert the Bruce and were rewarded with lands. Their cousin, Sir Walter, later the 6th High Steward, also distinguished himself as a commander at Bannockburn in 1314. He was knighted on the battle field by Robert the Bruce and later married his daughter. Fifty years on, their son became King Robert II. In 1607 James I made Sir Alexander Stewart Lord Garlies. Sixteen years later he created for him the Galloway earldom. Queen Elizabeth II is a direct descendant of the royal Stewarts through the female line.

The early bravery and military inclinations of the Stewart relatives – some destined to become the Earls of Galloway – continued through the centuries, right up until Randolph's birth. Some stood out. Lieutenant General Sir William Stewart, fourth son of the 7th Earl and Countess of Galloway, for example, co-founded the Rifle Brigade and fought in the Napoleonic Wars. His journals and papers, known as the Cumloden Papers and dating from 1794 to 1809, preserved at the family seat of Cumloden, contain a record of his achievements and include revealing correspondence from the Duke of Wellington and Lord Nelson.

Everything Lord Galloway knew and felt to be true about life derived from his family legacy. He was born on 21 November 1892, to Amy Mary Pauline, the only daughter of Anthony John Cliffe of Bellevue, County Wexford, and christened Randolph Algernon Ronald Stewart. His father, Randolph Henry Stewart, son of Randolph, 9th Earl of Galloway, had joined the 42nd Highlanders in 1855 straight from Harrow School. In his military career he survived some of the empire's most significant conflicts. He served in the Crimea and was present at the siege and fall of Sebastopol (for which he received a medal with clasp and the Turkish war medal) and also at the Indian Mutiny, during which he was present at the fall of Lucknow (another medal with clasp). He retired, as a captain, in 1876. He was fifty-five by the time he married, fifty-six when his first son was born, and succeeded as 11th Earl of Galloway, following the death of his elder brother, the 10th Earl in 1901.

Two harrowing events in early adulthood had shaped Lord Galloway's life. The first was the death of his younger brother, the Hon. Keith Stewart, killed during the First World War, and the second was his own experience serving in the Scots Guards during the first battle of Ypres. Wounded and close to death, he had been captured by the Germans and kept prisoner before finally being returned home.

Even before the Lieutenant Hon. Keith Stewart's death on 9 May 1915, when he was head of the leading platoon of his regiment, the Black Watch, in the charge on Aubers Ridge, near Festhubert in Flanders, he was regarded by all – family, friends, schoolmasters – as extraordinarily brilliant, a rather special boy who, had it not been for his brother's status as first son and heir, might well have eclipsed him in every way. At Harrow he was head of school, captain of the football First XI, had won the public schools' fencing competition in 1911, the Macnamara Prize for English three years running, and had passed second into Sandhurst in 1913, then fifth out a year later. He was gazetted to the Black Watch in August 1914, and went to the front in the December. (Lord Galloway – then 'Garlies' – had been at Harrow School only a year when his brother arrived and his own time there would prove to be not nearly so distinguished.)

It was inevitable that the tragic, early death of such a young man would shock the family. Keith Stewart epitomised all they stood for: brains, honour, courage, strength, and patriotism. It was some while before his body was recovered, but his popularity was so great that both commissioned and non-commissioned officers went looking for it at considerable risk to their lives. His corpse was eventually found lying within a few yards of the German trenches. It was brought back and buried by the British chaplain in the cemetery of Vieille Chapelle. In the months that followed the news his father received many tributes. Tommy Graham, who fought with him, sent back to Britain wounded, wrote to him:

He was young as far as his years are concerned, but he was old in wisdom . . . He never asked one of us to do something which he would not do himself: he shared our hardships and our joys; he was, in fact, one of ourselves as far as comradeship and brotherly love was concerned . . . We never knew who he was till we saw his death in the Press; but this we did know, that he was Lieut. Stewart, a soldier and a gentleman every inch . . . it's not every day one like Stewart joins the army. There was not a man in his platoon, or the regiment for that part, but would have willingly went through hell for him, and mind you we faced hell out there on more than one occasion.'

Graham had heard of the death from another officer, Lance-Corporal Alexander 'Sandy' Easson, who broke the news thus:

We have lost little Lieut. Stewart . . . the best man that ever toed the line . . . None of the rest of them ever mixed themselves with us the same as he done. He was a credit to the regiment and to the father and mother who reared him; and Tommy, the boys that are left of the platoon hope that you will write to his father and mother and let them know how his men loved him . . . He died at the head of his platoon like the toff he was, and Tommy, I never was very religious: but I think little Stewart is in heaven. We knew it was a forlorn hope before we were half way – but he never flinched.

The Galloway family motto is *Virescit vulnere virtus* – valour grows strong from a wound – and so it proved for Lord Galloway, who adhered to it throughout his life. As soon as he had recovered, both from injury and from the loss of his brother, he became honorary attaché to the British legation in Berne in 1918, and then, after the war, in 1919, ADC to the military governor of Cologne. A year later his father died and he succeeded to the title. That he would incorporate his brother's name into that of his son and heir shows how the legacy of Keith lived on. The military tradition into which the two brothers had been born sets in context the assumptions and expectations Lord Galloway would come to make of his own son, just as, one imagines, they had been made of him. It also explains the enormous sense of disappointment, bewilderment, and shame he would come to feel when he found that his heir could not live up to them. For now, though, Lord Galloway had no reason to suspect that when he married his beautiful young bride, their genes would mix so badly.

Lord Galloway and Miss Philippa Wendell pictured on their wedding day in 1924.

Lord Galloway's marriage to Philippa Wendell in 1924 was seen by society as a second splendid match for the Wendell family, descendants of the victorious American Civil War general, Robert E. Lee. The Wendell sisters were not just beauties – Catherine, the eldest, was blonde and graceful, and Philippa, 'a vivacious brunette' – they were American beauties, bringing with them the wealth that the British aristocracy so badly needed. In the fifth volume of *The Stewarts: A Historical and General Magazine for the Stewart Society*, the tribute to their union reads: 'To none of all the alliances formed in recent years between fair *Americaines* and members of the British

aristocracy does so much interest attach – historically and genealogi-
cally at least – as to that just celebrated by Miss Philippa Wendell
and the Earl of Galloway.' Two years earlier, in 1922, Catherine
had married the Earl of Carnarvon. That Philippa had followed
her into the aristocracy by marrying a Scottish earl, one whose
ancestry placed him at the head of the Stewart clan, was considered
another piece of good fortune. 'She comes on both sides of the
house from some of the very oldest New England families,' the
report in *The Stewarts* gushed, 'and, it may be added, of pronounced
Royalist sympathies.'

The new Lady Galloway was perfect in every way. She was a beauty
with fine, noble features. She had pale skin and dark, thick hair
(Randolph was to inherit her colouring), cut into a bob and worn
pulled back from her face, showing off to good effect the sharp
angles of her cheekbones and jawline. She enjoyed listening to and
playing classical music, which particularly delighted the musical
dowager countess, who in the past had held her own festivals at
Cumloden, and she wrote plays and poetry (the latter published in
Punch). Added to this her uncle by marriage, Mr Percival Griffiths,
possessed a fine and extensive private collection of Stewart relics.
There were wonderfully wrought royal layette baskets, miniatures
of Charles I hand-worked in silk; a lock of the 'Royal Martyr's hair';
the hawking outfit – pouch, lure, and gloves – of James VI and I;
the Bible of Charles II in its bag of Royal Stewart tartan velvet –
'probably the oldest example of that tartan in existence' – along
with rings, medallions, and trinkets.

Shortly after their marriage Lord and Lady Galloway took a house
in London which led the *Daily Telegraph* to speculate that 'Lady
Galloway would blossom out as a leading London hostess'. She did
not. Lord Galloway found that he preferred being on his estate,
for which he now felt a great responsibility. Although Lady Galloway
had chosen to have her baby in London, soon after Randolph's
birth they travelled back to Scotland.

Cumloden is situated in the county of Kirkcudbrightshire in the
south-west, close to the towns of Newton Stewart and Minnigaff. It
was not a stately home, but a converted hunting lodge, orginally
built in 1821 by Sir William Stewart. The family's main seat had
been the grand and imposing Galloway House, also in the south-

west, but that had been sold off in 1908 due to the family's dwindling funds. Cumloden was a low white house with black timbers, not remotely grand or imposing. At the front, there was a porch with a verandah, framed by trees, rhododendrons, laurels, box hedges and azaleas. Inside, to the right of the entrance hall, a couple of steps led off to the billiards room and the main telephone room.

Cumloden, the Galloway family seat since 1908 when Galloway House was sold off due to dwindling funds.

Along the south-west front of the house were Lady Galloway's sitting room; Lord Galloway's study; a bedroom called the Orange Room for important family guests; a little store room; and the drawing room, off of which was an ante-room leading to a conservatory always filled with flowers. Double doors led from the drawing room into the dining room, outside which was a hall leading to the bedroom of the head housemaid, and underneath was the wine cellar. A flight of stairs led off to the north wing where Lord and

Lady Galloway had adjoining bedrooms (Lady Galloway's room had a spectacular view). The dowager countess also slept in a pretty room in the north wing, despite it being considered the coldest room in the house. Across the passage was a bathroom and a set of box rooms where Lord and Lady Galloway stored their much-used travel bags. From here another flight of stairs led up to the bedrooms used by the gaggle of old Stewart aunts and American relatives whenever they visited. These rooms also ran along the south-west front of the house and were called South Room (with appropriately facing dressing room), Balcony Room, Blue Room, and Roof Room. The layout continued in this manner – a series of rambling wings connected by a rabbit warren of corridors and narrow staircases. The focal point of it all, close to the entrance hall, was the grand and central spiral staircase.

The beauty of the estate, however, lay not in the house, however comfortable the interior, but in the lands, which stretched beyond the eye could see and included a deer park that Randolph would grow to love. To the west was Kirkland, the nearest farm, and further beyond, up the Wood O'Cree Road, looking over the River Cree, sat All Saints', Challoch, the family's church and burial yard.

On inheriting all this Lord Galloway grew further into his new role and began applying himself to a myriad of public duties. He became justice of the peace for Kirkcudbrightshire and in 1932, four years after Randolph's birth, he was appointed Lord Lieutenant of the Stewartry of Kirkcudbright. This role lasted until 1975 and involved lunches with Queen Elizabeth II and Prince Philip, from whom – in terms of old-school austerity and iron backbone – he was not dissimilar. The same year as Lord Galloway began representing the Queen, he also embraced masonic life. He was initiated into Lodge St Ninian, No. 499, and became Right Worshipful Master when he took office in Grand Lodge as Junior Grand Deacon. (In 1945, he would become Grand Master Mason.)

Unsurprisingly Lord Galloway's responsibilities and his extensive travelling dictated the rhythm of the household. Randolph's early years were typical of a post-war childhood in a big house, at one turn privileged, at another, by today's standards, emotionally lacking. It would have been quite unthinkable by the standards of his class for Lord Galloway to make his many trips abroad without his wife. As a result Randolph spent much of his time with a succession of nannies, nurses, and governesses. The year was divided into time spent at Cumloden; a large house in Sandridgebury, near St Albans, where Lady Galloway had grown up following her father's death – a fine residence with butlers and footmen, chauffeurs for the two Rolls-Royces, cooks, general maids, and scullery maids; and London. The London trip occurred in late January, usually when Lord and Lady Galloway were abroad, and the children would travel up with the nannies to stay at 39 Lowndes Street, where they would remain until just before Easter. The children adored these trips. In the cold London air the nannies would walk them round Kensington Gardens and Hyde Park, where they would stand, eyes wide with delight, before Peter Pan's statue. Occasionally they would go to Bryanston Square, where Randolph had been born, and curl up with Nana, their mother's old nurse.

Just before Easter the children would be brought back to Cumloden where they would remain until July. The nursery toy box overflowed. There were puppets, clockwork cows, and the 'bunny express', an engine in lapine form that sounded a bell as it chuffed around the track. There was a toy cinema, countless picture books, and annuals – a favourite being the series of adventures of the Peek-A-Boos. Lady Antonia had a large and intricate doll's house, which in fine weather was moved into the play hut in the grounds of the house, and Randolph had three sets of trains with tracks, two containing green engines with chocolate and cream coloured coaches with multi-coloured roofs. The puppet theatre was a favourite. If Lord and Lady Galloway were in residence, the countess would make sure all adults attended performances, including the sombre dowager. Often Lady Galloway would go behind the puppet stand herself. There were picnics in the surrounding beauty spots, which brought the children much joy, but not always the adults, particularly the dowager. The sun annoyed her, any wind drove her frantic, and in the rain she would sit alone in the Rolls complaining of her misery and wishing she was by the drawing room fire.

Come July the children would transfer to Sandridgebury where they would stay until October. During these months Cumloden would be let out to rich holidaymakers and Lord and Lady Galloway would travel to Europe or beyond, announcing their departure in the broadsheets. The trip south was a complicated operation

Arthur Owen

LADY GALLOWAY: A RECENT PICTURE

Lady Galloway was before her marriage in 1924 Miss Philippa Wendell and is a daughter of the late Mr. Jacob Wendell of New York. Lord Galloway is a captain in the Scots Guards (Reserve of Officers), and was one of the unlucky ones who was made a prisoner of war in 1914

Lady Galloway in the grounds of Cumloden for *Tatler* in 1934, ten years after her marriage.

involving much luggage. At 8.30 a.m. on the dot Mr McGowan would arrive in the Rolls ready to drive the nannies and their charges to Dumfries station, the starting point of their long journey south. The nannies would then shepherd the children into the car while Mr McGowan struggled with the numerous trunks, hat boxes, Gladstone bags, books tied with string, attaché cases, and luncheon boxes, as well as the portable wireless and gramophone. At Sandridgebury they would be met by another Rolls, driven by Hubert

French, and in the back seat sat a delighted Mrs Percival Griffiths. Mr Griffiths was equally pleased by their presence in his large house, and often liked to take them to Whipsnade Zoo in the Rolls, although he would get cross if they made a noise during his afternoon nap.

All things considered, with old great aunts pressing upon him as many Fuller's peppermints as they could manage, Randolph thought himself happy at Sandridgebury. It was one long blissful summer of hide and seek, sardines, netball, rounders, tennis, croquet, and golf. And in October, on his birthday, there would always be a party during which his great aunt would stamp about the hall, much to the children's delight, shouting 'Do you know the Muffin Man, the Muffin Man, the Muffin Man? Do you know the Muffin Man who lives in Drury Lane?'

And so this was the cycle of Randolph's early life, spent largely in the bosom of extended family and in the care of familiar, loyal servants who were always on hand to ensure the smooth running of the houses. Cumloden had a large staff, most of whom lived on the estate with their families, so that as Randolph's anxieties began to take hold, and he became prone to wandering the grounds alone, these familiar, weather-beaten faces seemed part of his world even though they came from a quite different one. Mr Curry, for instance, who tended the grounds, tidied the woodland paths, cut the wood, and ensured the house remained heated, lived with his wife in a cottage in the deer park. Mr Malcolm Scott, the head gamekeeper, lived with his wife and daughter, Monica, at Cumloden Lodge, which sat at the south entrance (Monica was responsible for opening the gatehouse gate and waving in the Rolls). It was often the case that the house employed several members of the same family. The succession of cooks – Mrs Robertson, Mrs Cockie, Mrs Partridge, Mrs Bain, Mrs Clark, and Mrs McNabb – and the roll call of butlers – Mr Leashman, Mr Campbell, Mr Hopkins, Mr Sparks, and Mr Wright – tended to arrive alone, but the coachman's daughter, for example, was head housemaid and parlourmaid. Randolph's favourite servant beyond all others, the one he continues to talk of in adulthood, was Nan Dalrymple, the laundry maid and wife of the station hand at Newton Stewart railway station. Often he would seek her out in the laundry room and she would embrace him with vigour – an unfamiliar but very pleasant sensation.

Randolph and Lady Antonia were initially educated at home. They were woken at 7 a.m. by the school-room maid with a glass of hot water 'that tasted awful', as Randolph remembered later, and in the afternoon, after lessons, they rested for an hour before being taken for a walk around the grounds by their governess. There was rarely a shortage of company though. Children of family friends were always being invited over for parties and on Tuesdays in spring, after their return to Cumloden, the portable gramophone and a box full of records, including selections of Irish and Scottish country dances, would be carried down from the school-room and set up in the billiard room where Miss Border, the dancing instructress, would hold classes for them and their friends. But Randolph's fear of his father slowly began to overshadow all. His 'personality problems' began early, long before he left Cumloden for Belhaven Hill, one of the most fashionable Scottish preparatory schools at that time. He cried when he left Cumloden for Sandridgebury and he cried when he left Sandridgebury for Cumloden. He was often making a scene, 'either public or private or both', he recalls. This irritated and angered Lord Galloway, who expected his son to behave with dignity, composure, and formality. It did not help that Randolph was a slight, sickly child. Whenever he contracted a cold or the flu, the school-room was turned into a sick bay.

Years later, when he was an adult, Randolph wrote of a puppet show that his mother had performed for him during his childhood. She named it 'The Child in the Bath', and in tone it chimes rather tragically with the feelings Lord and Lady Galloway would come to have regarding their own son. In the show the mother puppet placed her infant child in the bath and left the stage. While she was gone, 'the Black Witch, an evil woman' entered and snatched the baby. 'No happy endings,' wrote Randolph, 'for both parents were so upset, they had no idea of the visitation of such a demonic and odious prowling spirit.'

For all the joyful innocence of the nursery, the picnics and the toys and the parties, Cumloden remained a formal household. Lord Galloway believed in the same values as his own father and his approach to child rearing was rigid and unbending. It was not an atmosphere suited to an increasingly odd and eccentric little boy. In 1935, for example, Randolph threw a tantrum at the news that a newly appointed governess would shortly be arriving in the schoolroom. Poor Miss Daisy Cook, who appeared armed with milk of magnesia and syrup of figs. 'Tears of wretched despair . . . and dejected despondency adorned my face in the schoolroom, when writing Christmas letters of thanks,' Randolph recorded. 'Miss Daisy Cook was not amused by my attitude.'

Randolph was not a good student and when he did badly, he would sob or scream, which would have Miss Cook shouting back

Randolph as a child in the grounds of Cumloden with his long-suffering governess, Miss Daisy Cook.

at him to bring himself under control. Other staff began to notice his oddities. On one occasion, following a telling off by the dowager countess, he displayed more peculiarity, fussing about and breaking wind (a habit that he never thought to control). 'I was swiftly removed by Mother to the schoolroom,' he wrote, 'wherein I became aggressive and threatened Winnifred [school-room servant] on her approach.' Mr Leashman, the butler, witnessed the incident and was 'deeply shocked'. But Randolph did not apologise for his behaviour. He broke wind again, which had the effect of 'bringing a dark frown to the butler's face'.

Randolph's eccentric behaviour was not confined to Cumloden. Reports would often drift back from outings with other children, and events would often occur at house parties that confirmed he was unlike the other boys. During one house party in June 1934, the housekeeper took the children to the coast of North Berwick (not far from where Lily lived). Randolph ran away and everybody got soaked in the rain while they looked for him. During one stay at Sandridgebury, the children were taken to a private tea party by their aunt. Randolph had promised to behave, but once there he found it impossible to rise to the challenge. He muddled up the names of all the guests – understandable in an eight-year-old child – but then went on to insult the host, Mr Parr, by telling him that his study smelt of rats and tobacco. 'It may smell of tobacco, Garlies,' said the surprised Mr Parr, 'but it does not smell of rats!' To which Randolph had rudely retorted, 'Yes, it smells of tobacco and rats, and is the smelliest house I have ever been in!' Throughout the rest of the tea, Randolph continued to break wind, which had his aunt slowly dying of shame. Back at Sandridgebury she told him that never in her life had she been so mortified. 'Signorita', who helped with the children when they stayed, told him wisely, 'If you do this at school, teacher will come and put you in the lavatory!'

These minor acts of bad behaviour only make sense in retrospect. At the time the puzzled Lord and Lady Galloway consoled themselves that their son would change with age. What he needed was to grow and toughen up. What he needed was the discipline of prep school. There he was sure to metamorphosise from cry-baby into a proper boy possessed of a dignity befitting his title, and a spirit strong enough for the future challenges of Harrow School.

In the summer of 1937, before Randolph was due to start at Belhaven Hill School in Dunbar, the headmaster, Mr Brian Simms, came to Cumloden for lunch. Randolph was petrified and thought him horrid. He did not like the way he 'fixed [him] with a cold and hard eye across the dining table'.

That September Randolph left Sandridgebury with his mother and father. They were met at St Pancras station by the dowager countess and together they travelled to King's Cross in order to catch the train back to Scotland. Randolph's behaviour during the journey was not encouraging. When a locomotive blew its steam, he began screaming. Lady Galloway became angry and told him to stop being so babyish. Once on board the train his behaviour changed completely and he became jolly, babbling a list of nonsensical words that his mother sweetly wrote down on some notepaper for him. They spent the night of the twenty-eighth in the North British Hotel in Edinburgh (to become the Balmoral). Randolph was 'as potty as ever, making the craziest of noises', and smelling and blowing his sweet wrappers. The following day they travelled to Dunbar where Lord and Lady Galloway delivered Randolph to Belhaven for the beginning of Michaelmas Term. As they disappeared down the drive, he stood watching them from the front porch. For the first time in his life, he was alone, about to begin a new phase of his life under 'the iron rule of Mr Brian Sims [*sic*]'.

4

Tea or coffee, ma'am?

'I hated it.' This was Lily's verdict on her new life of subservience. The first time she stood before a mirror dressed in her afternoon uniform, a black alpaca dress with muslin apron, starched cuffs, and cap, she felt a surge of disgust. She wanted to rip the dress from her back and throw it on the fire. 'I will not be a poor little servant girl! I will not!' Less than four years had passed since Alice Brockie had made her passionate playground declaration. Alice was now doing well at Berwickshire High, well on her way to escape. The same could not be said for Lily.

The household Sis found for her was on the other side of Duns. It was a large square, double-fronted home with steps leading up to a porch, on either side of which stood two mock Roman pillars. The ostentation was ominous. Her new employers (Lily refused to speak of them by name, referring to them only as 'they') were middle-class professionals, and her mistress, Lily soon saw, liked to maintain a lavish shop front when perhaps stocks were not as high as they might have been. 'There always seemed to be so much silver on the table, but to me very little food,' Lily wrote. That first day she was led up the back stairs to a tiny maid's room. The floor was bare and the bed coffin-like in its dimensions, topped with a lumpy flock mattress. Companionship presented itself in the form of a ferocious-looking old cook and a whiskery gardener. Her duties consisted of all that could not be cooked or weeded. She was to clean, tidy, clear the grates, and manage the laundry. All cleaning had to be completed by the time her mistress rose for breakfast, which meant beginning at 5 a.m., and certain rooms were forbidden her, except if she had work to do. She had to keep to the back staircase, and never use the main. She could not wear rouge or have boys loitering about, although this was not such a hardship – she was only fourteen.

Although Lily was already tall, taller than Rose and Etta, she was still a child, not yet built for the physical labour expected of her. Life was now dominated by loneliness and hunger. Had she been sent to a large estate, she would at least have experienced the hierarchical but friendly bustle of life below stairs as well as the relief of regular, sustaining meals. Instead she grew paler and thinner and her hands began to crack. When she was not working she would lie on her bed in the attic and fantasise about ways of making Sis see sense, but we have her word that Sis 'turned a deaf ear' to this misery. When Lily made her weekly pilgrimage to North Street, she went straight to 'my beloved Hannah', who sympathised but, like Papa, wisely refrained from facing Sis head on.

In time Rose and Lily would prove themselves extremely adept at bolting from Duns. For now, Lily tried to please her mother and her mistress, and wrote later, 'Although I wasn't happy, I did my job properly, in fact, they called me Miss Tidy, no one could find anything after I had tidied a room.' And yet she possessed an instinctive independence that prevented her from accepting her prescribed lot, a tension that was always to complicate her life. Her compliance was short lived. 'With help from no one,' she wrote later, 'I took the initiative and ran away.' It was 4 a.m. when she climbed out of a window. 'But', she added, 'I hadn't used much imagination.' She reached North Street by dawn and no sooner had she knocked on the door and encountered Sis's fury than she was walking the same road back. Her mistress took her back because of her age, her insecurity, and, no doubt, because she was cheap. A week later Lily bolted again, this time with the hope of travelling to London. She left in daylight, by the same downstairs window, and took the road out of Duns, which she hoped would lead to London eventually. It was a ridiculous plan – she had no food and hardly any money – and once on the road, it occurred to Lily that her ambition was beyond her. She lost her nerve and began to cry. When a stranger passed in his horse and cart, she accepted his offer to climb aboard and be taken home, weeping, to Sis and Papa, back, as she put it, to Duns to 'face the music'.

Presented with such abject misery, Papa displayed uncharacteristic resolve. '"She is NOT going back!" he told Sis. "Enough is enough! The child is desperate." I may add he won that round,' Lily later wrote, with obvious relish. Sis, furious in the face of being overruled and intent on exacting some kind of punishment, sent Lily to bed without supper. Victory, though, was sustenance enough.

Within two or three weeks of returning to North Street, Lily began working in Greenlees, a small independent shoe store in the town square, and it was here, among the racks of heels and Oxford brogues, that she made the physical transition from child to young adult. The once gangling limbs were now long and coltish, and her square jaw and jutting cheekbones, quite ugly in a small child, had matured to give her an arresting bone structure. Duns had little to offer a teenage girl interested in fashion. But Lily made the most of what there was. She bought her clothes off the rack from Mrs Saban, wife of the butcher at Manderston (her wages of seven shillings and sixpence for a sixty-hour week could not stretch to Aggie Johnson, the dress maker). When Betty, daughter of the town's one barber, opened a small room in her father's shop, Lily allowed her to cut off her hair and style it in the marcel wave using her new iron tongs heated up over the fire (electricity did not arrive in Duns until 1936, so even the dentist operated his drill by foot).

Mr Thomson's school productions began winning prizes again. One in particular – *Raggle Taggle Gypsies* – made it to the festival finals in Edinburgh until it was discovered that the 'leading man' – he with the marcel wave – was in full-time employment and the cast was disqualified. 'Much to my disappointment,' Lily wrote, 'my acting days had come to a halt – much to the relief of my mother, I may add.' Despite this, there are two periods of Lily's life where photographs record genuine happiness. The years between sixteen and nineteen are the first and the year immediately after her marriage to Randolph is the second. 'Life was good,' she remembered of her adolescence. She was between roles – no longer a child completely under her mother's rule, and yet not quite a woman with responsibilities of her own. She still gave Sis her earnings, but her pocket money was raised to half a crown. 'I felt rich indeed.'

Sis's disdain for pleasure had abated with age, but she permitted

Lily, aged seventeen, enjoying a rare break from Sis on
one of the Christ Church camping excursions to
Coldingham, near the Berwickshire coastline.

certain excesses of youth provided they were experienced within
the confines of the church. By now Lily was a committed Sunday
School teacher, and a regular on the Christ Church picnics and
camping trips by the coast. She looks happy enough in the photographs, but being constantly in the presence of Him must have had
a sobering effect, and only at the rare ungodly events that Sis
allowed her to attend, dances at the Town Hall, the Drill Hall, and
the Girls' Club, could she relax completely. There, she was more
flirt than church mouse.

Sis, Papa, and Etta, not to mention the sensible and hardworking
Alice Brockie, now on the cusp of becoming a nurse, came to rue
the day that John David Millar walked into Lily's life. Another forty
years would pass before Lily's friend, Lord Lauderdale, musing on
marriage, would comment that romantic matches are often dictated
as much by the needs and insecurities of the choosers as the merits
of those chosen. Lily met Jock, as he was called, at a dance. He
arrived, as usual, revving his motorbike with a cigarette hanging
from his lips.

A dance in Duns was a hot ticket. The most upmarket were held
in the Girls' Club, a hostel housing young ladies from outlying

areas in weekday employment, for the sum of £1 per week. The
rules by which Miss White ran her establishment serve as a succinct
metaphor for the aspirations of many Duns mothers. Only certain
boys were allowed inside. The son of Lady Miller's secretary at
Manderston was one; the son of the Manderston butcher was
another. These boys, associated by proxy with the gentry, were
considered safe, 'a cut above'. Jock Millar on his motorbike would
certainly have been a cut below. (Although his grandfather had
been a ship owner in Dundee, his father had been cut off after
falling in love with a servant girl.) He worked as a butcher in
Veitch's, the most prestigious independent grocers in Duns Town
Square, where every morning he could be seen neatly arranging
Mrs Veitch's meat on small trays in the window. He had orange
hair, a large forehead, and biggish ears. All this, combined with
the apron, did not make him an obvious Duns Don Juan. But he
dressed in sharp three-piece suits and had a way with women.

There were three things about him that attracted Lily: other girls
wanted him; he was older and therefore more sophisticated; and,
most alluring of all, he represented danger. He took her virginity
in the fields outlying Duns and afterwards she climbed on the back
of his bike and roared home to Sis, revelling in her act of defiance.
Being with Jock, confident, desired, *fast* Jock, provided her with
attention and physical affection – always in short supply at North
Street – as well as security by association. Lily's fatal error was to
mistake the euphoria this gave her for love. Did Jock love her back?
There are photographs of them lounging lazily in fields, he with
one arm draped casually round her shoulders, the other round the
plump and beaming Etta. Lily looks to have swallowed a happy pill.
Jock, too, appears to be enjoying himself, but if he did love her,
he had a novel way of showing it, for many more women continued
to climb aboard the back of his bike. Duns being what it was, none
of this escaped comment.

In February 1936 Lily became pregnant. The Miller family had
by now moved from North Street to staff quarters adjacent to a
large house in Langton Gate owned by Major Dees, a local solicitor
and pillar of the community. Papa was his chauffeur and would sit
bolt upright behind the wheel of Major Dees's racing green Bentley.
Occasionally the Major could be glimpsed in his tweeds, sitting in

the back. If the scandal of Lily's pregnancy unsettled her parents' new-found respectability, her mother did not buckle in the crisis. Intuiting that her daughter was about to saddle herself with a bad bet – Sis was naturally distrustful of men, but she particularly loathed J.B., as she called him – she made herself clear. Lily must keep the child, but not the man. She would help bring it up. Lily was horror-struck. Nursing a child under her mother's instruction while Jock went off with other women, leaving her behind, had limited appeal. She wanted to escape from her mother, and besides, she felt herself to be desperately in love.

Rose had long since left for Edinburgh, where she was busy making her own mistakes with men. Etta, on the other hand, heading for confirmed spinsterhood and growing ever more homely and cosy, was deeply shocked by Lily's news. Paradoxically she did the most to spread it around, reasoning that scandal was best heard from source. It was a choppy time and somewhere in its midst Jock decided to do the decent thing. Lily was thrilled but we can be less sure of Jock's true feelings.

Meanwhile Lily had lost her looks, almost overnight. By the time her wedding day arrived, she was gaunt and skeletal. The cause was lipodystrophy, a little-known syndrome that can cause fat deposits or strip areas of body fat and redistribute them elsewhere. In the worst cases, the sufferer is left with 'a buffalo hump', a Quasimodo-like pad of fat on the back of the neck. At first, Lily thought only that she was losing weight. But the muscle tone in her face continued to fall away and the wastage travelled down to the top half of her torso. Her face changed shape and her cheeks caved in. Her eyes now appeared even bigger. She had lost her youthful bloom. She had always been tiny – at dances boys had called her Pocket Venus on account of her eighteen-inch waist – but now she looked ill. '[I] tried everything I could to put on weight . . . I didn't have much success.' It was a devastating and cruel illness, all the crueller for the time it chose to arrive. It was identified at the local hospital but the doctor was at a loss. He had no idea of its cause and even less idea of a treatment. He sent her away with an apologetic shrug. She stopped looking in the mirror and began padding out her bra. Marriage and a child could only boost her dented confidence.

Lily on the day of her wedding to Jock. Second row from left, Sis, Jock, Jock's mother and Papa. Jock's black-sheep father was dead.

On 1 June 1936, at eight in the morning, in a ceremony at Christ Church conducted by the Reverend Richard Ford, Lily's name changed from Miller to Millar. All her early hope and ambition was now transferred to her future family. Her wedding dress was fitted at the waist with a simple A-line skirt to the floor. She wore a matching bolero jacket and a headband, and carried a large bunch of wild flowers. Etta wore a loose, sack-like bridesmaid's dress. Sis wore black and a grimace while Papa spent the day pensive and unsmiling. Photographs were taken in Major Dees's garden. There was no honeymoon and no big party. Lily went straight into married life, eleven grim years of it, beginning in Galashiels where Jock had a new job as a travelling grocer. His van was his freedom, a getaway car.

John Brebner Millar Junior arrived on 9 November 1936, shortly after Lily's twentieth birthday. His birth was the most important event in her life so far and it marked the beginning of the end of her marriage. Jock felt trapped. He began returning home long after dark and sometimes not at all. In that first year Lily spent miserable hours pacing the streets of Galashiels looking for his van. Her plan had backfired. The apparent lack of love she had from

Lily, Jock, and Brebner posing in front of Jock's 'getaway
van' shortly after their ill-fated marriage in 1936.

her husband only intensified the love she gave to her baby. Brebner
(they dropped the John) filled her every thought, and as soon as
he began to walk she paraded him about in a miniature kilt and
knee-high socks. A year into the marriage, Jock secured a job with
a grocer's store back in Duns. They found a small upstairs flat in
a pokey house in Gourlays Wynd and moved back, where Sis was on
hand to help and harm. Lily's marriage difficulties quickly became
family business. Now Jock and Lily quarrelled, Lily and Sis quarrelled, Sis and Jock quarrelled, and sometimes even Papa joined
in. Jock felt as if everybody was against him and he was right. Very
quickly the marriage descended into acts of spite and bitterness,
each one outdoing the last. Lily would complain endlessly about
his drinking – an echo of her mother's preoccupation – and once
even marched to the store where he worked and insisted to the
manager that her husband was fiddling the books to fund his drink
habit (a falsehood). In return Jock would tell her she was ugly and
impossible to live with. Just when it looked as if things could get
no worse, on 3 September 1939 Neville Chamberlain announced
that Britain was at war with Germany.

Picking over the remains of a failed marriage is a near impossible
task. All the atrocious acts, the resentments, and recriminations
pile up, one on top of the other, so that in the end there is nothing

left but a tangled and indiscernible mess. One thing is clear though. If the end of Lily's marriage to Jock began in peacetime, war finished it for good. Had Jock gone away to war and returned alive, perhaps the trauma of separation and threat of fatality might have reignited their brief passion. There were conscientious objectors in the town who chewed tobacco before their medical to produce the symptoms of heart trouble or wore dark glasses to create the impression of poor, infected eyes, but Jock was declared medically unfit because of an earlier bout of rheumatic fever. He was sent to work in the boiler rooms of nearby Charterhall, one of two airfields in Berwickshire used by the RAF (the other was Whinfield, near Norham). His boilers served the quarters of the Women's Auxiliary Air Force, so he had increased opportunities to stray.

The town began to fill up with evacuees from the Scottish cities, two of whom were housed in the back of Lily's house in Gourlays Wynd. Army camps changed the Borders landscape. The largest was stationed at Stobbs in the countryside south of Hawick, holding more than 100,000 men. The camps in Duns were much smaller but they swelled the population overnight.

Now that Britain was at war, the rules that had governed Duns for so long relaxed a little. With so many of the men away fighting, some of the women began to seek alternative stimulation. This sudden sexual liberation started with the arrival of the men from the British Honduras, brought in by the Government to cut wood. They were forward in their ways – or forward by Duns standards – and soon women began to visit them in their camp at Affleck Plantation, on the Duns Castle Estate. There is an extensive file still in existence which details how many of the local women visited the camp in secret. This led to clashes between local men and the woodcutters and raids, during which women were found in the bunks. Their names and ages are listed in the file. Eventually, the camp was closed to prevent civil unrest.

On 1 April 1940, Lily gave birth to her second son, Andrew. Unlike with some of the other wives, there was no suggestion of impropriety (Duns today has a small percentage of mixed race adults, conceived during the period with the woodcutters). She was twenty-four, although photographs of her at the christening give the impression of a woman almost twice that age. Life had become

Andrew and Brebner taken by Lily to Portobello,
Edinburgh, during the Second World War to be
photographed professionally.

rather a strain. The second baby did not bind Jock and her together
but instead drove them further apart. Jock had taken a mistress, a
WAAF he had met at work with whom he felt himself to be truly
in love. This heady conviction only made him even more resentful
of his wife. Lily leant constantly on Papa and Sis for support, regularly involving them in her battles with Jock so that he felt cornered,
persecuted, and doubly justified in erring from course.

There was an unfortunate incident when Papa, who also worked
at the boiler rooms, became directly involved in his son-in-law's
dalliances. Jock's mistress misread Miller for Millar on the nightshift
rota and dressed only in a raincoat, disrobed, and thrust herself

onto the old man's lap in naked glory. The next day Papa threw a punch at Jock, and they ended up struggling on the kitchen floor in a pool of water, having upended the kettle and knocked over pans, a grisly spectacle played out in front of Sis, Lily, and the children. The fight was probably the most unpleasant incident in the course of Lily's marital breakdown, but the scraps over the tiniest matters were more exhausting and destructive. They argued violently about everything – even about how best to peel an orange.

In 1942 the town changed shape again. Two thousand soldiers from the First Polish Armoured Division arrived and were placed in another camp on the edge of the town. The Poles were every bit as alluring as the woodcutters. As they drove their tanks through the town, the officers played to the crowd. The dances continued at the town hall, but with blacked-out windows, and when the women passed them in the streets, all giggles and sly looks, the troops bowed and clicked their heels and made to kiss their hands. Some of the officers wore hairnets after washing their hair, and their cologne was considered very avant-garde. The women, particularly those who were single, gasped and swooned. While all this was unfolding, the older Duns men such as Papa, who were protective and even a mite jealous of the soldiers' hold over the town's women, sat around grumbling about how the tanks were smashing up their pavements.

At some stage during the war, certainly after Andrew's birth, Lily fell ill. Doctors suspected that she had contracted tuberculosis. She was isolated immediately (no doubt to Jock's infinite relief) in Gordon hospital, where she remained for five months, beset by self-pity. Brebner and Andrew went to live with Sis. It is perfectly true that for a young woman Lily had experienced a good deal of bad luck when it came to her health, but it must be stated that she applied a degree of drama to her suffering that would not have gone amiss in one of Mr Thomson's school productions. In fact as an adult woman she had lost none of her childhood propensity for dramatising and displays of heightened emotion. So far as her health was concerned, her exaggerated sense of pain had started around the time of menstruation and developed to such a pitch that even Brebner, a four-year-old boy, dreaded her monthly cycle and the attendant crushing headaches of which she complained.

This latest health setback provided Sis with ample opportunity to get back into battle position and resume her recently challenged rule over her daughter's life. When matron eventually returned Lily home, Lily was ill-equipped to fight Sis's declaration that she was not physically fit enough to cope with her children and the stress of Jock. There was an element of truth in this. Lily would not allow Brebner to be taken from her – her bond with him was as intense as ever – but she acquiesced on the matter of Andrew. She told herself it was temporary. But the moment Andrew stepped out of her door and into her Sis's house, temporary became permanent. He never went back.

5

Happy Days Are Coming

Randolph, about to turn eleven, had been a pupil at Belhaven for two years when war was declared. At first the school made only a few adjustments. Lights were lowered and the classroom windows were blacked out with heavy curtains. But there was another change, less perceptible to the human eye. The ethos of the school, with its severe and unbending determination to turn privileged young boys, soft and fresh from the nursery, into hard young men ready for such military schools as Harrow, strengthened further still. Mr Simms, the headmaster, made use of the icy winter weather by throwing open classroom windows during lessons. Often, the temperature dropped so severely that the boys could not help but plead for reprieve, to which Mr Simms would shout back, 'Fusspots! If you enter the army or navy, you'll have oodles of fresh air to contend with, no matter how cold you are!'

There were other tests of character too, which had been in place long before Chamberlain delivered his speech to the nation. Bathing, for instance, if such a word can be applied to something approaching such torture, occurred at seven every morning, when Mr Simms would walk up and down the bathrooms issuing orders to the boys to jump into baths of icy Dunbar mains water. There followed prayers and early morning drill, now laden with extra significance. The school was divided into patrols: Lions, Wolves, Woodpeckers, and Owls. Each patrol would be instructed to jump up and down, arms swinging forwards and back, up and down, and over the shoulder. There were punishments, of course, which Mr Simms liked to deliver with one of two slippers, made all the more sinister for him having christened them with childish names. 'White Tim' was a large rubber sports shoe he kept in the junior classroom cupboard, whereas 'Painful Peter' was another rubber slipper but much smaller, enabling him to carry it round in the pocket of his plus fours. Boys were constantly being thrashed over desks and tables, and their first beating was ceremoniously referred to as 'Father's Hand'. It was not long before Randolph received that baptism.

Randolph was probably the most unpopular, most peculiar, unhappiest little boy who had ever had the misfortune to set foot in the school. It's hard to know what came first – his queer and disjointed ways, or Mr Simms's reign of terror and his clear disgust at having to deal with such an odd, unresponsive and seemingly backward child. Whichever way round it was, each fed the other. The more unsettled Randolph became, the stranger he appeared to his peers, and consequently the more he was loathed. Randolph's strangeness had its foundations in his insecurity and profound inferiority complex, but also in a certain arrogance that came from being his father's son. Paradoxically, it would be the understanding of his birthright and its privileges that would eventually pit him first against his father, and then against the lawyers seeking to deprive him of them. Given how his personality would develop, Randolph's greatest misfortune was to be born to a family of such achievements and to a world that expected so much of him. And yet he understood that this made him special. He was trapped between liking himself too much and too little.

Randolph admits that his behaviour in the years leading up to the terrifying, barbaric medical act performed on him as a young man, a last resort to bring about a change in him, was 'bolshy and obstructive'. He was, he remembers, prone to alarming his peers by 'running madly around in circles and falling down in a crazily bizarre manner, and uttering the most idiotic of monosyllables [*sic*]'. He was always crying and showing off, trying to get attention, which earned him the nickname of 'a baby, a babe, a bub, or a booby'. He also continued making what he called 'bare-bottomed noises', so that he was regularly making the dormitory reek and infuriating matron, who would enter and ask the boys, 'Somebody is needing a dose, Garlies, is it you? Are you stinking?'

Randolph had no friends. Not only was he considered anti-social and rather disgusting by the other boys, he also seemed to possess no particular talents, not for sport, nor patrol, nor academia. During patrol, for example – Randolph was an Owl – he flailed about at the back so that in the end Mr Spurgin, the Owls' drill master, had to move him to the front, so 'he could . . . deal with me when I failed to live up to expectations'. His academic failings hit Lord Galloway particularly hard. On one paper, Mr Simms scrawled in red pen, 'Lack of vocabulary makes you write nonsense!' and, as even Randolph saw, 'Mr Sims [*sic*] had no use for people who wrote nonsense in translation of Latin prose or History essay questions.'

Randolph did nothing to help himself. Believing that everybody around him burnt with hatred, he went out of his way to intensify those feelings, sinking into a well of self-pity and playing up to the part of school oddball. There was nobody to whom he could turn. He thought Mr Simms a bully and a sadist (the present headmaster, Mr Michael Osborne, an old boy, remembers him as 'a daunting dome-headed bald figure, more austere than an ogre'); Miss Simms, Mr Simms's spinster sister, who strode around in a milky coffee-coloured tunic with matching hat and feather, was guilty by association; even the maids 'possessed a severity that would freeze the softest hearts'. On one occasion, when his turn arrived to see the school doctor, who at the beginning of every term set up his examination bed in Mr Simms's study, he mounted such violent protest that he was dragged screaming and kicking like a wild cat by four boys holding his ankles and wrists. During school prayers he mumbled obscenities and made silly noises. Sometimes he giggled so maniacally and with so little apparent provocation that Mr Simms shouted at him in front of the other boys, 'Garlies, don't behave like a lunatic!'

We cannot know how much of this early behaviour had its foundations in a genuine and innate mental condition and how much of it was the result of profound unhappiness and childhood confusion exacerbated by a wildly inappropriate environment. If one were to hazard a guess, it would be a combination of the two. However bizarre Randolph's behaviour was at Belhaven, he seems to have been capable of self-examination. In his unpublished memoirs which are drawn on here, it is around this period that he first starts to refer to himself in terms of being considered 'mad' and 'a lunatic'. He uses the words freely, at times almost with a degree of relish. Shortly after his eleventh birthday, for instance, at the end of October 1939, he contracted the measles and his behaviour became what he calls 'distorted and 'slightly mad'. 'I was gripped to hypnotism with fright and terror,' he later wrote.

That Britain was once again at war with Germany raised Lord Galloway up to his full military potential. He had maintained a keen interest in the Territorial Army in the inter-war years, and now he raised and commanded the 7th (Galloway) battalion of the King's Own Scottish Borderers. (A year later he was to retire from the battalion on medical grounds. He was appointed Honorary Colonel but, undaunted, he would raise the local unit of the Home Guard.) Whenever Lord Galloway and Randolph were resident at Cumloden at the same time, Lord Galloway desperately searched for proof of some kind of development in his son. He was usually disappointed. During tea in the dining room he liked to fire general knowledge questions at Randolph, which Randolph could never answer. 'Don't pretend to be so silly, foolish boy!' the dowager countess would snap.

It was not long before the effects of war began to be felt at Cumloden. The house began to receive evacuees, who were housed in its outbuildings, and during the Blitz in the autumn of 1940 extended family from the south began to arrive. Sometime between 14 September and 14 October, 34 Bryanston Square, where Randolph had been born, received a direct hit. Lord and Lady Galloway decided that Lady Antonia was no longer safe in her boarding school in the south of England, so they pulled her out and brought her back to Cumloden. Randolph clung to the hope they would do the same for him. They did not. In light of the increased bombings, it was decided that Belhaven should be evacuated to Dinnet House, an ancient Scottish mansion with poor electricity near Aboyne on Deeside, in north-east Scotland. As a consequence Lord and Lady Galloway considered the location quite safe enough. Randolph was to go back to school.

It was, Randolph wrote later, 'rather awful'. The boys now worked mainly by candlelight, due to the antiquated and constantly malfunctioning electricity mains, and when it began to snow the school was cut off from all civilisation. Randolph felt more trapped and abandoned than ever. He wanted the comfort of his family. Matron would not do. From a window he would watch the snow fall, his cheeks hot and wet with tears, knowing that with every new inch piling up on the railway tracks, it was becoming increasingly unlikely that he would be able to go home for the holidays. 'Nevertheless,' he wrote, 'my attitude did not stop the snow from falling, the more I cried the heavier the snowfall turned, leaving me a tear stained wreck before the night was out.' Cumloden, home to his much missed mother and sister, the familiar and comforting faces of the staff and increasing numbers of relatives from the south, felt a long way off. Randolph began to dream of escape. In these dreams, he would be running down the school drive carrying his luggage, Miss Simms in pursuit, wearing the deerstalker hat that had suddenly replaced the coffee-coloured boater since they had arrived in the Highlands.

In December 1941 Lord Galloway decided to move Randolph to Chartridge Hill House, a boarding school near Chesham in Buckinghamshire, a decision that might very well have been shaped by the school's proximity to the London doctors Randolph was about to see, and his father's desire to get him into Harrow (Belhaven records state that Randolph 'went to a private school for special coaching'). In a final flourish of despair, Mr Simms wrote in Randolph's leaving report that he had driven him to the end of his tether. Another teacher added that Randolph would have to make more of an effort and keep his wits about him, and still another concluded that Randolph was extremely backward for his years and would have to learn to grow up. Randolph might well have been young for his years – he was thirteen – but that Christmas, the schoolmasters' counsel did not prevent Lord Galloway from pressing ahead with his own programme of development. He presented Randolph with a gun, and soon after Randolph began to go shooting with Mr Malcolm Scott, the gamekeeper. By the end of the holiday, he was accompanying Lord Galloway on organised shoots at Larg. Much to everybody's surprise, he showed signs of becoming a rather good shot.

Randolph's enrolment at Chartridge Hill House marked an important change in his family's approach to him. 'Through psychological and psychiatric causes that term I had injections inflicted on me by Dr Johnson, the school's Buckinghamshire doctor man,' Randolph recorded.

Given Randolph's perceived instability, it is most likely that Lord and Lady Galloway had decided that it was appropriate for him to be sedated, in order to curb his wild bouts of behaviour. Paraldehyde was the most used sedative in the first half of the twentieth century and could be easily administered by injection. It calmed patients down without impairing their intellectual capacity. But despite being under sedation, Randolph was to receive no soft handling. Lord Galloway instructed Mr Stafford Webber, Randolph's new headmaster, to forbid him from spending too much time with his southern relatives. Lord Galloway explained that Randolph had become 'spoiled, pampered and petted' and that he was still in need of toughening up.

It had already been settled that Randolph would attend Harrow School, just as three generations of his family had done. His passage to the school that had produced Sir Winston Churchill, Lord Byron, and Lord Palmerston was predestined. The full weight of family history had been pointing him in that direction since birth. *Virescit vulnere virtus* was the family motto and he would simply have to rise to it. That he could not frustrated Randolph deeply, and it made him even more terrified of his father. As is so often the case when the weak are terrified of the strong, the very fear itself feeds the problem, causing paralysis in the former and even greater fury in the latter.

In June 1942 the dowager countess died. She was buried in the graveyard of All Saints', Challoch, with the other Stewarts. A month later Randolph returned home from school and further irked his father. 'I gorged and guzzled at my food to grossest excesses, and ate far too much for the parents' conveniance [*sic*] and expense,' he wrote, 'The father man was truly disgusted at me, I was rude, discourteous, uncivil and impolite, not to mention greed [*sic*]'. Randolph's healthy appetite for buttered rolls, chocolate biscuits, and cakes had always infuriated the late dowager, who had called it 'vulgar and ungentlemanly'. Lord Galloway did not want to see a display of it either.

Three weeks after Randolph's fourteenth birthday in October 1942, he sat the Common Entrance exam for Harrow. It was a formality since the school would never have turned him down (his results were predictably 'abysmally low', even though he was a little old compared to other candidates). Randolph's inability to please his father was having a profound effect on his social development. 'My personality was slowly going to pot,' he wrote, 'becoming ever entombed in guilt, with the ever encroaching festoons of gloom entwined about complexes and phobias which had me a spectre's shadow before that term was up. The guilt was deep and intense, becoming ever more so. I gave up laughing, I dared not even smile, thinking both were wrong.'

If Randolph's propensity for overeating bothered his father, it was about to flip the other way and develop into a much greater problem, one that would threaten Randolph's physical wellbeing. Randolph's self-imposed starvation diet – a sign if ever there was one of just how deep-rooted his unhappiness had become – began towards the end of his time at prep school. The masters and subsequently Lady Galloway were once more at a loss as to what to do with him. And yet it was in the midst of the starving and the not smiling or laughing, the growing inferiority complex and the terror of the war, that the plans were finalised for Randolph to begin at Harrow School in the Easter term of 1943.

The memory of the First World War hung over Harrow School like a spectre, but now the school buildings themselves were in danger. That Harrow, merged with Malvern School since the year before, had chosen to stay on the hill placed it at great risk, not of direct attack, but of German pilots losing their way or dropping excess loads after bombing London. Parents, sensing the immediate danger, had begun to withdraw their sons, so that between the summer of 1940 and January 1941 the numbers in the school fell by almost a quarter. During the Blitz in the autumn of 1940, for example, all the boys were transferred to overnight shelters, with separate daytime shelters, and on the night of 2 October, thirty-three school buildings were hit. The first incendiary bomb fell at the feet of the headmaster as he entered the ARP control station in the war memorial.

In his definitive account, *A History of Harrow School 1324–1991*, Christopher Tyerman writes of how the school had been devastated and consequently shaped by the losses it had sustained during the First World War. Of the 2,917 Harrovians who served, 690 were wounded and 644, including Keith Stewart, were killed. In 1939 at least the school itself had been better prepared. The headmaster, Paul Vellacott DSO, had fought in the First World War and been gassed and taken prisoner. Air-raid precaution planning and classes on air-raid protection had started two years before the Second World War was declared, and detailed plans for dispersing the school during the anticipated aerial bombardment were in place by September 1938 when gas masks were issued.

If Lord and Lady Galloway had any qualms about sending Randolph to a place of such high risk, they did not change course. When Randolph unpacked his bags in the Grove, the same boarding house in which the 10th Earl of Galloway had been placed in April 1848, his parents had effectively placed his safety in the hands of the Senior ARP warden, H. L. Harris. Harris, greatly skilled at his job, would prove deserving of Lord and Lady Galloway's confidence, but there was no escaping the fact that bombing remained a serious threat to the school until the end of the war.

Randolph's housemaster was Mr Leonard Henry, a Scot and a first-rate historian who had been at the school for twenty-five years and housemaster of the Grove since 1935. During the First World War he had served in the Inns of Court Officer's Training Corps, from which he was invalided out. He was a classically educated intellectual of whom a former pupil wrote in the *Harrovian*, 'Joined to [his] power of breathing life into the facts of history was a genius for asking questions of them; this impelled one to think.'

Would the spirit of Harrow and the influence of such a man inspire Randolph? Would he learn to think clearly? Discuss and debate ideas? Would he acquire high standards and methods of scholarship? He would not, but Lord Galloway was not prepared to give up hope. Before Randolph left Cumloden for Harrow, John Edgar, Lord Galloway's head gardener, had taken him for a walk around the grounds and delivered a pep talk about how best to cope with boys tormenting and niggling him. It was a prophetic act of kindness. 'On account of my phobias and complexes as to what I did or did not do,' Randolph wrote, 'I was conspicuous beyond all proportion, and therefore a bit of a drip.'

It defies belief that Lord Galloway could ever have imagined that Harrow in wartime could have done Randolph anything but harm. Beginning life at the school unsettled and disorientated even the healthiest and most stable of boys. One such fellow wrote about it in the *Harrovian*, under the headline 'Random Impressions Of A New-Comer'. 'It was pretty alarming coming here in September, and the latter part of the summer holidays was somewhat clouded by the prospect. My first impression was that all the boys were very big and all the buildings very ugly . . . I shan't be sorry when I cease to be a new boy.'

Randolph was assigned a room with another boy, and they had had a view of the school chapel. The following day he joined the newcomers in the fourth form room where Mr Moore, the head-master who replaced Paul Vellacott, lectured them on the school rules, including the tipping of hats to him or any females connected with the school. There were countless others, which amounted to making Randolph's first week 'utterly wretched'. The Harrow in which he found himself was a long way from its halcyon pre-war days. This was not a place of exaggerated happiness and sunshine, where boys lazed about in their boaters at gloriously sunny speech days with strawberries and cream for tea in the house garden, or raucous bathing in 'Ducker', buying chocolate on the way. Now the boys – sixth formers and new boys alike – spent much of their time underground in the air raid shelters fashioned out of the school's cellars, where they would stay until dawn surrounded by a tangle of bedding. The school was blacked out, and its expenditure had been cut so that only essential purchases were made. The cars that had clogged the high street before 1939 were now barely a trickle. Sirens sounded constantly throughout the night and fire bombs scorched the roofs of the school buildings. 'I seemed to live in a hypnotized world of fright, terror and extreme infidelity,' Randolph wrote.

War and the threat of death and injury was everywhere. Each new issue of the *Harrovian* contained the roll of honour – as had been the case throughout the First World War – so the boys could read of the latest dead, the old boys missing, the prisoners of war, and the wounded. Most of the fresh intake of masters under Mr Moore had fought in the First World War, and were governed by the principles of bravery, patriotism, and honour.

The Corps continued with vigour. Randolph began Junior Train-ing Corps two months after he arrived. On Wednesdays and Fridays he and the other younger boys changed out of their grey flannels and 'bluers' (the Harrovian word for blazers, which replaced tails for normal dress after the First World War) into a khaki army uniform. The boys marched off, guns on their right shoulders, to the parade ground where they continued marching under the orders of Harrow's sergeant majors. As an antidote to this compul-sory activity Randolph joined the chamber concert club. Those evenings, when he would sit among the audience gathered in the music school listening to Mozart and Beethoven, provided solace, albeit brief. He was much happier there.

In all other ways he was profoundly unhappy. As he wrote himself, he was deeply frightened by his environment, and to exist in a state of such high anxiety was extremely exhausting. He grew even weaker for his determination not to take food: 'I never touched my share of butter and sugar and utterly disregarded and ignored my sweet coupons.' Whenever English relatives arrived, bringing with them a lemon Madeira or a canary cake, a small pleasure amid the gloom that surrounded him, Randolph would give it away: 'I was getting progressively thinner, weaker and paler, so the boys called me a rat and a worm, a drip and a twit, even a weed as my shoulders and cheeks hollowed with my immoderate fasting.' While the school marched onwards in its own way, clearing unexploded bombs and keeping watch for enemy planes flying over the build-ings, Randolph's weight dropped to five stone. It was hardly the spirit of strength the masters were looking for. On Friday, 5 November 1943, the epitome of that spirit arrived in bodily form.

The Prime Minister, Sir Winston Churchill, one of Harrow's most famous old boys, descended on the school for what was the fourth of his by then annual visits. Mr and Mrs Moore held a reception for him in the Old Harrovians' Room, after which he was enter-tained with a programme of Harrow songs in Speech Room. He then delivered his rousing speech to the school, intended to inspire future generations of soldiers. The path of the war was hard and long, he told them, with no fixed end. 'However long, however

hard, we shall go forward, and no one can tell at what moment the
resistance of the enemy may break, but that is not our affair; that
is theirs; that is for them.' He talked of the great responsibility that
awaited Britain when the moment of victory came, of the duty and
the 'burden of shaping the future'. Towards the end of his speech,
Churchill delivered a message Randolph had heard countless times
before, only spoken from different lips:

> You young men here, some of you may be in the battle-
> fields or in the high air, others will inherit, will be heirs
> of the victory which your elders and your parents have
> gained, and it will be for you to make sure that what has
> been achieved is not cast away either by the violence of
> passion or by apathy or by sheer stupidity. But let keen
> vision, courage, and humanity guide our steps so that it
> can be said of us that not only did our country do its
> duty in the war in a way which gained lasting honours,
> but that afterwards in the years of peace it showed wis-
> dom, a poise and sincerity which contributed in no small
> degree to binding up the frightful wounds inflicted by
> the struggle.

In Randolph's corner the rally cry fell on stony ground. It was
not 'the violence of passion' or 'apathy' or 'sheer stupidity' that
made him so incapable of stepping into the boots of his predecessors. It was more that the boots did not fit and were becoming
more and more uncomfortable. Randolph's fear of war intensified,
with good reason. In the early hours of Ash Wednesday, 22 February
1944, the school suffered a disastrous raid. A bomb hit the Old
Harrovians' Room, where Churchill had been received three
months earlier, and there were four fires in the east wing of the
Old Schools. The chapel was hit, setting the canopy alight. The
science schools, the Butler Museum and the school stores were
all ablaze. The wooden ventilator on the roof of Headmaster's (a
boarding house) was set alight, too, and the flames were so strong
that only firemen could put them out. The Grove was hit, as was
Moreton's and Malvern School House. While the boys remained
below ground in their shelters, parties of masters tried to bring each
blaze under control, while others combed the buildings looking for

more bombs. A bomb on the chapel stalls burnt itself out and two bombs were found in the gymnasium. Bombs covered the five courts and one had blown a hole near the squash court.

Randolph was in a state of high agitation. The school itself, however, remained strong under threat. Typically, by 9 a.m. the next morning, the holes in the terrace lawn had been neatly turfed over so that there was no sign of the events of the night before. Unexploded bombs were being loaded into wheelbarrows, tarpaulin had been laid over part of the roof of the school stores, and the chancel cleared up. The boys were given an extra hour in bed and then lessons went on as usual.

The following month Lord Galloway arrived at Harrow and took Randolph out to tea. The school stores were not yet restored so they went to the King's Head instead. Lord Galloway had been told of Randolph's unpopularity – often at breakfast the boys in the Grove sniggered at him and said, 'Give the weed some milk and sugar' – and once again he wanted to try and make his son see sense. He lectured Randolph on the importance of being social and cheerful. 'Does it matter?' Randolph responded. 'Yes, it does matter!' replied Lord Galloway.

One advantage of Harrow was that after the first year every boy was given a room of his own, with a coal fire and a wooden bed which let down from the wall. The boys were allowed to furnish the rooms as they wished. It was a domestic improvement, but in Randolph there was no improvement at all. Towards the end of June, escorted by the Grove's matron, Randolph boarded a train to London for a consultation with one of the many psychologists to feature in his life.

Cumloden continued to receive southern relatives. Lady Galloway's sister arrived (she had been thrown to the ground by the fallout of a doodlebug) as did Mrs Francis Jolliffe Raitt and her sister, Aunt Agatha, an ancient lady who repulsed Randolph and had 'the silver stubble of a greying beard beneath her ancient mouth'. After the war-torn landscape of suburban London, with its plumes of smoke and buildings with blown-out, charred windows, Cumloden during the holidays was an even greater relief. Randolph loathed the city – this never changed – and being able to walk through the deer park restored his spirits in a way his masters never

could. Towards the end of the summer of 1944 Lord Galloway
made an announcement. If he saw no improvement in Randolph's
attitude, he would be leaving the school at Christmas. Nothing
could have pleased Randolph more. As the new chauffeur drove
him out of the gates in the family Rolls, headed for the station, the
gamekeeper appeared from the front lodge and cried after him
'Good luck Lord Garlies!'

'I was ill at ease, upset and unhappy,' Randolph wrote of his
return. That term he began seeing a psychologist in south Harrow.
He was getting used to being asked questions by strange doctors,
and he made his way to his first appointment in the slashing rain
on his own. He returned dazed (in his memoirs there is no explanation of why this was; perhaps he had been medicated). He then
began to wander about in a disorientated fashion, alarming matron.
The sirens continued to sound. Randolph sheared off his eyebrows
with a pair of scissors, creating for himself a most curious expression: 'Harrow boys noticed that I had discarded my eyebrows, how
silly I looked . . .' He also became obsessed with having his hair cut
at the local barber's; he deliberately sat on the lavatory – 'the
throne' – back to front; and when faced with normal chairs, he
perched on their edges with a poker-straight back, a peculiarity
that made it into his school report and which Lord Galloway
observed 'must be awfully uncomfortable'. Two days after Randolph's sixteenth birthday, he went back to the psychologist: 'I told
him exactly how I felt, that I was being spied upon and watched,
followed and criticized by members of the school, especially boys.'

One of Harrow's master's, Sergeant Major Robert Banks, who
clearly had a poor grasp of Randolph's emotional state, told him
that if he wished to join the army, he would have to tighten his
shoe straps and behave the way any normal recruit would behave.
Then on 1 December, Sir Winston Churchill arrived at the school
again to deliver his fifth wartime speech, reminding Randolph once
more of all his failings:

> Now that we are marching into a period of great stress,
> of difficulty, now that you will go forward into a world
> where the problems will be made greater by the victories
> which have been and will be won, where duty will become

more compulsive because of the need to live up to what has happened in the past, now at this time, I say, you give to me, by your voices and by your aspect, that feeling that there will never lack a youth of Britain capable of facing, enduring, conquering everything in the name of freedom and for the sake of their dear, loved native land.

Confirmation that he was leaving Harrow came at the beginning of December in a letter from his father. In the New Year Randolph would go to live at The Rough, the Surrey residence of Lord Galloway's relative, Shane Randolph Chichester. There, it had been decided, as Randolph recorded later, he would 'do navvying manual jobs . . . to overcome this sensation of inferiority complex'. His health had become the concern of the whole family. Even Randolph's kind Aunt Catherine, who came to visit, gave him a talk about how he should focus on being an asset in life.

'On Tuesday 12th December before dark, I had my last appointment with Dr Wilson on psychological matters,' Randolph writes of his last week at Harrow. These last days were 'all eaten up in the misery of unpopularity and mocking, humiliating ridicule', but tinged with not an ounce of regret. Randolph tried to keep his departure a secret, but it somehow got out and the boys began taunting him that it was because he was stupid. At Christmas, he left, weighing 5st 11lb and three-quarters, bound for home.

Back at Cumloden his failings became increasingly domestic. The day after he arrived Lady Galloway gave him a talk, but it was to no avail. He showed himself up in the dining room and was considered 'rude, discourteous and impolite'. On another occasion, he attempted to sweep some crumbs off the table using the floor broom. 'In a gentleman's house,' Lord Galloway said, 'one does not use the dirty brushes of servants on one's dinner table.'

Randolph says today that everything his family did, every decision they made regarding his future, was always in the hope that it would bring about some kind of change in his personality. It is impossible to know whether that frightened, weak little boy at Harrow forgave them for this or indeed whether, at this stage, there was anything to forgive. How many parents of their generation and class would not have wanted to mould their heir for future responsibilities? Was their treatment of him simply a display of disciplined, responsible, illiberal parenting? That Lord and Lady Galloway came to rely on a string of expensive London psychiatrists shows how desperate they were becoming. There can be no doubt that Randolph's difficulties were as hard for them to bear as for Randolph. But their desperation would eventually lead them to make a decision with far more destructive consequences than a pair of lost eyebrows.

For now, fresh hope was invested in the influence of Shane and Madelaine Chichester. As planned, on 9 February 1945, Randolph left Scotland for Farnham Station and life at The Rough. Ten days later, Shane Chichester delivered his first homily: '[we] discussed my psychological situation, concerning the unnecessary phobias and complexes which had bugged me. I then had a low opinion of myself yet I was too proud and conceited to accept any criticism. Concentration, that of mine was another thing which worried Shane Randolph Chichester, and when people asked me questions I too often remained silent.'

At the beginning of March Shane gave Randolph a prompt card on which he had written his pearls of wisdom:

1. There are no reasons for fear
2. Happy days are coming
3. The truth, the whole truth and nothing but the truth
4. *Possunt quia posse videnta* [*sic*] – They can because they think they can
5. I shall pause and think before answering questions, then answer frankly
6. I can do all the things through Christ who strengtheneth me. Get into the stride of saying I can.

While Shane continued in his subtle and kindly efforts to correct Randolph's personality, a specialist in psychology and psychiatry began visiting the house. Poor Cousin Shane was continually tried: 'I entered the dining-room to pull down my brows at Shane . . . who then told me that he did not want to see a dark frown but a nice bright smile on my ugly face. I continued both to under and to overestimate myself.'

On V-E Day, 8 May, which Randolph describes as 'a day of magic', he was still at The Rough. Bolstered by the news, he moved his bed so he could lie on a platform outside his bedroom window and look up at the stars. By that August, when war ended with Japan, peace was finally restored to Britain. If only Randolph's life could have been as hopeful. Two months after Britain's victory he left The Rough accompanied by Lord and Lady Galloway. They were headed back to Scotland via London. Randolph was to spend a few days 'with family and psycho-annalists', a slip of the pen that reminds us how much Randolph's future medical treatment would reveal about the annals of psychiatry.

6

Becoming Mrs Budge

'By the end of the war I . . . had lost my husband, not in the horrors of war but to another woman in the Forces,' wrote Lily of peacetime. Her marriage to Jock, having limped through the war years, now gave up the fight. Jock eventually left her for his mistress. Bad luck had also struck Rose. Two years after Lily gave birth to Brebner, Rose, at the age of twenty, gave birth to a baby girl called Ann, an event shortly followed by the disappearance of her husband. She married again, only to find that her new husband liked to drink. She had produced two more children (his), and the family was living in near squalor in a flat by the docks in Leith, then one of the most dangerous and run-down areas of Edinburgh. Only Etta, harbouring no ambitions to leave Duns or escape her life of domestic service, gave Sis any hope. Out of the blue she announced her intention to marry a quiet and gentle shepherd, employed on a nearby farm called Blackerston. Following the wedding, she joined him in his quarters, a wing of The Retreat, a large, round hunting lodge and, just when Sis and Lily had ruled out the possibility of Etta producing a family of her own, in 1947 she announced that, at the age of thirty-seven, she was pregnant. Nine months later she delivered a girl, also called Anne. (If there was a compensation for Etta's comparatively uneventful existence in Duns it was that she remained married to the same man until she went to her grave.)

Lily's single status sustained the Duns gossips, not least because another woman was involved. But Lily shrugged off the talk. Her godchild, May Millar (no relation but the daughter of Sis's friend), then an impressionable child at Duns Primary, remembers being struck by how her godmother seemed wholly indifferent to what people were saying behind her back. She thought that this was either because Lily would not have wasted her energy on the opinions of those who did not know her, or because fresh problems had presented themselves on Jock's departure. Money worries loomed and they consumed Lily's waking hours. She did not expect, nor did she receive, any financial help from Jock. This left her with the sole responsibility of bringing up the boys, added to which was the worry over Andrew's health (he had contracted scarlet fever). Sis and Papa were 'wonderful', Lily later recalled – 'the only financial support I had was from them' – but their donations could only stretch so far and it became apparent that Lily would need to find a full-time job.

Lily later wrote, 'with a sad heart I made my way to the city', but it must be stressed that once again her sadness was not at leaving Duns – after all, it held nothing for her any more, if it ever had – it was much more to do with Sis's insistence that Andrew stay behind. His ear had been perforated and he was now partially deaf. He was also weak from the aftermath of his illness. As Lily observed, 'They were still young enough to look after him and give him the extra care he needed.' It was a decision made with his best interests at heart, but the consequences were to reverberate for years. Andrew was seven and broken-hearted. His father, as he saw it, appeared not to love him – he once shooed him away from Gourlays Wynd as if he were a stray – and now he was being left with his grandmother, who terrified him to the point of making him mute. The child adored his mother and could hardly bear the thought of her disappearing off for a new life with Brebner. But Andrew was a soft, delicate child, prone to tears, and he quietly accepted the situation. Brebner, on the other hand, created a scene. He wanted nothing more than to stay behind with his friends. As a result each looked to the other as having secured the better deal and this jealousy and resentment forced them further apart. (It was to last well into their adult years, when slowly they discovered they liked and then loved each other very much.)

Lily and Brebner arrived in Edinburgh in the spring of 1947, the inaugural year of the Edinburgh International Festival, conceived by Sir Rudolf Byng, conductor of the Glyndebourne Opera, as an optimistic and defiant response to Nazism. The plan was that she and Brebner would stay with Rose in Leith until they were on their feet. On this occasion Sis was right. A grim scene awaited them. Lily was completely unaware of the conditions in which Rose lived. As she walked up the stairwell she saw a mouse, which she thought a bad sign. She peered into the apartment with increasing dread. The walls flaked from damp and many of the floorboards were rotten or splintered. The flat had three rooms – a sitting area, a bedroom, and a kitchen, with a communal lavatory.

That night Brebner was given the sofa and Lily slept on the floor beside the cockroaches. The next morning she determined to find herself a domestic job that would get them out. She was, of course, returning to a profession she loathed, but servants were in demand after the war and needs must. By nightfall she had secured a position as a housekeeper in a large Victorian boarding house in Cluny Gardens, in the bourgeois and respectable area of Morningside, her accommodation provided. She returned to the tenement, collected Brebner and that night they slept in their new basement flat. She began her duties the next day, cleaning a house full of unappreciative students. It was an exhausting, soulless job, but it promised a modicum of stability. Brebner was enrolled in the local school, and just as their lives appeared to be acquiring a rhythm, an incident occurred that led to her tendering her notice.

It is important here to remember Lily's propensity to over-dramatise, but then the 'episode' is odd enough that one wonders how she could have made it up. A student boarder had, apparently, wantonly dropped his trousers and undergarments while she was dusting. Lily's reaction to this absurd display of masculinity (or lack of it) is telling. For all Lily's efforts to widen her horizons, there was still a streak of the Duns prude in her. She could not possibly stay on in Cluny Gardens following such an assault on her dignity, no matter how much trouble it caused her. And so off they went again, this time to the Hotel Marina on Inverleith Row, which was managed by a one-armed man. She did not stay there long – for unknown reasons – and they then moved on to lodgings in Hillside Street, where they lived while she worked in a snack bar in the city centre, frying up eggs and bacon.

The year that followed was the most itinerant of Lily's life. She was constantly moving in and out of jobs as she changed her mind about what was best for Brebner. She could not settle. Edinburgh then was a city of absolute contrasts – the rich and the poor, the New Town and the Old Town. The divisions and distinctions were there even in the architecture of elegant sweeping crescents and squares beside tenements black with soot. While serving up plates of food heavy with grease, she clung to her dream that Brebner would have the chance of a different kind of life. With each trying experience, the bond between them could only intensify. Andrew would later remember, poignantly, 'She loved me, of course, I always felt that, but Brebner was number one son. She adored him. You only had to watch her face when she looked at him.' Lily felt their connection was spiritual. Once when Brebner fell and split his head on the pavement, she recalled that 'the pain was so intense with me, at the same moment, that I couldn't see for a second or two'. On another occasion, when he was knocked down by a taxi, she maintained she felt a sharp pain across her chest. 'I knew he was in trouble but could hardly breathe,' she wrote, 'and a few minutes later he was carried into the house, he had bruises and his ribs were broken, the doctor had to strap my ribs up too, we recovered together.' One imagines the doctor was startled when asked to bandage Lily up, but the idea that she might have appeared comical, eccentric, absurd even, would not have occurred to her. Her feelings did not exist in half measure and for the most part she was quite unable or unwilling to keep her instincts and impulses in check.

With all the toing and froing Brebner fell behind with his schooling. When the results of his eleven plus examination were announced, Lily saw with dismay that he had failed, which brought back the memory of her own childhood disappointment. She understood immediately that if she did not take action, Brebner was in grave danger of treading her path. She had no intention of sending him to Darroch, a secondary modern, which she called the 'the drop-out school'. Instead she enrolled him in Trinity Academy, a semi-private school. Because she could not stretch to the uniform, she joined a warehouse clothes club that offered, for a weekly hire purchase charge of five shillings, £10 worth of clothing, which covered his blazer, cap, and tie.

Lily always had an atrocious grasp of finances and her first financial embarrassment remains murky, probably because it was murky

even to her. What is clear is that she overstretched herself by moving
from the lodgings in Hillside Street to a flat in Leith, which, with
Sis's and Papa's help, she hoped to buy, probably through the
services of a loan shark. Sis was now as sturdy and squat as a little
ox. Her face had fattened and slackened and on the end of her
nose sat round, black-rimmed spectacles. Her breasts had grown
to an enormous size and drooped towards her waist so that there
was a balcony effect dominating the top half of her frame over
which clothes strained at their fastenings. She paced about in
comfortable shoes and carried her handbag tucked under her left
arm, which she kept stiff at a right angle to her body. She still
cooked mutton stew over the fire and gossiped in the town square.
Papa, on the other hand, was as thin and wiry as ever, so that
together they looked like Jack Spratt and his wife. For all Sis's
instincts to control and dominate – now regularly exercised on her
grandson – and for all Papa's inertia, they remained loyal and
willing to help. Recognising Lily's need for security, Sis and Papa
gamely provided her with a deposit. Suffice it to say, the scheme
went wrong. Lily could not keep up the payments, and the bailiffs
arrived to carry away every piece of furniture for which she'd saved.
Brebner, sleeping on balls of their clothes, contracted nephritis.

Lily had no desire to return to Duns, but Sis's support had always
come at a price. She made her feelings clear and within a few days
Lily and Brebner were on a train heading towards the Berwickshire
coastline. In 1949 the Millers were living in the top part of a terrace
in Gourlays Wynd, bought by Sis's brother, Jock. There were Sis,
Papa, Andrew, Jock, and his brother Jim. Two years of power
struggles ensued. Brebner and Andrew fought constantly, but the
real battle raged between Lily and Sis.

The problem was not a new one. Sis persisted in treating Lily as
though she were a child, incapable of making decisions about her
life. Given the disasters that had occurred since Lily had left home,
and the fact that Lily had, when it suited her, fallen back into the
parental safety net, Sis had some justification in assuming Lily
needed her guidance. Her failure, though, was her approach. She
lacked the skills of tact or diplomacy and so her suggestions, however well-meant, were always delivered as orders. Lily felt cramped
and stifled, and this fresh exposure to her mother's domineering

nature reignited all the resentments she had felt during her child-hood. Had these quarrels been purely personal, a simple clash of personality, perhaps they would not have been so fierce, but what truly fanned the flames was that they often erupted over matters concerning the children. Sis had been raising infants from the age of nine and this, she believed, gave her the upper hand. There was also the indisputable fact that when it had suited Lily, she had been quite willing to leave Andrew in Duns in her mother's care. Sis was right about this, at least. But there was no getting round the fact that Sis's way of child rearing repulsed Lily. She was horrified by the idea of physical punishment (Sis once beat Andrew with a bunch of rhubarb), and rather than toughen her boys up, she preferred instead to demonstrate her affection. She liked to em-brace them and kiss them and tell them how much they were loved. There is no doubt that Brebner was overindulged, and that Lily was endlessly overcompensating for the fact that the boys did not have a father or any semblance of family security. But beyond these unconscious motivations, Lily had discerned from her own child-hood that children needed affection.

If anything could have driven Sis and Lily even further apart, it was the issue of Brebner's education. Sis could not imagine him remaining at school beyond an age when it was compulsory. Did Lily not understand he had a duty to contribute to the household? Was she quite mad? Lily saw red on this issue – in fact she possessed no more powers of diplomacy or tact than her mother. Her boy would not face the same indignities as she had. She was going to provide him with a proper education. During the rows that fol-lowed, Jock and Jim were monosyllabic and unfriendly, and the boys continued to fight like tomcats, biting and pinching after dark and bloodying each other's noses.

Life became intolerable. Lily decided to return to Edinburgh, this time for good. She had earnt her keep in Duns by housekeeping and by now had occupied a string of positions. These enabled her to secure a good post before she left. In 1951, she packed her bags and Brebner's – but not Andrew's – and boarded the train for Waverley Station. This time, the circumstances of her arrival were more ordered. She stood outside 42 Blacket Place, a large Georgian house in a sweeping crescent south of Princes Street, and pinched herself. She was to become housekeeper for the McIntosh family. Professor Angus McIntosh was Chair of English Language and General Linguistics at the University of Edinburgh. Lily's service flat was once again in the basement.

Almost immediately Professor McIntosh recognised Brebner's intelligence and engineered a meeting with his friend and colleague along the crescent at number eighteen, Richard Ellis, Professor of Child Life and Health. Brebner was fourteen and developing into a fine-looking boy. He was tall and fair-skinned like Jock, but with a quieter, more refined manner. He was naturally bright and intellectually curious, like his mother. Professor Ellis had married late, and his two children, a boy and a girl, were still too young to share their father's many passions, such as chess and oriental art, and the professor secretly yearned for a protégé whom he could 'bring on'. Brebner too had reached the stage when he needed a man in his life – not so much a stepfather to supplant him in his mother's affection, but a mentor, a guiding hand. He later cited the professor as one of the great influences in his life, adding that he had 'saved him'.

The professor's home was splendid, decorated with impeccable taste: oriental rugs on the polished floorboards, artfully hung oils on the high walls, and antique glass in display cabinets on strategically placed tables. Brebner had never seen such treasures, nor known such wealth. This was family money, and there were two further properties – a house in Hertfordshire and a country cottage twelve miles outside Edinburgh. The friendship began with after-school visits, while Lily was at work down the road for Mrs McIntosh. While she cleaned and shopped and ran the house, Brebner learned about art, antiques, and the rules of chess. Before long his visits to number eighteen progressed to overnight stays and in time he was joining the Ellises on their family holidays. Man and boy were even physically alike.

Lily quietly accepted Brebner's new attachment. She was never invited to join the party to the country cottage or the house in Hertfordshire, and she suspected that the professor viewed her with a degree of contempt that was born of her class and his assumption that she was failing her son. Considering the sacrifices Lily was making to safeguard Brebner's future, and the discontent this had caused within her own family, she would have had just cause to correct such a blatant underestimation of her character. But she said nothing, seeing the overall benefit of this civilising influence in her son's life. Instead, Mrs McIntosh's silver had never gleamed so brightly.

Nearly five years had passed since Lily's separation from Jock, but they had not yet divorced. Just as it had taken one pregnancy to begin their marriage, it took another to bring it to its official end. In September 1951 Lily became pregnant by a man called Jimmy Budge. Exactly how Lily met Jimmy Budge remains unclear. She liked to walk in Holyrood Park, where he was working as a gardener, so perhaps she met him there. It is no coincidence that he entered her life at a time when Brebner appeared to be leaving it. Jimmy was only twenty-eight years old, seven years her junior. He looked like Fred Astaire, only after too much dancing. Considering his youth, he had craggy, worn features, and a quiet, melancholic manner. He had been brought up in Abbeyhill, a rough area next to Holyrood Palace (Lily would go there occasionally, later with their son, Benjamin, and they would sit round the fire and eat squares of white bread covered in jam). Much like Lily, Jimmy was poorly educated. He was not a charismatic man – not the kind to juggle oranges or fly a bright kite – but he was not unkind to her, as Jock had been, and he was a hard worker.

The pregnancy was unplanned but Lily was delighted, once again caring very little about how it might look to anybody else. She had never relinquished her dream of a happy family, and now that Brebner was spending more time with the professor, and Andrew was back in Duns with Sis, Jimmy provided a second chance. He wanted to marry her, but first she had to persuade Jock to agree to a divorce. This became easy once she told him she was pregnant.

The lead up to their marriage was predictably fraught. The first blow came when Jimmy lost his job in the park, bad luck for which Lily was partly to blame. While out strolling one evening, she had dared him to scale a wall of the palace and pick her a flower. Eager to please, he obliged and was swiftly bundled into a police car and taken off to the station. He was not charged for trespass but he was promptly sacked. He then took a manual job with the Scottish and Newcastle Breweries like his father. The next problem to present itself was Brebner and the manner in which he discovered the pregnancy. Lily's condition hardly showed and she put off telling Mrs McIntosh. Brebner knew that she went to the Elsie Inglis Hospital, but he did not understand this meant maternity. It was a neighbour who filled him in. The McIntoshes took it just as badly. They could not keep a housekeeper with an illegitimate child. Lily was asked to leave.

Lily and Brebner moved to dingy lodgings in 19 Warrender Park Crescent in Bruntsfield. Brebner was furious at having to leave Blacket Place. As he later admitted, he was an 'absolute shit' to Jimmy Budge. He had coped well without the steadying weight of a paternal hand on his shoulder, and besides, what guidance he needed was provided by Professor Ellis. Jimmy was too young to win his respect and too diffident to command it.

Just as Lily's marriage to Jock had been on Jock's terms, so was the divorce. He petitioned, as the wronged party, citing her residing address as the maternity hospital. The decree absolute was granted on 6 June 1952, exactly one week before Lily gave birth to her third son, Benjamin Richard Ellis Budge, named after Jimmy's father and in gratitude to the professor. She held off registering his birth until after the marriage, which took place in a registry office in Morningside on 1 July.

Despite their marriage, Mr Budge has only a walk-on part in this story. He too liked to drink – it was to be his undoing – and to gamble, which also became an addiction. It is often maintained that men who need a woman to make a success of their lives rarely ever succeed, but still, it was Jimmy who helped Lily, not because he possessed any qualities of greatness – he did not – but because marriage to him enabled her to buy a house and because his failings fuelled her determination to succeed – to move further away from the past.

There is a photograph of her six weeks after Benjamin's birth. Her arms are thin and sinewy under the puff sleeves of her summer dress, and already her waist is back to Pocket Venus proportions. There is no maternity fat on her stomach and her chest is so flat it is hard to imagine her breast-feeding. Her face appears simultaneously thin and lumpy, rather like that of an old boxer. She could have looked better, to put it mildly, but despite this, she was happy. She had a purpose once more, and with Jimmy working, she could give up housekeeping and become a mother again.

Jimmy Budge with Andrew and Benjamin in Duns Public Park in 1953 during one of Lily's stressful trips home to Sis.

7

Lobotomised patients make good citizens

By 1952 Randolph had spent six years living with the label of schizophrenic. The conclusive diagnosis – rejected years later as hasty – had been made in 1946 at St Andrew's, a psychiatric hospital in Northampton. It is important to stress here that the method of diagnosis in the 1940s was different from that used today. Before the Second World War schizophrenia had already been identified by two psychiatrists using two competing models developed in the late nineteenth and early twentieth centuries. The first, Hans Kraepelin, looked for signs of precocious dementia, whereby young people became acutely disengaged from life, blunted, and withdrawn (*dementia praecox*). The second, Eugen Bleuler, who invented the term 'schizophrenia', looked for signs of a 'fragmented mind' and believed patients to be properly mad with the presence of voices and delusions. Today many psychiatrists believe that their predecessors diagnosed and treated schizophrenia from a position of ignorance. The problem was more that those psychiatrists were working to rigid models and they did not yet possess the knowledge or experience of other psychiatric conditions, which in turn would have equipped them to think laterally. As a result they were unable to come up with alternative diagnoses even if a patient did not quite 'fit' what they understood to be 'schizophrenic'.

If Randolph were diagnosed today, it is probable that he would not be labelled a schizophrenic at all. Certainly, psychiatrists would look for other explanations for his behaviour before settling on schizophrenia. For example, many of Randolph's early behavioural patterns are symptomatic of Asperger's Syndrome, a mild form of autism that affects one's ability to socialise normally. (Certainly Randolph's extraordinary memory and propensity for listing dates, names and birthdays throughout his memoirs suggest at least one symptom of autism.) But Asperger's Syndrome was not properly identified in Britain until 1981, when the original academic paper was finally translated from German into English.

Still, Randolph was a product of his time. A schizophrenic was what doctors thought him to be and a schizophrenic was how he was treated. Following the diagnosis he was subjected to insulin coma therapy, a procedure which is now regarded as an absurd quack remedy, highly dangerous, barbaric, and unsuccessful. When Randolph received the treatment it was just becoming known in Britain, although it had been written about as early as 1937 in Vienna, where experiments had been conducted on schizophrenics in the Vienna Clinic. The treatment, for which patients had to be admitted into hospital, involved injecting them with insulin – under strict medical supervision – and thus inducing a deep hypoglycae-mic coma lasting roughly twenty minutes, although this varied and most were drowsy for two hours. It was thought that the effects of this deep coma, if properly induced, could sometimes alleviate the symptoms of schizophrenia, although in the 1960s this was resol-utely rejected. The procedure carried the risk of brain damage and seizures, caused by a too rapid reduction in blood sugar levels, but at the time doctors dismissed these risks by maintaining that they were negligible with good practice. In Randolph's case the pro-cedure failed spectacularly. Thirty-eight years later, when he was once again in hospital and heavily medicated, he wrote what he called his 'testimony' – his own account of his psychiatric case history, which has been corroborated by various medical examin-ations conducted over the years. 'In my early adolescence I had a round of insulin,' he wrote, 'giving rise to behaviour of a turbulent origin, though outbreaks were few and far between.' Whether or not the insulin coma therapy damaged Randolph's brain is hard to say, since what was to follow was even more barbaric.

It was a time of anguish for Randolph and his family. Randolph periodically lost control and became violent. Later Lily was to main-tain that the final straw for his parents had been when Randolph became violent towards a woman, never named, within the grounds of Cumloden. The identity of the victim and the time of the attack has remained a secret, although Lily always said it was serious in nature and as a result very well concealed. Years later, when a new generation of Stewarts began to ask questions, they too found that the silence surrounding Randolph still existed. The few retainers left at the house refused to talk of the past, and for everybody else it was considered too painful, a closed chapter best left unexamined.

If Lord and Lady Galloway's haste at subjecting their son to insulin coma therapy seems inappropriate within the context of modern medicine, their decision to lobotomise him seems nothing short of butchery. That year, 1952, when Randolph was twenty-three years old, they asked him to pack a trunk for a stay down south. He assumed that he was going on holiday to the seaside. In fact, he was taken to St Mary's Hospital, Paddington, London, where he was lobotomised.

Three years before, in 1949, Professor H. Olivecrona, member of the staff of professors of the Royal Caroline Institute, presented the Nobel Prize for Medicine to Dr Egas Moniz, the first ever professor of neurology at the University of Lisbon, for his discovery of the 'frontal leucotomy', the proper term for lobotomy. 'Frontal leucotomy,' said Professor Olivecrona, 'despite certain limitations of the operative method, must be considered one of the most important discoveries ever made in psychiatric therapy, because through its use a great number of suffering people and total invalids have recovered and have been socially rehabilitated.'

Egas Moniz and his loyal assistant, Almeida Lima, had conducted the neurological experiments that came to be considered 'the beginning of modern pyschosurgery' back in 1936. With Moniz giving instructions from his wheelchair (he had been crippled and left shaky after a psychotic patient shot him), Lima drilled a hole into the top of the skull of their human guinea-pig, and with an implement similar to an apple corer, they had severed the leukos, or white fibres connecting the frontal lobes to the rest of the brain.

Certain psychoses, Moniz had observed, particularly schizophrenia and severe paranoia, involved recurrent thought-patterns that dominated normal psychological processes. The way to force them to be normal, he had reasoned, was to sever the nerve fibres between the frontal lobes (associated with psychological responses) and the thalamus (a relay centre of sensory impulses at the centre of the brain). Moniz's prefrontal leucotomy, as he called it, was considered brilliant. But in the din of the applause few paid attention to the professor's words of caution. The prefrontal leucotomy, he had begged, was to be performed only as a last resort.

It was too late. His psychosurgery had ignited the interest of too many other doctors. By the end of 1936 Walter Freeman, a neurologist at George Washington Hospital, Washington D.C., and his colleague James Watts, an American neurosurgeon, had already performed twenty lobotomies (as they were now called). They later modified Moniz's technique, making holes on either side of the head and using a steel probe with its end flattened, rather like a butter knife. The two doctors operated in much the same way as Moniz and Lima; Freeman, a neurologist and neuropathologist, had never qualified as a surgeon. Sitting in front of the patient, sedated with local anaesthetic, he would use his knowledge of the brain's geography to guide Watts's hands. In order to monitor the progress of their operations, while Watts fiddled about inside, Freeman engaged the patient in chatter, using its gradual deterioration to monitor how much of the lobes were yet to be destroyed. He often encouraged the clueless patient to sing 'Mary Had a Little Lamb'. Sometimes he joined in.

The transcripts of their conversations made it possible for the doctors to pinpoint the exact moment at which some aspect of personality vanished. Watts and Freeman were considered stars. They took the operation further and began promoting it as a remedy for all human sadness. They became rich, and from their considerable earnings published *Psychosurgery in the Treatment of Mental Disorders and Intractable Pain* in 1950. 'This work', it said, 'reveals how personality can be cut to measure.'

Following Freeman's further development of the transorbital leucotomy, many surgeons used an ice pick. For this the patient was anaesthetised by ECT shocks, the eyelids were lifted, and a sharp stiletto-like 'leucotome' was hammered through the orbital bone to a depth of 2.5 inches, one incision through each eye socket. Freeman's post-operative advice to his patients was to 'wear a pair of sunglasses'. He began to attract criticism as early as the 1940s.

He performed a total of 3,600. Even so, in the early 1950s, when
Lord and Lady Galloway made their decision – and it was their
decision, not Randolph's – the leucotomy/lobotomy had become
fashionable, pioneering even, and we must view their decision
about Randolph within this context. The lobotomy was thought of
as a tool to control undesirable behaviour in asylums, hospitals,
and psychiatric clinics throughout Britain and America. (In 1951
over 18,000 patients in the USA had been lobotomised.) President
Kennedy's sister, Rosemary, had been lobotomised. So, too, was
Tennessee Williams's sister, also called Rose, while he was away at
college. In his short story, 'The Resemblance between a Violin Case
and a Coffin', Williams describes the shock of seeing her drift away:
'I saw that it was all over, put away in a box like a doll no longer
cared for, the magical intimacy of our childhood together.'

By the end of the 1950s more than 50,000 people in America
and Europe had been rendered 'zombies'. These people were
apathetic and sad, with reduced drive and initiative. Thousands
were women who had been suffering from depression. A large
proportion were difficult children and rebel adolescents exactly
like Randolph, who more often than not had no idea of what was
happening to them.

Lord and Lady Galloway are no longer alive to defend their
decision. Sara Stewart, however, who is destined by marriage to
become the 14th Countess of Galloway, befriended Lord Galloway
two years before his death. She is deeply interested in the history
of the Earls of Galloway, not only those of the twentieth century,
and she helps make sense of a complex, somewhat extreme situation. 'The view was that Garlies, poor man, was incredibly unbal-
anced and that he was at risk of doing some very serious damage.
They were at their wits' end and frightened about his capabilities.
It's horrifying to think about him being so misunderstood,' she
says, 'I'm not excusing it, or condoning it. Today, he would have
been handled differently – care has advanced so much – but then
it was a taboo subject if your child was mentally disturbed. Who
knows how many children were shut away in darkened rooms and
never heard of again? After the operation, it was swept under the
carpet.'

On his death bed Lord Galloway avoided the subject completely

Lord and Lady Galloway at the coronation in 1953, a year after
Randolph was lobotomised.

– it was considered by everybody, including Sara Stewart and her husband, Andrew, the future earl, to be too painful to bring up.

'One has to remember that Lord Galloway was a peer of the realm and very, very British,' Sara Stewart says. She recalls Lord Galloway as a sick, lonely old man, but one prone to the occasional blast of humour.

> He was not an emotional man on the outside; he may well have been underneath, but he did not show it. I suspect he felt terribly let down – maybe he felt guilty himself that he had produced a son who wasn't up to the mark in simple terms, who couldn't possibly have carried on in that expected way. I think he was completely bewildered. He refused to talk about it. It was an enormous disappointment to him. Of course there were always rumours and the piecing together of bits and pieces, but there was a blanket of silence around Garlies. You simply did not speak out of turn, like I am doing now, you just kept quiet.

Within just ten years of lobotomies becoming a trend, they were discredited and are now hardly ever performed. As Randolph's GP wrote in a report years later, Randolph had been subjected to 'in present medical opinion . . . [a] totally unjustifiable treatment . . . under his father's orders'. He goes on to say that indeed Randolph 'may well have grounds for thinking that this crippling operation is bound to have affected him for the rest of his life'.

After Randolph's leucotomy in 1952 – following which he says he 'took a while to come to the day' – he spent fifteen years, except for a period between 1958 and November 1961, in the mental wing of the Crichton Royal Hospital, a psychiatric institution in Dumfries. The doctors were, he remembered later, 'indifferent to me', although, mercifully, 'they improved latterly'. The Christmas of 1952, however, was spent at Cumloden. On 27 December, Shane wrote to him from The Rough, a letter paradoxically full of love and compassion, but with all the old touches, such as 'Think only of doing your duty and helping others.' This had remained Shane's approach. Fulfilling his duty to his parents was the only way Randolph would be able to eradicate his doubts and fears – which seems an astonishingly crass and simplistic approach considering what he had endured. And yet it is so sincerely expressed, so indicative of a mentality that believes any problem can be overcome with the application of self-discipline. Randolph, 'old chap', as Shane addressed him, was expected to do his duty towards others at all times and when this was tough, Shane was there for guidance. The letter finishes with Shane reminding Randolph of his prompt cards. Forget about health and medicines, he counselled him, and on no account talk about them or write about them to anybody else – which is a measure of how terrified the family were of people finding out what had happened.

This letter set the tone for the subsequent years: a tragedy to be managed and not spoken of. Randolph continued to receive sweet, gentle, and affectionate letters from his mother, albeit written in the kind of tone a loving mother might adopt with her ten-year-old child. Most begin 'My Darling Garlies' and are signed off, in her loopy hand, 'Mama'. In one, Lady Galloway writes, 'Thank you so much for the delicious "chocs" and Dada and I are enjoying them enormously and also for the lovely card which has pride of place over the clock in the drawing room!'

A few letters from Lord Galloway to Randolph survive. They are more formal than those sent by his wife, but certainly not as bleak and loveless as Randolph came to remember latterly. In one, sent on 1 March 1962, on Royal Scottish Automobile Club headed paper (Lord Galloway's club in Glasgow), Lord Galloway writes, 'My dear Garlies, Just a line to remind you that we expect you for LC [luncheon] on Thursday 8th.' Following an observation about the cold weather, he writes, 'I hope you got safely back to Dumfries last Saturday. Looking forward so much to seeing you for LC on Thursday the 8th, Much love from Dada.'

It is hard to imagine the nature of their relationship now. As Sara Stewart observes, it is most likely that Lord Galloway's anguish over Randolph's inability to step into line had been replaced by a deep sadness. Randolph had not made the miracle recovery the lobotomy had promised and Lord Galloway had to live with the consequences of that decision. It cannot have been easy to bear. A letter sent by Shane suggests that after the operation a climate of tension prevailed, and Randolph attests to having suffered 'a multiple deterioration'.

Still, years later, the onus seems to have been placed on Randolph to pull round and behave. In a letter he received in November 1961, for example, Shane tells him that while he understands that his experiences must be a great source of worry to him, he must think of his 'dear Father and Mother', who were also greatly anxious and desired to see him happily at some work or other. Randolph must continue to try to make them happy, he writes. Randolph had taken up smoking a pipe but Shane told him that this must be confined to the garden since the smoke greatly irritated Lord Galloway. It was the same old story. Shane reasoned that even if Randolph could not see clearly about how to bring about his own happiness, he was surely able to see a way of helping those around him. Due to an injury to his left arm, Shane's typing skills were hampered, and it took him two weeks to send a follow-up letter (even then he was typing with one hand). In this letter of 26 November, he returns to the old theme of pleasing Lord and Lady Galloway. He types, using red ribbon, 'HAVE YOU MANAGED THIS?'

Twenty years after Shane posed this question, Randolph, by now married to Lily, was back in a psychiatric hospital, this time in the Royal Edinburgh. There, he wrote his 'Testimony', in which he recalled the aftermath of the lobotomy:

> I turned negative . . . more negative than I had ever been, not wanting to or feeling inclined to do anything useful or constructive . . . negation prevailed from time to time with intermittent spells of violence, which has happened from ten to twenty times within the last three decades, and often when under the influence of drugs . . . for years I have lived in an evasive and negative frame of mind, always seeking outlets from reality's challenge. This page and few lines will prove insufficient, insufficient fortitude as an account for a spirit of aggro on my part . . . For more than enough of my life has been wasted, in places such as the Crichton Royal Institution and the English Mental Home of St Andrew's Hospital, Northamptonshire, where I had insulin . . . To be in gaol

or an asylum would be the last thing wanted, shut off from the outside air and from society. Drugs and pills are worse than useless, if anything they are harmful. Melleril makes me feel worse, and the last couple of mornings I have awakened with headache giddiness through the drugs.

Today, when Randolph is asked about his lobotomy a haunted look crosses his face. It takes a long time to draw him to speak on the subject, and even then, great patience is required, since it is often difficult for him to articulate his thoughts. He usually drifts off with a sad, broken look in his eye, as if still trapped by the horror of the memory and still bound by Shane's advice: Keep quiet. Say nothing of it to anybody. When he does finally offer a few words – a sentence here and there – they are made all the more powerful for the effort of will, the courage behind them. 'They were, in several ways, embarrassed of me,' he said once of his parents. 'They wanted a change, but it was a change for the worst. I thought I was going to the seaside. It was flung upon me.' Randolph can see no further than the terrible effects the operation had on his life. When once asked to consider the idea that Lord and Lady Galloway, however misguided, might have thought they were acting for the best, he became agitated: 'It wasn't for the best! It wasn't!' he said, with great, uncharacteristic passion. 'It changed me for the worse. I was never the same again.' It is a sad truth to which there can be no adequate response.

8

Carnival of the Animals

In 1953 Brebner approaching his seventeenth birthday, found himself outnumbered by Budges: three to one. As he saw it, marriage to Jimmy had placed his mother in the enemy camp. There was baby Budge, too, a spoilt and indulged toddler prone to throwing tantrums to which Lily succumbed. This new domestic set-up pushed Brebner further into the ever-widening embrace of the Ellises (when Lily had gone into labour with Benjamin, Mrs Ellis had taken Brebner off to Skye on account of possible 'psychological damage'). He had since been given a room of his own at 18 Blacket Place, and a job working as a junior laboratory assistant in the pathology department of the university, a post secured on the basis of Professor Ellis's connections. The ties to Lily were loosening.

Still, after twenty years as a Miller and another miserable fifteen as a Millar, Lily greatly enjoyed signing her new name. It confirmed her new identity as wife and mother. The change was timely. It was the 1950s, after all, when women were depicted as domestic goddesses, capable of delivering to the table a delicious roast while somehow managing to look like debutantes. Lily did not quite live up to the image. She smoked heavily, usually John Players, which she let hang from her lips. Her granddaughter, Susan, has a lasting memory of her, smoking, ironing, and drinking tea, all at once. The cigarette would burn down dangerously close to Lily's lips and the ash would always teeter precariously, about to fall on the washing.

In the absence of polish, Lily still looked better than she had for some time. She and Jimmy now had a mortgage on a large flat in Marchmont Street in Marchmont (they were later to move to Gilmore Place, which had four attic bedrooms), which provided her with the long-awaited sense of security. Jimmy was a man of few words – theirs was not a marriage of minds or even personalities – but he worked hard, which in turn enabled Lily to spend time with Benjamin. Her playfulness and natural optimism returned. Sis remained the only blot on the landscape, and at times she rather blocked out the sun. The Budges visited Duns often – Lily liked to see Andrew and Sis liked to see the baby – but these trips never ceased to be a trial and afterwards Lily often suffered crushing headaches. Lily's headaches, both menstrual and premenstrual, had become so bad, in fact, that she was now under the care of the Bruntsfield Hospital, the Edinburgh hospital for women and children. Medication seemed to be having little effect, and so after a particularly violent headache following a trip to Duns, her doctor referred her to an almoner.

The interview was scheduled for 23 October 1953, and the almoner was briefed to identify any factors, apart from the physiological, that might be making Lily ill. Lily never talked openly about her feelings for her mother, or rather, whenever she did, she applied a positive gloss. For example, in *No Silver Spoon*, she wrote, 'My parents were wonderful people.' Her true feelings, never discussed, buried even by her, were far more complicated. On 23 October, however, under careful questioning, she could not keep up the act. She broke down and confessed. 'This patient seems to labour under a severe conflict over her relationship with her mother,' the almoner's report began, 'which may have a bearing on her headaches.'

The comments and observations that followed are extraordinary for the fact that had they not been preserved in Lily's medical notes, there would be no tangible record of Lily's true feelings for Sis. But here it all was, in black and white, for her doctor to see: Sis was making Lily ill. 'It seems the mother is of an excessively dominating nature,' the almoner continued. 'From childhood until the time of her first hasty and ill-considered marriage, patient was dictated to about every detail of her life. All friends and activities were prescribed by her mother and she was made to work after school hours from the age of 10. Any attempt at self-assertion was met by the threat that she "would be punished for it some day".'

Lily went on to confess that her childhood fear of expecting punishment for contradicting Sis still existed, although she acknowledged that now she could at least 'grasp the unreasonableness of her mother's attitude'. There was no question mark over her happiness with Jimmy, she insisted, it was more that Sis would not leave them alone, and 'consistently tried to interfere with the upbringing of the boys'. (It is worth noting here that when Andrew Millar met his father years later, Jock blamed the collapse of his marriage to Lily on her parents.) She went on to admit, too, that she felt Sis had never forgiven her for ensuring that Brebner had a full education. The headaches were, Lily thought, a direct consequence of a profound sense of guilt. On the one hand she understood perfectly well that Sis should not be allowed to interfere, but on the other she could not help feeling disloyal and guilty for her brewing resentment.

'This last severe headache followed a week-end at Duns,' the almoner concluded, 'where there had been the usual unremitting criticism by her Mother. The patient herself thinks that unconsciously she expected the headache as "a punishment for not liking her mother".' On the basis of this report, on 11 November Lily's physician at the Bruntsfield Hospital wrote to her G. P. There was no loss of weight; her facial muscles were noted as being very wasted, but the doctor added 'I remember seeing her at the Elsie Inglis and this apparently she has had for a long time'; her cardiovascular system was normal; and her chest was clear. There was nothing abnormal in her central nervous system, an X-ray of her skull was negative, and her retinae were 'quite normal'. In conclusion, the doctor wrote: 'I feel that there is a large psychological element in these headaches and I enclose a copy of our Almoner's report which might interest you . . . These headaches are no new thing and go back for at least 17 years. I think she would be greatly helped with a talk with Dr Young and I will try and arrange for this.' Whether Lily pursued ongoing treatment is unclear. Her medical notes show no further mention of the headaches. Perhaps after this cathartic admission they went away.

The following year, Brebner was conscripted and sent to Kowloon as part of the medical corps, which gave Lily something new to fret about. She missed him terribly, despite her second family, and she worried herself to distraction. 'I could hear the noise of gun-fire, and felt my son was in danger,' she wrote later. 'It turned out that there was an uprising in Kowloon, and the hospital where he was working was more or less under gun-fire, he and another boy were helping with the wounded in the midst of the fire.' She posted Brebner long letters full of protestations of her love, which he later burnt for being too embarrassing.

With life looking steadier and Brebner away, Lily called for Andrew to join her in Edinburgh. He was fourteen years old by now and one cannot help but think the request was long overdue. Andrew had had a miserable time growing up in Duns. Sis had reared him much as she had Lily, with a mixture of harsh discipline, limited opportunities, and fierce loyalty. Papa had remained quietly in the background, although in the absence of Jock, Andrew had come to think of him more as a father. Andrew contemplated Lily's offer but declined. He was not particularly content, but recognised that he cared even less to play substitute to the object of his greater resentment – Brebner. He remained in Duns.

Benjamin was growing up fast and Lily fixed on the idea of a private education, an ambitious notion given Jimmy's wages, and a sign too that there had been no let up in her fight against Sis's ideas. Jimmy had virtually no say in the matter. His diffident manner had gradually encouraged Lily into the role of decision maker, and Brebner, back living with them and working in the laboratory, began to see that his mother was becoming impossible in her relations with her husband – bossy, domineering, and determined to get her own way. In 1957 Lily enrolled Benjamin at Daniel Stewarts, a prestigious independent school in Edinburgh. Brimming with pride, she took a photograph of him in his prep school uniform. The ever-present Professor Ellis is behind him, with a guiding hand placed on his shoulder. Benjamin beams out of the picture, toothless and with a scabbed knee. A tie, striped in the school colours and far too long for him, dangles below his felt blazer. This son would make it to university. In the end, Jimmy and Lily were both right: the fees did cripple them and yet Benjamin was the first of the family to go to university.

Lily longed for another child. Gilmore Place was big enough, Jimmy was in work, and wouldn't it be too lovely for Benjamin to have a sibling near his own age? She fell pregnant, a stroke of luck considering she was over forty, smoked, and complained constantly of unspecified 'gynaecological' problems (a foretaste of her hypochondria). But in the first trimester of her pregnancy she miscarried and then suffered a haemorrhage. She was heartbroken, and for years afterwards spoke of the baby as The One I Lost.

By way of compensation, she put her name on a list to foster children born to unmarried mothers. She began by taking on one or two infants, and then decided to start an independent day nursery where working mothers could drop off their children for a morning of play. Lily jumped through few administrative hoops to achieve this (a marvel considering the stringent laws enforced today), although she took what she referred to as 'a crash course in child psychology and child care'. Her charges adored her, probably because in many ways she was as childlike and unselfconscious as they were. On one occasion, Brebner switched on the television set to find Lily's face peering from the screen. She was surrounded by a group of children dressed as woodland creatures, mostly badgers, squirrels, and moles, bearing names such as Tufty Fluffy Tail, Minnie Mole, Naughty Willie Weazel, Mrs Owl the Teacher, and Policeman Badger. Tufty badges were pinned on their fur. They broke into the Tufty song advertising to Scotland's young the importance of road safety (24,500 clubs operated across Britain – 'I ran the largest in Scotland,' Lily boasted) and at the end of the bulletin, Lily and the smiling creatures handed the presenter a hedgehog and waved to the camera.

Towards the end of the 1950s, with her little nursery flourishing, Lily fell in love with a house, a large Edwardian sandstone villa that sat at the foot of Liberton Brae, an Edinburgh suburb built in the inter-war period to accommodate the growing middle class. It had four public rooms, four bedrooms, and an annexe for a maid: too big for a family of four, but it carried much potential for Lily's twin business ventures: to expand the nursery into a larger kindergarten, 'one of the first in the city', as well as running a bed and breakfast for the growing number of foreign students in the city. Jimmy agreed, of course. She named it The Cisandra and no sooner had they moved in than she began making changes. The large morning room was to be the nursery and the bedrooms upstairs were assigned to paying boarders, students, or foreign tourists attracted to the city by its famous festival, which had been running since 1947. She acquired three cats and three dogs, two of which were beloved toy poodles that soon bred a litter of pups (a favourite was later mown down by a van which devastated her and moved her to doggerel). In the spirit of expansion, she also took from the RSPCA a cluster of hedgehogs, two red squirrels – 'the only two in captivity, they were found injured in a net in the Lake District' – a lame duck, a rhesus monkey, 'huge like a gorilla!', and a variety of injured birds who lived in an aviary she erected in the corner of the morning room. There were also an injured fox cub, which bit her and sent her to hospital, and six incapacitated owls, including Boo Boo, 'the most intelligent and lovable of all', also supplied to her by the RSPCA. The children loved being in such close quarters with the birds of prey, and Lily shared their delight. 'I was always sad when they finally left,' she wrote of the owls, 'they were given complete freedom, some decided to stay longer than others.'

She took her menagerie extremely seriously. She loved the birds quite as if they were human, and would become morose and preoccupied if one fell sick or made no progress. She sought advice from anybody she thought might help. Once she wrote to Mr J. J. Yelland, curator of birds at London Zoo, about one of her owls, 'an adult bird badly injured'. 'It is nearly always difficult to diagnose illnesses of birds,' he wrote back, 'but if your bird is breathing and the bowels appear normal, it is doubtful whether you can do more than tempt the bird to eat natural foods such as mice, voles, young rats, beetles, woodlice and so on.'

'I nursed him back to health and he became very tame,' she later said proudly. She adhered to the veterinary advice relating to their care, learning how roughage in the form of fur, feather, and small bones aids a bird's digestion; how warmth revives a sick bird, particularly a temperature 'of up to 80°F inside the cage'; how to assist a bird that has trouble nesting ('sometimes the cramp of the oviduct occurs and this can generally be relieved by heat treatment, leaving the bird quiet in a very warm place').

Often, her duties were grisly. The mice had to be 'freshly killed and still warm' and when fed to a bird that had not yet learned to pull them apart with its claws, they were to be cut into small pieces (complete with fur and sawed-up bones). One might wonder how she went about finding a rolling supply of vermin. As with so many other things – babysitting the nursery in a crisis, dealing with run-away dogs, burst pipes, and other such domestic trials – Brebner was always at her beck and call. He was about to marry a pretty young nurse called Dorothy, who over the years would display astonishing patience with Lily's demands. During his visits to The Cisandra, Brebner delivered dead mice and warm carcasses of chicks from the poultry farm, which Lily stored in the fridge next to the sausages and bacon she served to the bed and breakfast guests.

As Lily went from strength to strength, Jimmy diminished in confidence, no doubt sensing he was now on the periphery of his wife's chaotic life. Lily was always in demand, either from the pets, the children or the lodgers, and this left very little space for anybody else. Despite her endless drive – she was absolutely determined to make enough money to ensure they could all remain living in The Cisandra while continuing to educate Benjamin privately – sometimes even she failed to keep pace. On such occasions Brebner, often busy at work in the laboratory, would receive a frantic message saying she urgently needed to leave the house and could he please come round immediately and mind the infants.

The household began to develop a tendency to descend into farce. It was for this reason that Lily's sudden announcement that she intended to adopt a small, sick child was met initially with comical disbelief. But it soon became apparent that she was deadly serious. Little Henry Phillips Jones, born on 25 September 1956 to a woman keen to be rid of him, was terribly poorly. He had severe coeliac disease and had come to Lily as a foster child with the prognosis that he was not long for the world. She had become so attached to his plump little face, his sad eyes and the way he had of clinging to her as though his life depended on it (which it did) that she saw no reason why she should not make him her own. The memory of her miscarriage continued to pain her, but she was now reconciled to the truth that her childbearing years were over. She needed a baby and this baby needed her. Was this not good reason enough? The more opposition she faced, from Brebner, Professor Ellis, and the social services, the more determined she

Brebner, Lily, Benjamin and Paul Budge in the sitting room of
The Cisandra.

became. As she did on countless other matters during this time,
Lily got her way. Henry Phillips Jones became Paul Anthony Budge.

It is difficult to get a clear idea of the exact point at which Lily's
marriage to Jimmy collapsed. At some point he moved out of their
shared room and into a small maid's room at the top of a flight of
stairs leading off the kitchen. Lily never talked about this marriage
breakdown in the way that she had her marriage to Jock, in fact
much later she erased Jimmy's presence in her life completely and
made it appear as if her three boys had been born to the one man.
If one were to hazard a guess at a reason for her silence – most
uncharacteristic – it would probably be that by the end, her opinion
of Jimmy was so low that she could recall no happy memories and
had not a good word to say about him. Unlike her mother, she was
not one for retrospective bad-mouthing (she bore no grudge
against Jock), and so it fits that she preferred to keep quiet. Jimmy's
problems were various, but underpinning all of them were signs of
alcoholism. Rose too was encountering a similar strain with her

second husband. The difference between Rose and Lily was that Rose liked to drink herself. The similarity – and experts in addiction would maintain this was not a coincidence – was that alcohol in some form had come to dominate their adult lives in much the same way as it had dominated their childhood (when it was conspicuous by its absence) and, for that matter, the childhood of their mother.

Domestic unhappiness at The Cisandra was not helped by an accident Jimmy suffered at work. He had changed jobs to become a passenger shunter on the railway and had been clipped by a railway carriage. This affected him badly and he found that his recuperation in a home thronging with animals and children did little to aid his recovery. This seems to have been when he started drinking 'rum by the bucket'. Under the influence he would sometimes become violent, hitting Lily and the children (Paul Budge remembers Benjamin jumping on Jimmy's back and trying to knock him out with a frying pan). He was gambling, too, and the house started looking lighter in knick-knacks.

Jimmy walked out in 1961, shortly after Brebner's marriage to Dorothy. He left behind a mountain of debt but little regret to speak of. Lily divorced him in 1968, and heard no more until March 1981, when she received a call from the Royal Infirmary informing her that he had been picked up on the streets, homeless and close to death. On his deathbed he asked to see Benjamin and Paul Budge. Neither wished to see him again. He died soon after that, his weak will no match for the combined onslaught of bronchopneumonia, hypothermia, alcoholism, and self-neglect. On the death certificate, his brother, George, listed Jimmy's address as his own, an act of kindness to ensure that there might be some aspect of dignity about his death where in later life there had been none.

9

A Crazy House

By the summer of 1965 five years of growing competition had forced Lily to close down her kindergarten. She decided instead to concentrate on turning The Cisandra into a proper bed and breakfast, one that advertised abroad. Even though The Cisandra was operating on a professional scale, there was no question, ever, that she would re-house her creatures, or even reduce their living conditions by placing them outdoors where they belonged. The owls were quite tame and flew overhead in the morning room. Boo Boo, her favourite, liked to perch on the top of the door so he could peer down at the guests eating their supper. Between 9 p.m. and 11 p.m., he was permitted to waddle about in front of the fire playing with Dinky toys and balls of wool. Sometimes he even watched the television beside Lily on the sofa. She was edgy about Boo Boo. She feared his claws would become trapped and broken if the doors slammed shut. Guests were therefore instructed to keep all doors propped open with stops, which meant howling gales blew through the house. There was also a lame duck, which she exercised twice a day in the bath, and the pups born to her poodles, Candy and Pip, who danced about underfoot and threatened to send her guests and tea trays flying. There was a problem with the hot water, which took such an age to heat up that boarders were forced to strip and bathe in the icy Edinburgh air only to scald their hands later when the water bubbled to near boiling point. And to cap it all, there was one resident boarder, an octogenarian called Mr Hamilton, who knocked back whisky and tried to trap Lily in the airing cupboard.

Lily had nine beds and, all things considered, she was lucky to fill them. She ran The Cisandra alone and a climate of chaos

Lily in the garden of The Cisandra in July 1964 with Boo
Boo, her favourite owl, now on his way to enjoying rude
health after being found 'starving and badly singed with
a broken beak' two months before.

prevailed in the house in much the same way as it had when it had
been half-used as a kindergarten. There were not enough hours in
the day, and it was quite normal for the steam iron to be hissing
in the middle of the night and her cigarette smoke to be seen
curling beneath the kitchen door. Lily's life was not made easier
for the fact that she could not drive, although in the spirit of
optimism she later owned a motorcar. She bought the car with
good intentions but in time it became clear she was a poor learner,
and that driving was another casualty of her infinite capacity for

distraction and excitability. She was tolerated at first, but once too often her car veered off towards pavement strollers and caused her passengers to roar 'Lily! Eyes on the road! *Please*', or 'Lily, we usually drop a gear when we take a bend!' Sometimes a passenger would lunge for the wheel. In the end she concluded quite correctly that it was doubtful she was ever going to sit behind the wheel unattended. She kept the car anyway, working on the principle that if she supplied wheels, she'd have a better chance of finding a minder driver to ensure they turned in the direction of her choice. (The hunt for new gratis chauffeurs continued until the day she died, although the car packed up years before that.)

Paul Budge at Willowbrae House School for children with learning difficulties.

By now Benjamin, aged thirteen, was doing well at Daniel Stewarts, and during the holidays he spent much time with Brebner and Dorothy. Often they would return to Duns and stay with Etta and her family at The Retreat, where they could fish and enjoy the countryside. Paul Budge, on the other hand, was faring less well. He had severely tested Lily's natural instinct for mothering. It had been one long battle from the start. While at first he had been a flaxen haired toddler, he had developed into a dark haired child, thin and pale, and always on his guard. In the five years that had followed the arrival of his adoption papers, Lily had ferried him from one hospital consultant to another, grimly determined to find a way of controlling his illness and ensuring he lived as normal a life as possible. He was on a gluten-free diet and had begun to gain weight. From here on, though, the struggle was not purely medical, and she was advised to place him in Willowbrae House School, a residential school for mentally and physically handicapped children.

It was this summer of 1965, between 27 July and 7 September, that Lily experienced six weeks of girlish delight. The object of her joy was Jean François Garrison, a nineteen-year-old French student with a passion for Carl Jung and seances. He had been sent to The Cisandra by his father, via an agency in Paris called Bureau de Voyage Scolaires, in order to brush up his English. Lily and Jean François did not have a love affair, but the episode does demonstrate Lily's flirtatiousness and her endless appeal to those more than thirty years her junior (male and female). She was fast approaching her fiftieth birthday and the menopause, but there is no doubt that, with Jimmy gone, the French guest turned her head. She liked men, particularly if dark and handsome. Among Jean François's letters to her which she preserved carefully in a white drawstring laundry bag, there is a photograph of him standing in his parents' home in the fourth arrondissement of Paris. He is wearing a woolly jumper knitted by Lily and beside him is a human skull. It sets the tone of their friendship.

Lily arranged by letter that she would meet Jean François off his plane. It landed at Edinburgh Airport at 4.40 p.m. on 27 July and she identified him immediately because there was a yellow badge pinned to his lapel and a sticker on his luggage. He instantly thought her 'mediumonic' with 'an intense gaze, a keen look', physically much like his idol, Edith Piaf. It boded well, he thought, although he did notice that she was 'even more than slim, skeletal to some extent', 'old enough to be my mother', and 'more like a gypsy than a Scottish woman'. They travelled back to The Cisandra on the number thirty-one bus. As it rattled down Princes Street, then along the North and South bridges, past endless buildings caked in soot, towards the respectable outlying suburb of Liberton, he declared with a swivel of his heavy-lidded, ink-black eyes that he did not much like Edinburgh. The Scottish men, he observed, were horribly oversized and rough looking, with 'huge red faces' and features without refinement. And the city! *Alors*, such ugly, black buildings, quite different from those in the fourth arrondissement.

Jean François's disdain for the city was quickly overshadowed by astonishment at his landlady. Mrs Budge – this was how he addressed her at first – was unlike anybody he had ever met and The Cisandra was unlike anywhere he had ever stayed. Jean François (now a successful tax lawyer in Geneva) has never forgotten the Ealing comedy-style scenes that unfolded before him. His attraction to Lily was, he says, purely platonic, but he does concede that she was 'quite orientated to men', and that night after night they would sit 'gazing at each other, fascinated by the other's different worlds'. Sometimes they went out, to watch the military tattoo or for a rare spot of sightseeing, but Jean François realised that after his two or three hours of book work, he really preferred to stay in The Cisandra. He thought Lily 'lovely', 'alive', 'eccentric', with 'a great sense of humour', and 'so much energy'. It is easy to imagine the extent to which his attention flattered Lily's ego. She became girlish and skittish and kept him amused with impressions of the other guests. In the evenings, when they were alone, she would fix him with puppy dog eyes and encourage him to tell her stories about the accomplishments of Mesdames Garrisons, the Parisian aunts and other old lady relatives who snapped spoons and broke table-tops during the family seances back in Paris. All this fitted well with her own growing fascination with the occult and what she referred to vaguely as 'unexplained phenomenons [*sic*]'. She possessed, Jean François told her seriously, immense psychic powers. He could tell.

Very quickly they began to discuss the possibility of holding seances in The Cisandra. Lily became carried away, displaying an enthusiasm and an energy that both attracted and frightened her French lodger. She was desperate to connect with the other side, he remembers, to the point where he grew increasingly worried that he might have given birth to an unhealthy obsession. She was, he recalls now, very keen to call forth spirits and 'levitate the table'. He was unsure, fearing the consequences of unleashing on the world the united force of their psychic power. But he continued to tell her about Paris and Jung and she told him of her childhood

in Duns, particularly of Hannah and her gypsy ways. It thrilled Lily
that he thought of her as a gypsy. In the end, no tables moved,
and no spoons snapped. Jean François wisely desisted. But the gusto
with which Lily had embraced his ideas about spiritualism was a
sign that she had begun to search for another dimension to her
life, one beyond the corporeal, which would soon come to be satisfied more conventionally by her devout Anglo-Catholicism.

It was inevitable that she would have to say goodbye to him. They
promised to write, which they did, sometimes by return of post.
Lily clung to the friendship. On 10 October 1965 Jean François
wrote telling her that he was troubled by how frequently she wrote
to him: 'Don't misunderstand me, it isn't because it annoys me at
all in contrary, it is because my father becomes suspicious.'

Professor Garrison was responsible for distributing the mail every
morning and had become alarmed at how often this 'Mrs Budge'
was sending missives from Edinburgh. 'I told him that you send
me back my own letters after you corrected their mistakes. I don't
know if he was convinced,' Jean François explained. 'I think it would
be safe if you would send this letter back with some corrections, so
I should have something to show him . . . I hear here in France
your favourite record almost so much than in Scotland. You know
the one whose words make one so happy and sad together. You
understand the strange feeling?' He signs off 'your servant, Jean
François', and as if to prove their minds were still running on old
themes, adds cryptically, 'PS: In my last message I wrote that the
lines of your hand didn't lie, they said the truth.'

Three days before Lily's forty-ninth birthday in October 1965,
Jean François wrote promising to buy her a comb for her handbag.
She wrote back saying she found him unnecessarily 'formal', to
which he responded, 'It was not with intention . . . I think English
is not a very good language to say nice and sweet things.' Lily
worried that his affection was cooling. Her letters (which Jean
François threw away) began to take on a needy tone, and to judge
from his responses it seems she was spoiling for a fight in order to
push him to admit what she wanted to hear. 'You asked in your
last letter if I like a formal writing rather than an open one,' Jean
François wrote back, 'No, of course, but there is a right middle to
find. I am sorry but you are not twenty years old.'

It was an intelligent response, and painful to read. Lily was not twenty years old and never would be again. These bare facts silenced her. Five days later, Jean François wrote once more this time beginning 'Dear Mrs Budge'. He was desperate – 'so depressed that my pen stays dry. I don't find anything interesting to say. It is probably better to stop here and write soon again when the inspiration comes. I hope that I shall get some news from you because you didn't write to me for a long time.' They overcame this hitch. Around Christmas, she sent him a parcel containing a pair of pyjamas, some Scottish jewellery, and 'the famous pullover' she had knitted for him specially, despite a hurt wrist. 'It is much more beautiful than I thought,' Jean François wrote back on 16 December. 'It is really marvellous . . . The only thing is that it's

Jean François Garrison, 19, at home in Paris
wearing the oversized jumper Lily knitted
him for Christmas.

perhaps a little too big, would you give me the advice to wash it to make it smaller?' In this same letter, he informed her that since returning home, the Bureau de Voyage Scolaires had been in contact to ask how he found his stay at The Cisandra. 'I don't know what I shall reply . . . Would you like to suggest me what to tell? I would like to write something about "a crazy house", "bad receptivity" and something like that (he! he!).'

Their correspondence continued for two more years. She would moan about her 'boy boarders', all lazy good for nothings who refused to make their beds, and he would write back saying that making nine beds every morning was just impossible; French boys would never act like this, and he wished he could fly to Edinburgh during the Christmas holidays to give them what for. The following year, he signs off one letter 'XX' and then 'May I?', but it was harmless and, as a consequence of distance and time, the intensity dissipated of its own accord. Reflecting on that time, Jean François Garrison understands now that Lily was beset by loneliness. Soon after she struck up another relationship with a man remembered only as Rob and connected with the docks at Leith. The relationship was extremely brief, a few months, and if it were not for the fact that he played a part in the sale of The Cisandra and for the fact that he treated her badly, it would hardly merit a mention.

The Cisandra was flourishing and Lily saw no reason why she should not expand to a proper hotel. In preparation, she went on a course in bar and hotel management, and secured a job with the brewers, Thomas Usher and Son, where she became a trouble-shooting relief manageress visiting some of the roughest pubs in the city. Lily was well into her middle age, but she loved this job. It made her feel important. In the autumn of 1967 she travelled to Paris for the first time, taking Rob with her. She contacted Jean François and was received for lunch by Madame Garrison. She blew into their Parisian home like a galleon in full sail. It was the first time she had been treated as an equal by the professional class and she enjoyed the sensation greatly. 'It would appear that most of my best friends are French,' she wrote later, breathlessly. 'The hospitality of the French people, is, I am sure, the finest in the world.' The Garrisons remained a constant presence in Lily's life. Rob did not.

Shortly after returning from Paris, Lily sat Paul down and broke the news that he was adopted. He was eleven, and about to begin at Coltness House, another children's home. He was stunned and left reeling from an increased sense of being on the outside, made worse by the arrival of Rob and his children at The Cisandra. Lily had not let go of her dream of a hotel and around this time she found a house in Minto Street in Newington, close to Blacket Place, which fitted her image. She put The Cisandra on the market, found a buyer, and exchanged only to learn that she had been gazumped on Minto Street. Then Rob disappeared. What follows, Brebner remembers, was 'a very low period'. He agreed to take Benjamin while Lily began looking for somewhere to live. Much like the hard years following the war when she had first arrived in Edinburgh, she continued to work and tried to remain optimistic. But Jimmy had left her with a pile of debt and Rob's abandonment had hurt her terribly. The lovely big villas of Liberton were now out of her price range. She house-hunted around Newington. She eventually settled on a large first floor, four-bedroom flat at 4 Bernard Terrace, in the district of St Leonards, between The Meadows and Holyrood Park. The flat was in a tenement, unattractive from the outside, and certainly a comedown from The Cisandra, but it was big enough for her to house boarders and it was close to the Royal Hospital for Sick Children where Brebner worked.

The stress of her life took its toll on her health. In 1969, Brebner received a call from the Prom Bar in Leith informing him that Lily had collapsed. Her age, her smoking, the stress of her personal and professional life had all combined to send her blood pressure up to a dangerous level. She was advised to slow down and give up the job, which she did with great regret.

Once recovered she needed another source of income, a job less physically demanding than bar management, but demanding enough to occupy her mind. And so she found one. With a deep breath and a toss of the head, she stepped into the closed world of Edinburgh antiques and declared herself a dealer. It was far from the last time she would change her life completely. She did it very well, and there began a new, brighter phase, for which, once again, she had only herself to thank. If there was one skill Lily truly mastered in her life, it was this ability to bounce back. It is what gave her, in years to come, a glinty look.

'Out of each experience, we become better people,' she wrote, which could have been her epitaph. The consequence was that she became watchful over her own happiness, always on guard to fight for it, tooth and nail, should it ever be threatened again.

10

Anglo-Catholic with charismatic overtones

Until the mid-1960s Edinburgh did not have a thriving or even established antiques quarter. Dealers sold mostly to each other and had narrow tastes. They would, for example, turn their noses to the wall if offered a piece on which Mozart could not have placed his bottom. Casual browsers, those that existed, were tolerated, but only just. The city had its upmarket antiques shops, Janet Lumsden on George Street, and Wildman Bros on Princes Street, for instance. Some belonged to ladies with grand names, such as Jan Struther, owned by Lady Anstruther. There were two auction houses, Dowells, on George Street (later bought by Phillips and then Bonhams) and Lyon & Turnbull, established in George Street since the nineteenth century. But this was the sum total. In 1963, however, a young, relatively inexperienced dealer called David Letham hatched a plan to create a street full of specialist shops, each specialisation complimenting the rest: oils, good brown furniture, china, jewellery, anything and everything that might entice London and international dealers to the city. Thistle Street, a narrow, cobbled lane between Queen Street, where the New Town begins, and George Street was then, like so much of the central Old Town, a virtual slum. The three-storey buildings were run down and without running water, and the inhabitants came straight from a Dickens novel. It was said there was a brothel, a communist who had stripped his walls back to stone, an old woman and her son living in one room with a blaring gramophone, and behind an open window the decomposing corpse of a man who had been murdered by a cuckolded husband.

It was here that David Letham saw a chance of fulfilling his vision. He bought an upstairs room of a house, refurbished it, and began to build up what became a legendary antiques business. A Russian aristocrat often accompanied him to auction rooms and house sales, where he pointed out fakes and the finest European gems. It was not long before every piece that went through Letham's door was of museum quality. The antiques started to come and go at quite a pace, and Letham began to buy up some of the other properties in the street. The only properties he could not acquire were those owned by Lyon & Turnbull in the block between Frederick Street and Hanover Street, which backed on to the auction house. Soon another young antique dealer from Aberdeen, Aldric Young, arrived in the street and together they began recruiting other dealers whose work they respected. Very soon a tight-knit community was established. The men were gentleman dealers and they took their profession seriously. There was much heavy drinking, too, usually whisky, so that if one of them returned from an auction at 9 p.m., the rest would be relaxed enough to try to buy the new acquisitions on the spot.

By the time Lily began looking for premises in 1970 Thistle Street was on its way to becoming an established antique centre. However, it was still bohemian in feel and affordable, unlike George Street. Lyon & Turnbull was offering its buildings, now shop fronts, for a peppercorn rent. This was how Lily edged herself into Thistle Street. She named her shop The Magpie's Nest and decided to fill it with antique dolls, Staffordshire china, pottery, and textiles. She made little impression on the gentleman dealers, except that one noted that she had 'raven, lacquered hair and wore white vinyl knee high boots and a mini skirt to match, quite short for a lady of her age'. When it came to the quality of her stock, Lily did not make it onto their radar. Whatever the vintage of her china or her textiles, the men judged it 'fairground and garage stuff', hardly worthy of the label of 'antique'. They would nod to her out of neighbourly politeness but that was where the connection ended. They were in a different league.

Despite the professional snobbery that surrounded her, Lily began to make a living. Her timing was superb. She was starting when stock was in abundance and public interest was beginning to pick up. She attended the Lyon & Turnbull sales, sometimes six a day, as well as 'lane' sales on the trestle tables outside. The sales themselves were curiously hierarchical affairs, she found. The gentleman dealers were placed around a long banqueting table with the auctioneer at its head. The most established dealers had the best seats while she had to stand at the back. Still, she enjoyed bidding for the antique dolls. The notes she made to herself during these sales make for odd reading, but they give some idea of the kind of figures turning her head. 'Kilted doll, walks with aid, eyes and head move side to side' is one of her jottings. 'Cosmopolitan doll "Marie", British' reads another. Sometimes she recorded items of clothing such as 'beaded mitts' and 'art nouveau night cap, pink with lace'. She soon began buying. Each doll, she learnt, was valued on the worth of her name, incised on her skull and indicative of her pedigree: Schleswig and Holstein, Jumeau, Steiner, Bru, Gesland, Simon & Halbig, Armand Marseille. The older dolls she bought had moulded hair and eyes and closed mouths, while the young ones possessed glass eyes, either inset or lead-weighted to create the impression of a doll inclined to sleep or flirt. Some had moulded ears, teeth, and tongues, others had teeth 'made separately and glued into the mouth before the dressing of the head'. Lily's favourites were the fashionable lady dolls – stylish representations of elegant young ladies in haute couture – and the large, pert-faced bébés who lent themselves perfectly to the miniature and intricate period costumes she would make for them out of old silk and lace while sitting at the back of her shop in an old armchair. The finished 'girls' were lined up in the window so that foreign dealers strolling past The Magpie's Nest could be in no doubt of what they might find inside.

If the desire to amass a collection of dolls, albeit of antique quality, strikes one as a strange indulgence for a grown woman, it has to be stressed that Lily was far from alone. The market was growing, particularly abroad. 'Some of my dolls landed as far away as Japan, Australia and America,' she wrote later with some pride. Every successful bid brought with it the promise of a new attachment. Her heart would lift and flutter at the sight of a 'finished' doll standing before her in restored bonnet and mitts. It was a joy always tempered by the knowledge that it would not be long before the figure would disappear through the door, on her way across the Atlantic, never to be seen again. 'I . . . really got more joy out of collecting than selling,' Lily wrote. It was purely economics that forced her to deal, and had she won the lottery her inanimate family would no doubt have eventually crowded her out of her own shop.

Ultimately, though, she knew to keep her sentimentality in check. She saw that her dolls provided the bulk of her income, as they continued to do throughout her life. It was not uncommon for an Eileen or a Mary, hitherto perched atop a tallboy, to vanish suddenly, usually around the time of the arrival of a household bill. ('Oh well, I suppose she's going to have to go,' Lily would say with a sigh.) Business was good. 'I was keen and happy to meet all the different people and I received many invitations to visit other countries.' And Lily knew that to be maudlin over a doll's inevitable departure was pointless. She may not have been dealing in museum pieces, but she soon developed a good eye and a gift for getting a bargain (Sis's influence, no doubt). Day after day she would sit in her shop, wearing her white vinyl boots, smoking her John Players and making tea from her Nambarrie teabags, a remnant of her childhood in Duns. Lily was obsessed with tea-making. Her family would make her two cups of tea at once, holding one back to present to her when she inevitably complained that the first was too weak, too strong, too cold, or too hot. At auctions, she carried her teabags with her in her handbag, the auction house tea being far too wishy-washy. In her shop, at least, she was mistress of her own teapot. Whenever the bell sounded over her shop door, she would lay her cup down, smile brightly and ask, 'Now, dear, how can I help you?'

One day in this first year of business, an arresting looking young man walked through the door. He was twenty-one, short in stature, had a black bouffant, a black beard trimmed and clipped to perfection, and wore groin-hugging flares and jewellery at his wrists and neck. His name was Joseph Bonnar. He was a fledgling antique jewellery dealer and had been in Edinburgh five years after leaving his adored mother in Fife, at the age of sixteen, determined to make his way. Lily liked what she saw. 'Do come in, dear! Now sit down here and tell me all about yourself. I want to know everything.'

The feeling was mutual. From the moment Joseph Bonnar set eyes on Lily, needle and thread in one hand, Nambarrie brew in the other, white boots tucked under the desk, he knew he had found his Best Friend.

Joseph presented Lily with her first true vision of 1970s counter-culture styling and she loved it. Since arriving in Edinburgh, Joseph had come out as a homosexual and consequently he moved in an arty demi-monde. One of his closest friends – to become one of Lily's friends too – was an aesthete called William Mowat Thomson who owned a drama and dance school in St Stephen's Street and who dressed in Mandarin suits made from homespun linen. He drove around the city in a vintage Rolls-Royce, often accompanied by his mentor and substitute mother, an eccentric woman called the Countess of Mayo, who had picked him up in the Festival Club in 1952. Both extolled the virtues of yoga, having spent time in an ashram in India. While William was a classically-trained dancer and an increasingly successful businessman, Lady Mayo's influence meant his thoughts ran mostly on the importance of chakras and manicures.

Amid a sea of bibulous men in brogues and tweed, bellowing at each other about the delights of eighteenth-century Chinese porcelain, Joseph seemed heaven-sent, a soul mate at last. It was to become a great source of debate among Lily's close family whether or not she really understood the mechanics of homosexuality. Dorothy once spelt it out to her, when Lily was in her eighties, which produced cries of 'No! Don't tell me any more! Stop it! That's shocking!' This was nothing more than an artful ruse. In the company of her three unequivocally heterosexual sons Lily contrived to appear more innocent and naïve than was the case. She suspected her sons considered her rather camp, slightly ridiculous, 'a fag hag', a label she disliked, although there is no question that she adored gay men. The fact remains that at the beginning of the 1970s, with Joseph Bonnar as a loyal and close friend – the first of many friendships she was to form with flamboyant homosexuals – Lily could have been in no doubt about the pursuit and pleasures of gay love. There was not yet the horror of Aids (she later lost a friend to the disease) and Joseph enjoyed a florid night-life, much of which was recounted to her over the morning brew,

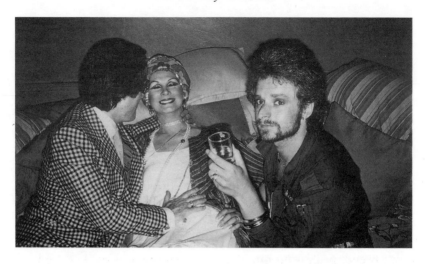

Joseph Bonnar (right) with William Mowat Thomson relaxing at an
Edinburgh party with the transsexual April Ashley in 1977. Full details
relayed to Lily later.

poured and drunk at the back of her shop. Joseph's liaisons provoked in her barely a flicker of surprise. Lily was, he saw, utterly
modern, quite ahead of her time, and possibly the naughtiest, least
self-conscious woman he had ever encountered. One can't help
but feel a twinge of sympathy for the attractive males (always young)
who suffered the misfortune of entering The Magpie's Nest when
they were both inside. They did, at least, have the good manners
to refrain from comment until after the door had closed behind
him. Then Joseph or Lily would cry 'Ooh, I wouldn't mind that
one!' and both would erupt in peals of scurrilous laughter.

When they were not discussing sex they would often parody the
other antique dealers, giggling like a pair of schoolchildren if
subjected to pomposity or flourishes of grandness. Two years into
their friendship, or thereabouts, Joseph came rushing in to Lily's
shop to tell her that David Letham and Aldric Young had visited
him at his stand in the antiques market in St Stephen's Street.
'How's biz?' they had asked him. Within weeks they had moved
him into one of their shopfronts in Thistle Street. As he was erecting
some glass panels in his new shop, Aldric Young had loomed large
and said, 'Oh dear, I'm afraid you are going to have to rethink
those.' 'I mean, my dear,' Joseph moaned to Lily later, 'they'll be

controlling the pearls in my display cabinets next. It's too much!'

Lily had always placed great importance on her physical appearance, even though circumstances had challenged it. But now this new genteel profession of hers permitted some restoration. She simply refused to go grey, as had been noted by the gentleman dealers. It was thanks to the dye bottle that her hair was as jet-black as it had been in childhood. She wore it short, parted on the right and set in curls around her face. She was still close to eight stone, her teenage weight, which meant that as well as the white vinyl mini, she could carry off stylish pant and skirt suits in chocolate brown and bottle green velvet. Her bust was still minuscule, but the padded bras continued (until death) and served her very well under tight fitting blouses with wide 1970s collars. She sometimes wore tweed, preferring pinks and blues to fusty browns and olives, although the thrift-shop velvets remained her favourites despite the fact that some of them had seen better days. They suited her pale skin. If one were to sum up her style, it would be 'subverted classic'. For example, she wore her chiffon scarves tied on the side of her throat, and often opted for slim belts around tailored military style jackets. The overall effect, combined with her new enthusiasm, made her appear younger than she was – fifty-four years old by the end of 1970 – which allowed her a flexible approach to the question of her age.

Materially Lily's life had turned another corner. Using the proceeds from The Magpie's Nest, particularly the dolls, and her access to the auction rooms, she slowly built Bernard Terrace into a proper home. Her tenement rooms were high-ceilinged and the large, hexagonal reception hallway contributed to a feeling of spaciousness. Her taste in decor was traditional: furniture successfully bid for at various sales, complemented by the dolls, small armchairs, and the odd sofa upholstered in mint velvet. It was not The Cisandra, but it was home and she liked it.

On 20 February 1971, at 7.10 p.m., Papa, aged eighty, died of renal failure and chronic pyelonephritis, at the Royal Infirmary, Edinburgh. Once his death had been registered, Lily travelled back to Duns and stayed with Sis in the small house. At the burial of his ashes at Christ Church, Lily was uncontrolled in her grief. She

could not walk unassisted and had to be helped by Brebner and
Andrew. By the time of his death, Papa and Sis had been married
for more than sixty years. Sis stood quietly by his grave, for once
silent. Lily's loss was profound. She had looked up to him throughout her life, and during her childhood he had been her ally, if
a passive one. She could not grasp that he was gone. It was an
uncomplicated kind of grief, built of love and loss. The kind of
grief that she would feel on Sis's death, three years later, was far
more complex, much less visceral, and in many ways more debilitat-
ing. In *No Silver Spoon* Lily does not distinguish between the bereave-
ments. She handles them as if they were the same event. 'The death
of my parents . . . affected me greatly,' she wrote. 'I knew I had lost
part of myself as well, and the links in the family chain were broken.'
But it was Sis's death that finally forced years of ambivalent emotion
to the surface, which was to set off a short-lived crisis to shape the
rest of her life.

The same year as Papa's death, Paul Budge left Coltness House,
institutionalised, undereducated and 'very insecure, like a baby'.
He had become, by his own admission, 'the black sheep of the
family'. He was fifteen years old but did not move back in with Lily
at Bernard Terrace, choosing independence instead: a cheap room
in Leith and a job in a shop. From here on Paul Budge began to
roll in and out of Lily's life like a bad penny. Leaving Coltness
House marked the start of years of petty crime. He was constantly
in trouble with the police. He thieved from Lily's purse and from
the electricity meter, and became involved in gang violence in
Leith. Once he was hospitalised with a knife wound. At first Lily
refused to banish him. And then one day, after he had left Coltness
House, she arrived at The Magpie's Nest to find much of her stock
and till contents gone. Brebner and Benjamin blamed Paul. Lily
dithered. The break-in had shocked her and she could not understand why only her shop had been targeted. Paul Budge admits to
taking money from Lily's purse, but to this day denies robbing her
shop. He offers as a defence that he knew nothing about antiques
or how to 'get rid of them'. The police believed him. However,
Brebner, who had no emotional connection with the adolescent,
became determined to protect his mother from her inclination to
believe the best. He issued her with an ultimatum. She could choose

between Paul visiting the house or him. He knew perfectly well he would win hands down.

After a decade of estrangement (he still has no contact with the brothers), Paul Budge tracked Lily down to tell her he was trying to make something of himself as a chef. She was, he says, very supportive and full of encouragement. She even agreed to attend his wedding. When, at the last minute, she sent her apologies, Paul Budge sensed the return of an old pattern. If he has one regret now, it is that he never made his innocence clear to her. In *No Silver Spoon*, Lily makes no mention of her adopted son.

On 3 March 1974, at 7.30 p.m., Sis died in Whitchester Hospital in Duns from a cerebral thrombosis, aged eighty-three. After years of living in Sis's shadow, Lily felt terrified at the idea of life – her own and life in general. It did not seem possible that the world might continue without Sis in it. Later Lily wrote, 'my world collapsed'. She meant it. She had, as she identified, lost part of herself. For all her efforts, she had never managed to disentangle herself from Sis's idea of her. Sis had watched, judged, sometimes hampered, often assisted everything Lily had done. What made the loss all the more painful was that Lily's grief was laced with some relief, which in turn summoned all those old feelings of intense guilt. As the arrangements for Sis's cremation began, Lily's sons prepared themselves for another display of grave-side hysteria. But when the day arrived, Lily remained quiet and in full control of herself. Brebner was open-mouthed with astonishment. Lily did not so much as shed a tear.

Once Sis's ashes were buried with Papa's at Christ Church Lily carried her emptiness back to Edinburgh where it grew worse. Apart from Joseph Bonnar she had few close friends. Even the gossip of Thistle Street could not lift her spirits. She was confused and sought escape, mostly from herself: 'I used up my free time helping old people, visiting people who were lonely and working for Charities.' She was applying to her life exactly the kind of philosophy Shane had encouraged in Randolph following his leucotomy: forget your troubles by helping others.

On Easter Sunday Lily experienced an epiphany. It was the moment she understood she had a saviour:

> I was walking with my dogs in the park, my thoughts
> were with my Mother as she had always loved Easter
> Sunday. It was then I heard a voice loud and clear telling
> me what to do, it was the name of the Church, that
> evening I attended the service and I knew that it was in
> that church that I would find comfort and strength to
> carry on.

The drama is quite in keeping with her character. Lily was not
the sort to undergo a quiet, slow-burning conversion, born of hours
of book reading, inner reflection, or religious instruction. It was
always going to be sudden and unexpected. Her experience on The
Meadows that afternoon was mystical, too. Lily was not well-read.
Perhaps Sunday school teaching had introduced her to the lives of
the saints or mystics such as Teresa of Avila or Julian of Norwich,
but it seems unlikely. A scientific, secular explanation would be
that the 'voice' was a cry for help from her subconscious. Whatever
it was – the Lord, her psyche – the voice was real to her. It promised
her what she was looking for: salvation, solace, and unconditional
love, a whole greater than the self.

Signs of her 'search for meaning' can be found in her earlier
fascination with the occult, as witnessed by Jean François Garrison.
But it was this religious experience on The Meadows that was the
most important moment in her spiritual life. Conventional Christianity plugged the hole left by Sis's death, it absolved her of her
guilt, and it framed her natural compassion. In the name of her
faith, she would dedicate her life to helping others. That evening
she attended evensong at St Michael and All Saints' Church, the
church to which the voice had directed her. It was situated on the
edge of The Meadows, in Tolcross. St Michael and All Saints',
affectionately called Spiky Mikes by its eclectic congregation, is
an Episcopalian church of high Anglo-Catholicism. Fittingly for a
church of flamboyant worship, its construction had been part-
funded by the sale of diamond tiara, donated by the well-heeled
wife of Alexander Haldane, Bishop of Argyll, at the turn of the
twentieth century. 'Religion was nothing new to me,' Lily wrote
later. 'I have always been connected with the Church since my early
days and recall with love the Mission Hall in Duns, where as children

we spent many happy hours and where we learned by heart so much.' At Christ Church in Duns, though, the worship had been low, 'below floorboards', as she acknowledged later. St Michael and All Saints' was high church, an altogether different kind of worship. The Latin, the music, and the choreographed movements of the clergy mesmerised her; the heavy incense made her slightly dizzy. She found the whole experience overwhelming and each time it reached further and further into her soul. She began attending services morning and evening, which drew her to the attention of Father Gordon Reid, the priest who is now Canon Reid and Rector of St Clement's Church, Philadelphia, Pennsylvania. 'Every time I looked up, she seemed to be there,' he recalls. He found her a welcome addition to his flock, recognising that she had the kind of nature that always wanted to help:

> She was always there, for me and for the parish. If we wanted something done, whether it was carrying a collection can, polishing the pews or cleaning the church before Easter or special events, there would be Lily, as happy as a lark. I found her remarkably caring and a great example to the rest of us. If only we could all behave like that. She was always looking at what was next to come and how she could make the best of it. She began to make a lot of very good friends who helped her, because she would help them if she could.

The nature of Lily's devotional life, her approach to Mass and the sacrament, was as close as she could get to Roman Catholicism without a conversion (like Father Reid, she believed that her church could be reunited with Rome). In the meantime she prayed through the Virgin, which Father Reid recognised as being 'quite wrong, because God understands all and everything and, of course, Protestants do not pray through anyone to get to God, they go straight to him, but she found it helpful to go through Mary'. The Blessed Virgin was everything to Lily. Mary was a normal woman, a mother, a sublime model of chastity who, as Marina Warner puts it in *Alone of All Her Sex*, 'with her mercy, her sweetness, her overflowing goodness . . . was incapable of withholding her favour if approached with the right courtesies and the correct salutations'. She was, in other words, everything Sis was not.

As Lily's faith grew stronger, she became almost fanatical in her desire to share it with others. Her family found such conversation dull, and Brebner, not remotely religious himself, was often vexed and fatigued by her opinions. She talked incessantly of the Virgin and once told a stunned acquaintance, 'A church is not a church without Our Lady!' Rose, now bringing up a fourth child by a different man, found Lily's new conversion absurd. The two women had proved to be very different in their attitudes towards life, as had Etta, who had remained exactly the same as ever, content in Duns. Rose, on the other hand, would often tell her children, 'I had four of you and I didn't want any of you!' Her approach to them had been much as Sis's had been to her. She found it impossible to display affection. She was also antagonistic to religion and niggled by the fact that her eldest daughter, Ann, had become a member of the Pentecostal church. (Before her death, Sis had referred to her granddaughter as 'a hallelujah!') Once, spoiling for a fight, Rose asked Ann for a definition of a Christian, and thinking her mother to be serious, the girl had delivered a long explanation at the end of which Rose had retorted 'Balls!' Lily did not talk about God to Rose, but she did to Ann, and probably Etta too. She had a poor grasp of the nature of the Pentecostal Church, and years later, when sometimes she would pray with Ann and her husband, Ann's son had explained that it was 'charismatic'. Lily was later heard describing her own church as 'Anglo-Catholic with charismatic overtones', which made the family smile. Lord Lauderdale, whom Lily was soon to meet, remembers how she was for ever 'blurting out her opinions on religious matters in the most inappropriate context to the most inappropriate people', and how she would 'pour out her heart and her convictions to a total stranger'. It was behaviour he judged to be 'as scatty as hell'.

Through the strengthening of her faith and the community of the church, Lily was restored to her old self. In October 1974 she turned fifty-eight. Her faith illuminated her, physically and mentally. Through St Michael and All Saints' her social life picked up considerably. There were coffee mornings, evening soirees, and church concerts. Within a few weeks Lily encountered a young man called Michael Chinnery, a server at the church whose hobby was genealogy. He took great pains to master the lives and the family trees of the titled in Scotland. His subjects were often dead, but he was especially enthralled by the living. If they were willing to provide him with high tea in their grand drawing rooms, so much the better. He had, he told Lily, befriended many members of 'the top aristocracy'. He was always talking about the dinner parties or the hunt balls he attended. Lily thought him very posh. He did have a very posh voice, and a very jolly face, buried as it was in *Burke's Peerage*.

Michael Chinnery's attention was first drawn to Lily by her shoes. They made click-clacky sounds as she walked down the aisle to take her seat at the front on the left-hand side of the church. When he was introduced to her he thought her 'colourful' and pursued the friendship, working on the idea that she might present another possibility for 'a howf', a Scottish expression for a spread of snacks and tea and coffee or, if after 10 p.m., as was often the case with him, a nightcap. Michael Chinnery judged the situation correctly. Lily did not have the allure of being upper class, but she proved to be an exemplary hostess. The doorbell at Bernard Terrace often rang at midnight, but she never complained. She was, as Chinnery saw, 'one you could always drop in on'. Chinnery considered those who went to bed early 'so boring', and in Lily, a single woman, he found a kindred night bird, one always willing to provide a dram.

Once Lily penetrated Michael Chinnery's accent they settled into friendship. He appeared to like her, provided company, and also guided her through the complicated tenets of Anglo-Catholism, about which she was hazy. Shortly after she joined the congregation, Father Reid established a branch of the Ecumenical Society of the Blessed Virgin Mary, dedicated 'to the working for fulfilment of God's will here in Scotland'. Lily and Chinnery were among its founding members. Soon Father Reid's lease-hired, battered old charabanc became a firm fixture in the car parks of famous shrines such as those at Walsingham and Haddington and this was how Lily was to come to meet Lord Lauderdale, and subsequently benefit from his kindness. In 1970 Lord Lauderdale had inherited a side chapel in St Mary's Kirk. He subsequently learnt that in the fifteenth century it had accommodated an 'Altarage of the Blessed

Virgin and the Three Kings', thought to have been intended as a replacement for a medieval shrine of Our Lady. From then on Whitekirk and Haddington had become the centre of an ecumenical pilgrimage attracting thousands. It was a favourite among Father Reid's flock.

Lily liked nothing more than a pilgrimage. It made a nice day out for her and her faith, and multiplied the potential for 'love and friendship'. The outings took on a familiar pattern. They would meet at the church, motor in the bus to the shrine of choice, and jostle around with the other pilgrims. Then they would attend a service (when it came to the peace, she would often embrace her fellow pilgrims with great enthusiasm); pray; eat lunch out of sandwich boxes – on the grass if the weather was fine or in the bus if it was raining. Sometimes it would be possible to buy bookmarks and postcards bearing messages of religious guidance. And then it was back on the bus for the bone-rattling trip home, with everybody thanking Father Reid for his trouble.

Lily revered Father Reid. When he spoke or delivered a sermon she fixed her eyes on him intensely. She carried his sermons in her head for days. 'It has always been God's way to take a few people and give them something special to do for Him,' he preached in one of the early sermons she heard, 'not for their own benefit only but also for that of all His children.'

On this occasion, Father Reid had been making a political point about the restoration of unity between his church and Rome. But these were Lily's sentiments exactly and she applied them to life in general. She was about to fulfil this teaching in a way that surpassed anything she had done yet.

PART TWO

Viola: I pity you
Olivia: That's a degree to love

WILLIAM SHAKESPEARE, *Twelfth Night*

II

Poor Love

By 1975 Lily was twice married, twice divorced, and doing very
nicely. She had been without a man in her life for more than ten
years. It was beginning to appear as if she had a chance of easing
into old age – she was to turn fifty-nine that year – a single and
contented woman, not quite of significant means, but certainly a
woman free of the dramas and hardships of earlier years. The
Magpie's Nest was ticking over; Bernard Terrace was comfortable
and she could pay the mortgage; she had her sons and also four
grandchildren, who brought her so much pleasure. But throughout
her life Lily had shown an extraordinary capacity for turning it
from good to bad, or perhaps it would be fairer to say, from a state
of calm to a state of emergency. She was due for some trouble to
upset the equilibrium. Lily met Randolph in March 1975. Seven
months later she was his new bride.

Lily was accustomed to bolting through her nuptials with one
eye on the calendar, but in speed and secrecy this third marriage
far surpassed the other two. There were two forces responsible for
the collision of Lily and Randolph's lives. The first was Our Lady,
the second was Michael Chinnery, who had befriended Randolph.
While Lily worshipped God the way others worship rock stars –
climbing on and off tour buses; proselytising in the hope of conversion; investing in memorabilia – Randolph, by now out of the
Crichton Royal Hospital, was quieter in his devotion. In fact, he
was silent. The Monastery of the Transfiguration into which he had
been placed by his parents at the beginning of the 1970s was not
a monastery in any formal sense, more a community of three or
four brothers existing by vows made according to the Cistercian
rite, which includes that of poverty. Their house, which they called

The Sanctuary and then The Hermitage, was a single building in Roslin, Midlothian, and their chapel was fashioned from a corrugated iron outbuilding. Randolph did not wear the charcoal grey flannel habit secured with a leather belt because he was not one of the brothers, but he did join them daily to pray, to eat sheep's heads, and to dig potatoes. The monastery observed time according to Mount Athos, which meant rising during the night. 'I note from your letter,' a relative had written on 13 April 1973, 'that you are now "living on SPACE TIME". Don't you find it rather confusing when you have to catch buses or trains?'

The Brothers of the Order of Transfiguration, an alternative title, is included on a list of Anglican Benedictines, although the brother superior has converted to Roman Catholicism and been ordained a Catholic priest, and is registered as being 'engaged in work with the poor and destitute'. It provided an agreeable solution to Lord Galloway's problem of how best to remove his troubled son from society while keeping him in a safe country environment. The Order promised an obscure and hermitic existence. Life there was simple, austere, and, most importantly, private. It was not well-known. As it happened, Randolph was not the only titled inhabitant. Brother John, who showed him particular kindness, was Reverend John Walter Brook Halsey, 4th baronet and great-grandson of Sir Charles Brooke, the second White Rajah of Sarawak and grandson of Bertrand Brooke, the Tuan Muda of Sarawak.

The brothers rarely left the confines of the Order, although occasionally they went on day trips. In April 1972, for example, Randolph and the brothers went out for the day. It had tipped with rain, which drenched their habits and forced them to take refuge in a café where Randolph resorted to a cup of black coffee to perk himself up. When he told his mother this story, which she called 'a vivid and dramatic account', she wrote back, 'We laughed and laughed – which was very unfeeling of us because it was hard luck to have your outing ruined by such ghastly weather.' In the same letter Randolph returned to his old preoccupation with 'bottoms', only this time they were 'flying bottoms'. Of this, his mother responded on behalf of Lord Galloway too: 'We were fascinated by the "flying bottoms" – I wonder what they are? Do tell us when you write again.'

It was fondness and love expressed at a distance. Their approach was to humour him, as though he were still a child. Letters Randolph wrote at the time indicate that he seemed quite content with his life with the monks. But then, as Michael Chinnery observed whenever he paid a visit to the monastery, Randolph appeared to be heavily drugged. 'He was kept quiet,' he remembers. 'He didn't say very much. It was an absolute hovel there and all that eating of sheep's heads and bloody cuckoo clock time – I felt very sorry for him from day one.'

Chinnery saw clearly that the brothers did not entirely approve of Randolph leaving The Sanctuary without them. But as they were gentle, charitable men who were not the kind to create a scene, they allowed Chinnery to take Randolph off in his car, which was often filled with other well-connected young people. One boy was called Johny Chute and was a law student at Edinburgh University. He played chess with Randolph and invited him on the occasional shoot on a nearby estate. On one occasion the boys tried to teach Randolph to drive, but he slammed the car into a tree. Miraculously, nobody was hurt.

It was while living with the monks in February 1974, the year before he was to meet Lily, that Randolph learnt of his mother's death (coincidentally, Sis died six months later). It came as a huge blow for the Stewarts. The countess had been younger than her husband, and in all the correspondence sent to Randolph during the early 1970s the news was always of Lord Galloway's health and how well he was recovering from various complaints. Lord Galloway never really recovered from the loss, while Randolph, sedated and digging potatoes, was now more alone than ever.

The Society of Mary continued to flourish and Lily had been elevated to the post of chairman. In March 1975 she heard that Lord Lauderdale was organising a pilgrimage to Coatbridge, on the outskirts of Glasgow, where there were to be two services in aid of Our Lady of Walsingham. There was no question but that she would galvanise her society into attendance. Michael Chinnery agreed to attend the trip, scheduled for the middle Saturday in March. Beside his name, he added another, Randolph Stewart, a friend of his, he said. On the Friday before Michael Chinnery arrived at The

Sanctuary to pick Randolph up. The following morning they rose early to catch Lord Lauderdale's bus. On the other side of Edinburgh Lily was applying the finishing touches to her coiffeur and dressing, as usual, in velvet. The story of what happened next has been retold so many times by Lily that it has become a kind of myth. Michael Chinnery, who was the only friend present, says that he led Randolph towards Lily, who was sitting at the back of Lord Lauderdale's bus. 'I said, "By the way, Garlies, come and meet a friend of mine from church. Garlies, this is Mrs Budge, and to Lily, "Lily, this is Garlies." '

Years later Lily was to tell another friend, the journalist and writer Michael Thornton, that Chinnery played no part in the meeting and that she had approached Randolph of her own accord, thinking that he looked tragic and unhappy. Later in life Lily was prone to going into huffs with her friends, and it is more than likely that she was in a bait with Chinnery at the time she cut him out of the story. However it happened, everybody agrees that Lily and Randolph met at the back of a bus. 'Part of the spirit of a pilgrimage is to welcome everyone and stretch out the hand of friendship to any stranger,' Lily explained. On a different occasion she wrote, 'I was asked to sit next to Randolph Stewart whom I found at the back of the coach looking scruffy and rather sad. My sympathy went out to him.' There was no woman better equipped than Lily to stretch out the hand of friendship to a stranger. 'I wasn't certain how I could help him,' she recalled. 'I talked merrily about the church and invited him to a concert.'

Randolph was a bird with a broken wing. Lily would always maintain that she thought him a tramp. His clothes were so tatty and his confidence so eroded that she could not imagine where he fitted into society. He walked with a stoop, his head hung low, his eyes trained on the floor. When he lifted them to look at her as she attempted to engage him in conversation, there emerged from his mouth stuttering speech before he retreated back into impenetrable silence. He was not much used to talking. And yet, even on that first meeting Lily saw beyond his defects to all that was good. She was particularly struck by his soft accent, which was a gentle, clipped purr compared to the fruitiness of her own. His manners, even with the effect of medication, were impeccable, quite unlike

Lily and Randolph, centre, second row from back, with Father
Gordon Reid and the devoted members of the Society of Mary
on one of their day trips.

anything she had encountered before (even in Professor Garrison).
Lily would come to say that Randolph had always possessed aristocratic breeding worthy of his lineage, it was just that it needed
somebody like her to encourage it to flourish.

A few days after the trip Randolph wrote to Lord Galloway. 'My
Dear Father,' he began, 'I will start by giving you some information
about what happened at the weekend. On Friday evening I was
picked up by Michael Chinnery . . .' The letter gives a brief outline
of the pilgrimage, before ending, 'Bitterly cold weather here of

late but as long as the snow stays away I do not mind. Hope you are keeping better and this brings you very much love. Garlies.' There is no mention of him meeting a Mrs Budge. Only when Michael Chinnery saw Randolph again did his mind start whirring. 'I never thought any more about it,' says Chinnery of the first meeting, 'but when I saw Garlies, I asked "Did you enjoy your trip out Garlies?" and he replied, very courteously, "Yes, tell me, Lily Budge, how is she?" I thought, "Good heavens! That is the first time I've ever seen Garlies have any reaction to a woman." I replied, "Oh well, you should write to her or ring her up." I provided him with her details. Unbeknownst to me, they began to correspond.'

Lily's life went on as normal. She spent her days at The Magpie's Nest and her evenings either at church or at home, running an open house for the needy: 'My home was open to all church people, · or in fact to anyone who was in need of friendship, so I suppose this was how it started. He became a regular visitor and I knew little about him.'

Over the following weeks Randolph visited her for coffee at 4 Bernard Terrace and accompanied her to a handful of concerts at the church. She never illuminated the exact details of this court-ship, except to say that it was absolutely platonic. One can imagine her pressing upon him hot food and treating him much like an orphan. These meetings were facilitated by Michael Chinnery, who picked Randolph up in his car, saying nothing to the monks of the kind Mrs Budge. He now admits to being motivated by an element of mischief-making, as well as pity for the bleakness of Randolph's life. The significance of Randolph's childlessness had not escaped him, although the prospect of Lily, however sprightly, providing an heir was out of the question.

According to Michael Chinnery, he informed Lily of Randolph's background 'very quickly after the first day', which would seem normal between two friends. But Lily was always coy about exactly when she learned that Randolph was titled. She maintained that it was at a late stage in their friendship. 'I didn't question Randolph about his family or circumstances,' she wrote in *No Silver Spoon*. 'To me he was a lame dog, a terrible introvert who could do with-out nosiness. All I gathered was that he was 48 [a miscalculation], unmarried and living in some sort of community. I felt so sorry for him, he seemed so poor but I thought it was something to do with the "vows of poverty".'

As their friendship progressed, Randolph's life remained unchanged in all other ways. His health and mannerisms gave no clue of what was to come. On 17 April, for example, Randolph wrote to Lord Galloway informing him that he and Lady Antonia had gone to see *The Desert Song*, a show being performed by the Musselburgh Amateur Musical Association at Brunton Hall. Once again, he began fondly – 'Dearest Father' – and wrote, 'The synopsis of the scenes is as follows. Act 1, scene 1, Retreat of Red Shadow in mountains. 2. Outside General Birabeau's house . . .' He continued in this manner until act two, Scene five, after which he listed all the musical numbers. 'We all thoroughly enjoyed it and afterwards Mrs Guinea kindly gave us a meal at the lodge where she now lives.' The letter continued the following day. 'Yesterday evening I cut the grass here and was surprised how dry it was after so much rain. It was very nice to see you that day. It took about three hours by car and we got back at approximately 2 p.m. Bible Time. Well I do hope you are keeping better and this brings you very much love.'

At some stage, though, Randolph must have begun to talk about Mrs Budge and the visits he paid her. Quite out of the blue, Lady Antonia contacted Lily to say she desired a meeting. Lily found it 'a curious phone call' but agreed to the meeting. 'I assumed her title was through marriage only, and suspected nothing,' Lily wrote later. 'It was an odd visit. She said: "I hear you've been to the concert with Randolph." But, for some instinctive reason, I refused to be drawn.'

It was as if Lily guessed that Randolph's family would not approve of their friendship. At this stage she had nothing to gain or lose. She certainly was not in love with him. Her evasiveness was born more out of her desire to protect him, to prevent him from losing something that seemed to bring him happiness. In addition she took exception to Lady Antonia's questions: 'We parted amiably enough, though I was left feeling puzzled. Never in my wildest dreams would I have thought that Randolph had a title – he owned only one suit, which I had begged him to buy for church. Even then someone took me to one side and whispered: "You dinna want anything to do with him, he's a poor soul." ' This kind of response to Randolph horrified Lily. She could not comprehend it. If Randolph appeared to need her help, who was she to withhold it? Such compassion was at the root of her Christianity: 'I felt so sorry for him . . . that's what Christianity is all about, helping people who need help, not those who are doing well. Randolph shared my interest in music and was a Christian person, which was all that mattered to me.'

It is one thing that Randolph became Lily's friend, but quite another that he became her husband. Just as their meeting has become mythologised, so too has the moment when they decided to marry. To some people she claimed that he arrived on her doorstep one night in a storm. There was a thunderous knock at the door, she said, and she had found him standing there like a drowned rat. 'All he said was "I've come to stay" and we married within a month.' In this version of events it is this moment that Randolph tells Lily the story of his family: that he was an aristocrat and that he had never experienced affection from anybody except Nan, the laundry maid, who would sit with him on the back stairs. In *No Silver Spoon*, the drama of the occasion is taken down an octave or two:

> One night he told me he had been ill treated from the time he was seventeen, and had undergone surgery in 1952 for a leucotomy, ordered, he said, by his Father to change his personality, and the reason why he was staying in the community was that he was not allowed to go home.

Michael Chinnery believes they corresponded by post and that perhaps Randolph proposed in a letter. Randolph was always better at expressing his feelings on paper, but there is no trace of such a letter or correspondence in Lily's extensive archive. There were other people, too, who believed that Chinnery had encouraged Randolph and that he had engineered the whole thing for his own amusement, something he vehemently denies. Certainly, following the wedding Lord Galloway never forgave him.

In another version of the story, Lily wrote that Randolph proposed to her one night after a concert: 'He said he wanted to talk to me. "Would you marry me?" he asked softly. I was stunned. It was the last thing I had expected – our relationship had seemed simply platonic. "Marry you?" I gasped, "I couldn't."'

But plainly, she could. Randolph says now that 'they asked each other, on a pilgrimage bus to Govan', but this too seems strange. In all that Lily wrote afterwards, at least, she talked always of her initial horror and confusion at the idea of marrying Randolph and her friends' accounts seem to back this up. Brebner remembers her in the back seat of his car in a distinctly 'shall I, shan't I?' frame of mind. 'Nothing she did was ever surprising to me,' he comments dryly.

Lily's eventual capitulation had its foundation in pity. 'The pain on his face was unbearable,' she wrote, recalling the moment when she originally declined the offer. 'I carefully explained that I couldn't marry him because I didn't love him in the way a woman should love a man. He seemed lost, wounded, as if he'd found in me a companionship he'd never known before. I'd realised he was lonely but before that moment I'd never grasped to what extent.'

After hearing 'the horrifying story' of his life, Lily became less sure of her refusal. By her own admission, his tale had confused her feelings. 'Perhaps it was at that time, pity turned to love,' she wrote later. 'I don't know, all I know is that he was a quiet, gentle, loving man, someone who was desperately in need of love and more than that, to belong to a family.'

She approached Father Reid for advice. 'Pity, well Lily, there's nothing wrong with that!' he recalls telling her. Chinnery, meanwhile, counselled, 'You'll have lots more friends with a title, people you don't know will come flocking around you and you'll be a queen bee amongst them all.' He also warned her of the possibility of meeting disapproval in 'the top aristocracy'.

Lily was muddled. She had gone from knowing that she did not love Randolph to thinking that she now might. Randolph was due to holiday in Spain with Lady Antonia, which bought Lily more time. She would think about the proposal while he was away, and if her answer was yes, she would be at Edinburgh airport to meet him on his return. While he was gone, she went on a pilgrimage to Walsingham, looking for guidance:

I never prayed so sincerely as I prayed at Walsingham. I
knew myself well enough to be sure that Randolph's title
would not influence my decision – such things never
really have made an impression on me. But I believe that
we are only human and need help in examining our
consciences. I also had to find out if I did love Randolph
or not – and if I did, would I be strong enough to take
on someone who had been through hell on earth?

There was an internal struggle at Walsingham, but it was not
protracted. Lily changed her mind within a few hours. Praying to
the Blessed Virgin, she realised that she did indeed love him. 'I
can not explain how or why I reached that decision in logical terms,'
she wrote later, 'it was just a realisation of the truth . . . the blinkers
came off . . . It was easy to love him for his sweet self.' When he
returned from Spain she was waiting for him, as promised.

Throughout her life Lily remained extremely touchy about her
motives for marrying Randolph. This was not so much from a guilty
conscience, but rather because so very few people seemed to be
able to understand. To the outsider, to one who did not know her
well, the whole thing would have looked questionable. After all,
Randolph was a lobotomised and drugged virgin with no experience of women or the world. He could barely hold a conversation.
Why on earth would she want to marry him? The only thing Randolph appeared to have in his favour, her detractors, including his
father, would come to say, was his title and perhaps his inheritance.
For a woman of humble birth and meagre means, was this so incon-
sequential? Was this the reason why she said yes?

Retrospectively Lily went to great lengths to provide proof that
she was not an adventuress, concerned only with acquiring a title.
This is the reason why there are so many versions of the timing of
the marriage proposal. She had to make it look good and to look
good meant delaying the moment when she discovered who he was.

There is no doubt that Lily's decision to marry Randolph was
hasty, instinctive, and, looked at from one angle, foolhardy. But
behind it lay a complex weave of reasons. There must have been
a small part of her that was excited by the title, although Lily had

shown no previous tendency for social climbing beyond wanting to experience financial security. It had been Chinnery, after all, who had told her that life would be very different if she became Lady Garlies. A title promised a passport into a new world, although Lily, possessing no knowledge of Edinburgh society, might not have known this instinctively. But there were other motivations, more deeply rooted than whether or not Lily desired to mingle with 'top aristocrats', as Chinnery called them. To Lily, Randolph was always her 'poor love'. Much like the owls, the squirrels, and the coeliac child who had filled her life before him, Randolph was another dependent who needed her love and care. The love she said she found kneeling beneath the statue of the Blessed Virgin was interwined with Randolph's need. There was a spiritual component – she truly believed that it was her mission to be good and worthy and to help others – and a psychological one too. The reason why Randolph's story had affected her so profoundly was that it touched some buried emotion of her own. She later said of Randolph and of herself that they were 'castaways'. Both had grown up with parents they simultaneously loved and disliked, whom they feared and revered; both were left with a sense of not belonging. It was only with each other that they found a fit. She identified with him. She was the only person who did.

Once it had been settled that they were to marry, Lily and Randolph feared, quite correctly, that should Lord Galloway get wind of the preparations, Randolph would be carried off and locked back in his tower, and they would be heartbroken, star-crossed lovers for ever more. It is a nice reversal of the fairy tale – strong woman saving frail man from his wicked father – and this exaggerated notion of endangered romance and lip-quivering fear shaped the mood of the occasion. Michael Chinnery posted the banns in Roslin, not Edinburgh, listing Lord Garlies as Randolph Stewart. He figured that the news was far less likely to be picked up by the monks in Roslin than the press in Edinburgh. Lily went to Joseph Bonnar for two antique gold wedding rings. 'You sly old thing,' he told her.

Michael Chinnery admits that he did whip up a certain amount of hysteria. He remembers that by the day of their marriage, 17 October, three days after Randolph's forty-seventh birthday and eleven days before Lily's fifty-ninth, nobody would have been at all surprised should Lord Galloway have charged in on horseback leading a private army through the corridors of Newington Registry office. This did not happen. Very few people knew of the event. Chinnery was unofficial best man to Randolph and the second witness was a female churchgoer called Euphemia. Brebner knew it was taking place but did not attend. So far as Lady Antonia and the monks were concerned, on the eve of the wedding Randolph was thought to be attending 'a grand ball' with Chinnery, with whom he would stay before being dropped back in Roslin the following morning. In fact, he spent that night in Bernard Terrace with Lily. By the end of the following day it did not much matter that the monks were wondering where he was since by then he was married.

Michael Chinnery has two clear memories of the wedding day. The first is of Randolph dressed in a cream suit with a red tartan tie, 'beaming', no doubt feeling the force of his personal triumph, and the second is of Lily, now Lady Garlies, nervous, quiet and

Lily and Randolph following their secret marriage at Newington Registry Office in October 1975, flanked by best man Michael Chinnery (far right) and Euphemia in leopard print.

unwilling to be left alone with her new husband after the small gathering of church friends finally dispersed from her flat in Bernard Terrace.

There was also the matter of breaking the news to Lord Galloway, who Chinnery thought would 'play silly buggers'. Eventually he grabbed the phone and bit the bullet. 'I thought "I'm not going to let him get the better of a happy day",' he remembers, 'so I phoned him, got through and said, "Yep, by the way, just ringing to tell you that Garlies is now married to a Mrs Budge. So there we are. They'll be living in Edinburgh." He blurted back, "What! Has she got money?"'

While Lord Galloway was reeling in his sun porch, Chinnery was plotting how best to claim a large and valuable Galloway diamond ring for the newlyweds, bequeathed to Randolph by his mother in the unlikelihood that he should ever marry. 'I then stormed off to the lawyer's office,' says Chinnery, 'produced the marriage certificate and said "Randolph is now married. Can you hand the ring over, please?" And I returned with the diamond ring, three rocks of Gibraltar. On reflection, perhaps I wouldn't handle it quite like that if the situation arose again.' It was the first of many mistakes they made. To Lord Galloway the snatching of the ring did not bode well for Lily's motives.

There was no question of Lily and Randolph consummating their marriage yet. Randolph told her plainly that he would not consider them man and wife until Father Reid had blessed their vows in church. There was also the fact that he was still taking sedatives, although Lily was already thinking about how best to wean him off them. The gap between the civil and church services gave Lily a chance to get used to the idea of having a man in the house and to think of how best to handle the matter of Lord Galloway. Within two weeks of the civil service she urged Randolph to write to his father telling him in his own words that they were now married, and that he was invited to their blessing on 17 November followed by a wedding party at the Caledonian Hotel.

On 1 November, the same day as their wedding announcement appeared in the court and social pages of the *Daily Telegraph*, Lord Galloway responded on Cumloden paper. 'My dear Boy,' he wrote, 'At long last I hear from you personally about recent happenings.

I can not conceal from you how bitterly I am hurt and how much I resent the deceitful and underhand way in which the marriage was carried out.' After such an unpromising opening, the letter took a surprising turn. Lord Galloway seemed to have absolved Randolph of most of the responsibility (an indication of how vulnerable he believed him to be) and instead laid the blame at Lily's door. 'My dear boy,' he continues, 'I do not blame you too much. I am quite sure that the idea of practising this hateful deceit on your ill and ageing father was not yours. It originated from and was carried out by certain others who knew quite well what they were doing and whom I shall *never* forgive.'

The letter continued, 'I was, however, so very pleased to read in your letter that you now feel so secure and happy. That is indeed good news.' The optimism was tempered with his final lines:

> These, however, are early days. I can only hope that once the 'first fine careless rapture' has passed that disillusion will not set in. If, as I hope, things continue to go well I shall hope eventually to be able to see you again, but it will need a *long time!* The arthritis in my right hand and wrist is very bad and makes writing almost impossible for me, but I do hope you will be able to read this letter.
> With my sincere hopes that things will turn out well.
>
> Much love from Father.

It was not an encouraging response, but the letter demonstrates clearly that Lord Galloway cared about his son's happiness. There was also the glimmer of hope that sometime in the future he might be able to accept them as a couple. This is the hope to which Lily clung. Fortunately she had the distraction of her wedding party. While the exchange of vows had been covert, Lily and Randolph viewed their nuptial mass at Spiky Mikes, followed by the 3 p.m. reception for sixty at the Caledonian Hotel, as a way of coming out into Edinburgh society.

In her dress, at least, Lily chose safely. It was long and cream, with a high collar, lace trim, and full sleeves nipped in with wide lace cuffs. She held a white antique evening bag, fastened with an old clasp and embroidered with gold flowers. Her jewellery was the newly acquired 'three rocks of Gilbraltar' and her gold necklace, on which hung a crucifix. Her make-up was subtle and her nails were unvarnished. Randolph appeared well groomed and wore a new kilt. A few months later, a photograph of them appeared in the *Edinburgh Tatler*. Nothing appeared to be at all amiss. They looked happy and healthy.

Lord Galloway and Lady Antonia did not attend the church blessing or the party. Instead Lord Galloway dispatched a telegram bearing the message, 'My thoughts will be with you both on Saturday.' The staff at Cumloden sent a message too: 'Best wishes to you both.'

Others were more effusive. One acquaintance they had made through the pilgrimages, a young trainee at theological college, wrote, 'I offer you my warmest well-wishes, my heartiest congratulations, and my sincere and fervent prayers for a future endowed with every possible blessing, both spiritual and material! God bless you both! As you can see, this news has quite taken my breath away, but if I can think sensibly for a minute . . .'

As the new Lady Garlies, and without the support of Randolph's family, Lily went on the defensive. She felt she had two priorities: 'To show the world that Randolph was a normal human being, and to prove our love.' Randolph challenged the definition of 'a normal human being', but Lily blamed many of his oddities and unsocial behaviour on the huge doses of drugs he had taken over the course of his life. She was convinced she could rehabilitate him. She took Randolph to her GP – whose opinion confirmed hers – that the doses were too high. Lily threw away his pill pots without further ado. 'When he stopped taking them, he began to be ill,' she wrote. 'Within weeks the weight fell off him. He almost died. But it was a risk I had to take because they were killing him slowly anyway, so my doctor told us.' The process of rehabilitation was not easy. Lily might have done better to reduce his dose gradually.

Although Randolph was not at all well, Lily was still required at The Magpie's Nest. She somehow managed, ferrying between Thistle Street and Bernard Terrace, where Randolph liked to sit in a chair smoking a pipe (she did not mind his smoking in the way that Lord Galloway had). He preferred silence to speech. Chinnery and his friends regularly dropped round for chess or to

take him out for a pint, and Lily started buying and cooking
sheep's heads for him, so that he would not feel too disorientated
in his new environment. Visitors to the flat in those early days found
the scene touching. She was a mixture of nurse and mother, they
saw, running about after his every need, ensuring that he was as
comfortable as could be. The relationship was more than that,
though. In response to gossip and speculation about the exact
nature of their relations, she let it be known that they enjoyed a
full marriage and relished telling the story of how she had first
suggested to Randolph that they might begin to share a bed. He
had responded, 'When my father required my mother, he rang a
bell.' 'And I told him, well Randolph! There'll be none of that in
this house!'

Lily was smart. She quickly grasped the power of her new title.
She had calling cards printed up on which 'Lady Garlies' was
embossed in gold. The days of 'Mrs Budge' were over. Christian
Orr Ewing, a privileged young man working in the antiques trade,

A long way from the monks: Lily and Randolph settle
into married life in Bernard Terrace.

remembers her placing her card in front of him with a flourish. 'She's either new to the title or married to a "Sir",' he thought, eyeing her quizzically.

As their first Christmas together approached, Lily and Randolph received an invitation from Colonel Robin Stewart and his wife, Lady Daphne, daughter of the Marquis of Tweeddale to attend their Christmas house party at Middle Blainslie, their home near the Borders town of Lauder. It was an important moment for Lily. It acknowledged her existence, she thought. They accepted. The guest list also included a woman called A. J. Stewart, who, Lady Daphne told Lily, would also be travelling by bus from Edinburgh on Boxing Day. Maybe they could travel down together? Lily went one step further. She was planning a pre-Christmas soirée for her friends at the church. It provided the perfect excuse for an icebreaker with her travel companion. She obtained her telephone number and extended an invitation, which A. J. Stewart readily accepted. A few days before, a friend telephoned A. J. to say, 'You may think them an odd couple but they are very, very happy and I am sure you will be gentle.' The intermediary said nothing else but the tip-off served its purpose.

Lily had given her Christmas party much consideration. She was keen 'to bring Randolph out into society'. He had been hidden away for too long. Now was his moment in the sun. She truly believed that the restoration of his confidence lay in social acceptance. While she wanted him to meet as many people as possible, she recognised that he would need considerable prompting and jollying along. How could she possibly mind him and circulate with the canapés at the same time? She came up with the idea of having him answer the door. There he could introduce himself formally as Lord Garlies without being drawn into protracted conversation. On the night of the party, Lily ensured he looked the part in black tie. When A. J. Stewart arrived, she found Randolph 'deeply handsome', having made an introduction 'in the most beautiful voice'. He took her cloak and then froze, clueless of what to do next, like an actor who had forgotten his lines. Lily appeared as if from nowhere – she became very good at this – and covered up the impasse with ceaseless chatter. A. J. Stewart was waved through to the sitting room while Lily showered Randolph with soothing

words of encouragement in the reception hall. A. J. Stewart understood immediately what her friend had meant.

When faced with the spectacle of Lily, Randolph, and A. J.
Stewart, one wonders who the guests thought the more curious. It
is a testimony to Lily's open-mindedness that when she met A. J.
Stewart that night she did not bat an eye lid at her attire, although
she must have realised immediately that they were destined to
become good friends. Like Lily, A. J. was not the sort of woman to
blend with a crowd on Princes Street. This was mostly because
she dressed always in early sixteenth-century costume, not musty
originals, but copies she ran up for herself on her sewing machine.
Her attire was a floor-length black kaftan, belted with a gold chain,
worn over a white blouse to create the overall effect of medieval
surcoat and sark. On her cloak she pinned various Royal Stewart
memorabilia and on her small feet she wore gold slippers. Her hair
was dyed bright orange and her face was powdered a chalky white.
She was fond of red lipstick and Gauloise cigarettes, but not of the
gout or the celebrity her appearance had created for her. The nub
of the matter was that A. J. Stewart was grappling with two identities.
She was, she told Lily, the reincarnation of James IV, King of Scots.
'Queen Margaret, my mother', she recollected in her published
book, *Falcon: The Autobiography of His Grace James IV King of Scots*,
was 'a charming dark-haired lady in a green silk gown stitched with
pearls upon its bodice'.

Considering Lily's early interest in psychic matters, she was quite
willing to accept A. J.'s identity dilemma, and even sympathised.
As A. J. made clear in *Falcon*, 'I must stress that at no time was I
deliberately searching for knowledge of an earlier existence for it
seemed to me that to have passed once through this world was
adequate punishment for anybody.' It was a view that chimed with
Lily. In the years that followed A. J. asked no questions of Lily
regarding her marriage to Randolph, and Lily refrained from
pressing A. J. on the unique nature of her circumstances (A. J. was
always a little surprised, however, when Lily demonstrated such a
poor grasp of Scottish history). Their friendship was based on
loyalty, discretion, and a love of style. A. J., who was blessed with
considerable beauty, somehow avoided looking as if she had
stepped off a museum plinth, and she appreciated the care Lily

gave to her own appearance too. One of Lily's most cherished possessions was *Falcon*, presented complete with a loving message from the King.

Christmas 1975 passed in a whirl of socialising and present giving. It was unlike anything Randolph had known, at least during the previous twenty years of his life. In marrying Lily he had not only gained a wife, but an entire family: three stepsons and four step-grandchildren. For the first time, he told her, he felt part of a proper family. The party at Middle Blainslie was a success, too, although there had been a hiccough with the transport when the bus, carrying A. J. in full fig, had sailed past Lily and Randolph, before screaming to a halt under A. J.'s orders.

Lily charmed her hosts. Lady Daphne, a charitable and refined woman, could recall Randolph's early years clearly, when he was at his most unwell (secretly, she had been appalled at the leucotomy and had been of the opinion that he could have been better helped by therapy). What she saw now in the drawing room was that he had a wife who seemed devoted to him. Lady Daphne and the Colonel consequently gave the marriage their blessing. Perhaps as a result of this a few months later Lord Galloway decided it was time he gave his estranged son and new daughter-in-law an audience. He bade them to Cumloden to stay for Easter. It was an opportunity for Lily to work her magic, to repair the damage, and build bridges for the future.

12

My home is my castle

An audience with a peer of the realm, especially when he was a former Lord Lieutenant and one's new father-in-law, required forethought and preparation, as Michael Chinnery advised Lily as Easter 1976 drew closer. But despite the enthusiasm with which Chinnery sought to play at being Pygmalion, he noticed that Lily did not share his enthusiasm. He sailed on regardless, talking of the importance of speaking U over non-U and how she must eschew her velvet trouser suits in favour of a staid skirt. She seemed to have an inherent confidence in her marriage, Chinnery thought, and was not at all hampered by feelings of social inferiority. He found this startling and concluded, rightly, that Lily had no idea of what awaited her. She was aware that the visit demanded a degree of bridge-building, but she understood this only in terms of proving to Lord Galloway how genuine her feelings were for his son. And because they were genuine she felt no fear. Her confidence was much like that of the innocent man who finds himself in the dock. But Lord Galloway lived by an entirely different set of values, and by these she would be judged harshly.

While Lily chattered on, talking in terms of 'reaching new understandings' and 'enjoying brighter futures', Randolph, who had not seen his father for at least half a year, perhaps even longer, became increasingly agitated and morose.

When the day arrived for them to travel to Dumfries, Lily and Randolph had contrasting emotions. She was filled with hope, he with terror. He was nearer the mark. He was also suffering from the flu, which made him appear gaunt and ill. Lily had little idea that she was headed for the eye of a storm. Lady Antonia, for instance, had always appeared to be friendly and welcoming. But

Lily was hampered from the start: by who she was; by who Randolph was; and by her naivety in thinking that none of this would matter.

Randolph had often talked of Cumloden and his love for the deer park. As a result Lily was full of eager anticipation and as the car that brought them from the station rounded the last bend in the long driveway leading up to the house, she was greatly impressed. 'It took my breath away,' she wrote later, adding, 'There were dressing rooms adjoining the bedrooms, which overlooked a terrace and the rolling gardens. There was even a billiards room on the ground floor.' As Lord Galloway's housekeeper led Lily and Randolph to their room, she could barely take it all in. There were robes and swords, and everywhere she looked were the fruits of Stewart achievement. Jewels and medals were displayed in cabinets, then there were regalia relating to Lord Galloway's position as Past Grand Master of Scotland, regalia of the thirty-third degree of the Scottish Freemasonry, rings, the past first grand principal of the Royal Arch Jewel, and sixty-eight volumes of Sir William Stewart's letters and correspondence, the Cumloden Papers – easily one of the most valuable assets in the house.

Paintings, drawings, miniatures, and prints hung on most walls, many of them capturing Randolph's serious-looking forebears. If, as Chinnery suspected, Lily had not really understood the significance of the family into which she had married, she could be in no doubt now. In the drawing room, for example, were a portrait of Randolph's father as a young boy with his brother; a three-quarter length oil of Randolph's grandmother Amy, Countess of Galloway; a three-quarter length oil of Anne, the 7th Countess with her child; a half-length oil of Alexander, 1st Earl of Galloway; a three-quarter length portrait of Mrs Cliffe, Randolph's great-grandmother, in a blue dress wearing a red cloak; a bust-length oil of Mary, Queen of Scots in red dress; and a half-length oval portrait of Alexander, 6th Earl of Galloway wearing a red coat.

Faces from the past peered down wherever she looked; the 2nd Earl of Galloway; Lady Mary, daughter of the 2nd Marquis of Salisbury; Lady Susannah, daughter of the 6th Earl of Galloway, playing the lyre; the 9th Earl of Galloway; the Hon. Keith Stewart; a three-quarter length portrait of the Hon. George Stewart, son of

Alexander, 6th Earl of Galloway; a half-length portrait of George, 8th Earl of Galloway; James, the 5th Earl of Galloway; Lady Jane, daughter of 1st Earl of Uxbridge and wife of the 8th Earl of Galloway; and John, 7th Earl of Galloway.

The paintings displayed the calibre of countesses who had preceded her, young, beautiful women, the daughters of dukes and earls, titled and wealthy from birth, destined to help continue the line. Like them, Lily had become a Stewart, a 'great lady', just as the snowy haired Hannah had predicted more than half a century before.

Lord Galloway awaited them. Today, more than twenty-five years on, the memory of that encounter still sends Randolph into an agitated state. Pressed for the details, he becomes nervous and frightened, as if more admonishment awaits him. Lily wrote of it, 'I shall never forget that day . . . I walked round the grounds . . . before we left, comparing the beauty of the place with the sadness of its occupants . . . for all its finery, [it] was not in my eyes a happy place.'

Lord Galloway's opening remark was a comment on Randolph's appearance. He was wearing a new suit, a silk tie, and a crisp shirt, chosen and pressed by Lily. This passed Lord Galloway by. 'My God he looks ill!' he observed correctly, given that Randolph had flu. 'What has happened to him?' The atmosphere was stiff but just about bearable. Lord Galloway was trying his best, but he still bore a grudge about the secret wedding. He made this very clear. After Lily and Randolph had collected themselves, it was suggested that they accompany Lady Antonia on a walk around the grounds. It was during this walk that the situation worsened. Whether out of nerves, bad judgement, or both, Lily let Lady Antonia feel the hurricane force of her religious fervour. Her grave error was to speak of what she and Randolph would do to Cumloden when it eventually became their home. They would open it up, she said with great excitement, 'to people less fortunate than ourselves', convert the stables into a retreat 'where those with troubles could find some peace'. Lily was later to refer to these plans as 'a baseless fantasy' but her conviction then had been solid.

It is difficult to think of a worse indiscretion. It was not that Lord Galloway was unused to the pull of religion, for his late wife had been a devout Anglo-Catholic too. His repulsion was more to do with the inappropriate way Lily sought to apply 'God's plan' – which was how she spoke of her marriage – to the future of his family home, about which he felt deeply protective. Worse still was the fact that this latest development of 'God's plan' was unfortunately predicated upon his death. After supper Lord Galloway instructed Randolph to go to his bedroom. He obeyed, leaving Lily behind to experience what she took to calling 'that dreadful scene'.

'At first I mistook it for a friendly gesture and chatted on about antiques,' she was to recall. But Lord Galloway cut her short, saying, 'We're not here to talk about antiques. We're here to tell you you shouldn't be the countess. You've married into the House of Stewart, and you'll be the Countess of Galloway one day – if you're still together. But you wouldn't know how to be a countess. You have not been brought up in the same sort of family as us.'

Lord Galloway, convinced that Lily had married Randolph for his money, saw money itself to be the solution to the problem. How much would it take for an annulment? he asked, flipping open his cheque book. Just as her display of vulgarity had offended him to the core, so was she was offended by having to answer his question. Lily's friends tell different versions of this encounter, each one impossible to corroborate. The one consistent detail is his attempt to buy her off, which suggests that it did happen. Did he not realise, she told him, that she loved Randolph? 'But how can you love him?' Lord Galloway retorted – a comment that perhaps says more about his own capacity for emotion than hers. 'It is not love you feel,' he told her, 'it is pity.' But Lily had already worked out where she stood on that distinction. As Father Reid had told her, 'Pity, Lily, well, there is nothing wrong with that.'

Lily's response to Lord Galloway's spectacular insult varies from version to version. To some friends she maintains that she spat back, 'You may be a belted Earl, but you're not fit to lick my boot-straps'. This is a highly unlikely story. At this stage Lily still wanted to win him round, proved by a letter she wrote to him soon after. Still, retrospectively, she told others that she had pointed at some of the portraits and informed Lord Galloway that they were fakes. All these supposed retorts are almost certainly embellishments, a kind of artistic licence taken latterly to create the impression of a personal victory, all the more desired after years of bitterness and anger. Perhaps they are how she would have responded had it not been for her shock. 'That night, hurt and confused,' she wrote, 'I clung to Randolph, sustained by his love. No, I have never known luxury. But if I had been like them my husband wouldn't have fallen in love with me. But at the moment I couldn't explain our love.'

Lord Galloway on Easter Monday, 1976, in his sunroom
at Cumloden after meeting Lily for the first time.

The following day they left for Edinburgh with Lady Antonia behind the wheel of her small car. As they prepared to go, Lord Galloway concluded with cold resolve, 'Well, he's your problem now.' This was spoken in Randolph's earshot. The memory has never faded.

The truth was that Randolph *was* Lily's problem. He had become so reduced by withdrawal symptoms and so dependent on her that she had decided that she had no choice but to wind down The Magpie's Nest and care for him full-time until he made a recovery. The pattern was starting all over again. She had enjoyed her shop for five years now, but Randolph came first and that was that. She would close it down in June, she decided, by which point she would have cleared her stock. Randolph had only £3 in the bank and she was already overdrawn, with a huge VAT bill looming. She could have had little idea of how they would survive – by income from boarders, perhaps, or by selling her dolls. At this stage, though, Lily must have been consoled by the thought that security lay in the future, when she would live out the autumn of her life helping the unfortunate amid the relative splendour of Cumloden.

On their return to Edinburgh Lily decided that she and Randolph must write to Lord Galloway independently expressing their thanks and their hopes for the future. On 23 April Lily sat down and composed the following letter, displaying how she wrote exactly as she spoke, rarely slowing down to honour the demands of punctuation.

Dear Father

We had a pleasant journey home, the countryside was so beautiful and the sun was shining until we got to within a few miles of Edinburgh. Antonia drives very well, I think we all felt a little weakened and everything was beautiful, to me it was like fairy land. I want to thank you so much for allowing me to visit Cumloden and for your hospitality. I appreciate the worry and disappointment Garlies must have caused you and his mother over the years, and I know from experience when one has been terribly hurt its [*sic*] difficult to forgive, and one can't ever forget. We must all help him now before it is to [*sic*] late the next few months will be a storm on him just as the last few months have been. For the first time in twenty years he is without the help of drugs, which in the past may have kept him sedated but have at times nearly driven him out of his mind. I assure you Father with love, understanding and help over the bad patches he will get well.

He is full of fear over certain things, built in inhibitions and regrets over the things he has done to hurt you and his mother in the past, we must help him to get rid of all that.

He relies on me a lot I know, but as long as I have his

love and confidence, return love with love, be firm when necessary and put my trust in God I will not fail.

This will take time Father, I can not undo all the harm the drugs have done for twenty years in a few months but I have faith it will happen, Garlies will be mentally and physically fit.

Please don't worry about him father just try to understand how difficult it is not to have a guilt complex when he is with you. This makes him unable to tell you all things he wants to.

Thank you again for your kindness

Keep well father

Love and Gods [*sic*] blessing

Lily.

If Lily was furious with Lord Galloway for his suggestion that she had her price, this letter was her olive branch. There is no doubt that it was well-meant, honest, and, considering how badly he had insulted her, admirable. But it was also spectacularly misjudged, a disastrous attempt to push herself into the family and align herself with Lord Galloway in order that they could become a united front, partners in the mission to bring about Randolph's recovery. There was too much talk of 'we' – 'We must all help him now before it is to [*sic*] late' – a lot to take for granted considering Lord Galloway had told her he did not want her in his family. Worse still, considering the formality that ruled the Galloway household, was that she seemed to have abandoned any semblance of etiquette. When with her own family, Lily always referred to Lord Galloway as 'Father', which Brebner felt to be a touch artificial. However, when he questioned her about why she insisted on such informality, Lily always responded that Lord Galloway had asked her to address him this way, another curious detail in their fraught relations. Lily's letter was also tin-eared to the sensitive issue of how Randolph's health had been managed over the years, and in trying to convey her commitment to make Randolph well again, Lily had instead come across as a kind of self-styled disciple of Christ, working to achieve what normal mortals had not yet managed – 'I can not undo all the harm the drugs have done for twenty years in a few months but I have faith it will happen . . . I assure you Father with love, understanding and help over the bad patches he will get well.'

Poor Lily. What she and Randolph needed more than anything was a mentor to guide them through such matters, at the very least somebody to proofread their letters. She would have done well to ask the advice of Lady Daphne, for example. Lily did not yet understand that public expression of feelings and emotions were anathema to Lord Galloway. For a man who had spent his life maintaining a stiff upper lip, the tone of this letter would have cut like a knife, and forced him to confront all that he found abhorrent and painful – 'He is full of fear over certain things, built in inhibitions and regrets over the things he has done to hurt you and his mother in the past.' This extraordinary document must surely have put Lord Galloway off his breakfast. If it did not, there was the letter from Randolph, just to finish him off.

23 April 1976
Dearest Father,

Thank you so much for our lovely visit to Cumloden. We had a pleasant journey back, the dogs gave us a great welcome but the weather changed it was cold and dull. Yesterday it was like winter again and we had a set back. Lily was just going off to the shop, and Candy, one of the dogs was hit by a car, we were all very upset but it turned out the vet said she was badly bruised only, and although she seems very stiff the injection helped to ease the pain.

Lily did not go to the shop as she was too upset, but Brebner came along for lunch and we told him all about our visit to Cumloden. He and his family love the country and hope to see Cumloden one day. Brebner has helped me such a lot and I always feel relaxed with him and able to confide in him.

As a medical man he understands why I have problems, and why, although I want so much to confide in you I just can't. Believe me Father I want to, but it is the guilt complex I have of the things I did in the past to hurt you, and dear mother. I am deeply sorry Father and I suppose the guilt I feel, is part of my punishment which I am sure is well deserved.

Lily assures me that Mother is very near to us and knows and understands.

The rehabilitation from the drugs is a long process, when it is complete it's only then that I will improve physically, and will look and feel less tense.

Brebner has every confidence in me that when the cure is complete I will be able to work, in a garden, have a greenhouse and watch things grow, or with animals, the country certainly.

I love it and feel I could be a success, if only I could work with someone like Brebner, who seems to bring out the best in me.

I have told him about the Financial side of things and he said both Lily and I have problems like everyone else these days, and does not think we should worry you about them. Lily has an overdraught [*sic*] and I have just £3 in the bank but we have some unpaid bills. Electricity, telephone and part of a roof repair but Lily hopes to get enough from the shop to pay these. Lily is giving up the lease at the end of June but to close the lease alone, it is £474 which she will have to recover from stock, so over the next few weeks it will not be easy.

I want to thank you again Father for having us to Cumloden, and please forgive me for all the things I have done in the past to hurt you.

This brings you very much love in which Lily joins me.

Garlies.

There can be no doubt that this letter is not the work of Randolph alone. For a start, he did not like Lily's poodles. They aggravated him. Everything about the letter – its tone, the points it makes – reads completely at odds with every letter Randolph had ever written before, or would write in the future. It was not that Randolph did not express his emotions in his letters – he would come to do this constantly in years to come – it was more that he would never have expressed them in this way. Randolph's writing style is quite unique and at times wild. There is something far too calm and measured about this letter for it to have been written by him. For example, it is inconceivable that Randolph would have written, 'The rehabilitation from the drugs is a long process, when it is complete its only then that I will improve physically, and will look and feel less tense.' 'Tense' is not a Randolph word. His reference to 'the guilt I feel, is part of my punishment' picks up from Lily's letter and it also seems pretty clear that Lily's bill of £474 is mentioned in the hope that it might prompt Lord Galloway to help. If it was not a gallant attempt to scrounge on her behalf, then it is exactly the kind of reference that an independent reader should have told them to omit.

Lord Galloway responded immediately. He had, understandably, picked up on the mention of money and it had made him furious. As far as he saw, Lily was already trying to dip her fingers into the Stewart coffers. He did not write to Randolph to express this. He wrote to Lily, informing her in no uncertain terms of how much he disliked her, how little he trusted her, and how she would never be a part of his family. She had tricked Randolph into marriage, he wrote, and not only that, she was making Randolph ill by taking him off his medication. Did she understand what she was doing? He also saw quite clearly, he continued, that she was attempting to turn Randolph against his own family and that it was quite evident that she expected him to bale her out. True to form, Lily destroyed this letter. Lord Galloway, however, kept the letter she wrote in response, in which she answered point by point the criticisms and accusations he had levelled at her.

'Dear Lord Galloway,' she now began (such formality is much more in keeping with her Duns upbringing): 'I received your letter this morning and as intended it gave me quite a shock. I am sorry that I accepted your invitation to Cumloden, If I had known how you felt about me I would have refused.'

She had, she retorted, absolutely no regrets about marrying Randolph secretly. The reason they had done it in that way was because they had set their hearts on being together and did not want to risk the marriage being stopped. 'You are wrong if you think it was a trick,' she wrote: 'you have mentioned for the second time how I would have felt if any of my sons had married secretly, that would never have happened. I had their love and confidence from a very early age, they came to me with their problems and we worked them out together . . . I am glad that I know you will never forgive me, because now I know where I stand.'

She was fiercer still on the subject of Randolph's health, delivering to Lord Galloway harsh truths about his treatment of his son. 'As I said before Garlies served his sentence by being away for far to [*sic*] long . . . There must be a reason for his fear of you . . . which was there long before he met me . . . I got the best medical advice I could about Garlies . . . You obviously don't know about the side effects of drugs, it's a wonder he is alive, after the amount of drugs he has had over the past twenty years. As you said when I was at Cumloden Garlies is my problem now, its [*sic*] strange I never considered it a problem, if you love a person enough, and accept them for what they are you are not afraid of the future.'

Next she turned to his assumption that she desired his money. It is unlikely that Lily and Randolph would have refused financial help had Lord Galloway offered it. But now that Lord Galloway had brought it out in the open and levelled it as a criticism, Lily could afford to protest her innocence. 'The other matter which I feel I must mention is the matter of you "baling me out" if I get into financial difficulties. My financial problems have nothing whatsoever to do with you. I am giving up the shop for two reasons, one is that I am not making enough profit to survive. My business has suffered since my marriage because I can't devote enough time to my husband if I put in the hours at the shop, and my husband comes first.' Lily concluded her letter triumphantly:

> I am fortunate, and thank God for it that I am capable of hard work. I have scrubbed a floor for half a crown to give my son his lunch. I could do the same again for your son if the need arises, and may very well do it, to prove a point. You are surrounded by beauty and treasures which you inherited. My home is my castle which was acquired by her [*sic*] hard work and determination to survive, some times against great odds.

Her closing remark was simultaneously dignified and patronising: 'As a convert Christian I shall pray for you, to God to soften your heart. To our Blessed Lady to intercede for you.'

This was Lily at her absolute best, defending herself from the heart, more than a match for Lord Galloway. She emerged with her pride intact but there was no going back now. If the consequences of Lord Galloway's rejection of Lily had not been so desperate, so upsetting for her, and so damaging to Randolph, the retelling of it might raise a smile. After all, it was so close to cliché – a good old-fashioned struggle between rich and poor, with Lord Galloway cast as the cold aristocrat and Lily the working-class servant with a heart of gold. But far too much damage ensued for it to be comic, and besides, the situation brought out the worst in everybody concerned. Lily had been very unwise mentioning her plans for Cumloden, and she had been very heavy-handed with Lord Galloway and Lady Antonia. A gentler, more considered approach – not claiming the ring and steering clear of money talk, for example – might have led to eventual acceptance. On the other hand Lord Galloway was, from the outset, searching for confirmation of his fears. He saw only the worst in her and nothing of the good. With every cross word spoken, every letter sent, the chasm became ever more yawning, the prospect of a reconciliation ever more remote.

13

A Shoddy Day and Age

Gossip travelled fast in Edinburgh and some of it found its way to Fleet Street. At the end of June Lily received a telephone call from Olga Maitland, Lord Lauderdale's daughter, who worked as a diarist on Town Talk, the gossip column in the *Sunday Express*, then edited by the indomitable diarist, Peter McKay. Town Talk was intending to publish a story on what had happened at Cumloden. Would Lady Garlies care to comment? Lily was startled. She had no experience of journalists and could not imagine how they had found her (such was her naïvety then). Still, she remained cross and hurt by Lord Galloway's insults and she spoke openly of these feelings. It was not a calculated step intended to grieve Lord Galloway further, although she had more than enough reason to behave in the manner of a woman scorned. It was more the consequence of unknowingly submitting to the diarist's skill. With expert prompting, Lily remained talking on the telephone far longer than was wise. When she finally placed the receiver in the cradle, Lady Olga had a good story in her notepad. As McKay attests, 'We've had dukes admitting to all sorts of things on the telephone. It is amazing what can happen when you catch people off their guard.'

On 4 July, 1976 news of the rift was published in full detail in Town Talk, under the headline 'An "unsuitable" marriage in the House of Stewart'. After a brief summary of the facts, the article moved straight into quotation. 'I am afraid that neither my father-in-law nor sister-in-law Lady Antonia Dalrymple will ever accept me. Lord Galloway is clearly not pleased about my marriage.' The article went on to recreate conversations conducted at Cumloden. 'I had the most upsetting meeting with him ... After dinner the night we arrived, Lord Galloway ordered my husband to his room, and

ordered me to come and see him alone. He told me to sit down
and then asked straight out, "Why did you marry my son?" He
suggested that I married him for his title and money. Nothing is
further from the truth ... They were most unfair allegations. I am
not ashamed of my humble birth. My husband has not been well
for years, and all this time has been under the care of doctors.
Lord Galloway is now criticizing me over the way I look after my
husband.'

The article repeated many of the sentiments Lily had outlined
in her letter to Lord Galloway. She did not want his money; she
had a capable pair of hands; she'd scrubbed floors before and
would do so again. And she wished Lord Galloway would stop
sending her 'most upsetting letters'. Why could they not just leave
them alone? She and Randolph would manage alone in 'their
simple flat in Edinburgh'. 'I have always had great faith that the
Lord will provide,' the article concluded.

There was a long-running joke between McKay and Michael
Thornton who often provided McKay with copy. 'How did they take
it?' McKay would ask the following morning. 'Ah,' Thornton would
say, 'they were fit to be tied.' 'It was a wonderful way of describing
the extent of somebody's anger,' McKay recalls, 'so overwrought
and juddering that they were in need of tethering.' On the morning
of 4 July, Lord Galloway was indeed 'fit to be tied.' To have aired
the Stewart's dirty laundry in such a public way he saw to be yet
another sign of Lily's supreme vulgarity. It fortified his prejudices
and did nothing to aid diplomatic relations. Lily mounted her
defence by pleading to have been clueless as to the consequences
of the conversation, but it was a lame excuse and it got her nowhere.
In any case, the sentiments expressed in Town Talk were quite in
keeping with those she felt. The day after the article had appeared,
Lord Galloway received a letter from a reader of the _Sunday Express_,
who was writing in response to the article. 'Having read the _Sunday
Express_ report of your son's marriage to a commoner, I would not
hesitate to disown him,' the letter read. 'The House of Stewart has
played such a tremendously important part in Scottish history, and
though I am English and a commoner, I was sad to think that
generations of Stewarts should be lightly dismissed by your son and
heir. In this shoddy day and age, where children are taught not to

respect tradition – or their parents' wishes, then they themselves must take the consequence. You owe it to the Stewarts to leave the title to a more worthy successor – even if you need to invoke the sex discrimination act to leave it your daughter.'

It was a prescient letter. It reflected Lord Galloway's thoughts exactly. If Lily would not accept his offer of cash for an annulment, and if Randolph persisted in his loyalty to her, he would have no choice but to disinherit him. Lily recalled of this time that there were 'constant phone calls, constant attempts to part us'. She also recorded that somebody – and she does not say who – tried to suggest that Randolph was 'incapabable of living a full married life'. 'I'm afraid my answer offended this person but I was so angry at attempts to part us,' she said of the exchange.

Lily felt it was important to give Randolph a purpose in life and so she secured him a job as a voluntary gardener working for a charity hostel. He liked working in the outdoors and they both felt this would be good training for when he eventually ran Cumloden. Meanwhile she set about closing down The Magpie's Nest. She sold off her china and packed her dolls in boxes ready to take back to Bernard Terrace. Just at this moment, Lord Galloway was in the process of changing his will. He had asked Lady Antonia if she might like the estate, as the cross *Sunday Express* reader had suggested, but she declined. (Following the death of her husband, Sir Mark Dalrymple, she had inherited Newhailes, a stately home in Musselborough famous for its library.) This left Lord Galloway at rather a loss as to what to do next. As his health was declining he wanted the consolation of knowing that his family's land and heritage would be safely shielded from the force he felt would lead to its destruction. Cumloden meant everything to him, far more than the laws of primogeniture. So Lord Galloway looked over the head of his only son towards a steadier man, one who could steer the estate into the future and ensure its safety.

Although Lord Galloway's concerns for Cumloden's future were quite reasonable, he was not prepared to compromise. Randolph was to be cut out completely, with not so much as a cottage in the grounds in which he could spend his old age. It is impossible to know exactly how Lord Galloway felt about disinheriting Randolph. The only evidence of his thinking lies in his paperwork, particularly the passage of the codicils attached to his will. Lord Galloway was not a man given to hysteria or self-pity. Outside the business of Lily, he approached his affairs and conducted his life with the utmost composure. It is inconceivable that the will he made in June 1976 – two months after Lily and Randolph visited – was his first. The only clue about his intentions before Lily arrived on the scene that now remains is a letter sent in 1974 by Lord Galloway's trustees to Randolph's psychiatrist at the Crichton Royal Hospital in Dumfries, in which they requested an opinion as to Randolph's capabilities. Randolph's psychiatrist had not examined his patient for three years, but he responded saying that he doubted if Randolph was mentally fit enough to understand what was required of him and that he would be much happier if there was an appointment of a *curator bonis*, a third party appointed by the court to look after the financial interests of one who is deemed incapable.

If, in 1974, Lord Galloway was concerning himself with how best to ensure the safekeeping of his son's interests, by 27 June, 1976, he had all but eliminated the need to ask the question. He swore, in this new will, 'to pay my son Lord Garlies only such a sum out of the capital of my moveable estate as shall equal the value of legitim and any other legal right or rights which my son may have in my estate on my death.'

Cumloden, its contents, and its land, were made over to Lord Galloway's distant relative, Alexander Stewart, a Suffolk farmer in poor health. The wisdom of finding a younger man soon became clear and on 8 September, 1976, Lord Galloway signed a codicil that shifted his entire fortune into the lap of Alexander Stewart's son, Andrew Stewart, an Old Etonian stockbroker, whom he had not met. It was a gamble, but Lord Galloway was desperate. Andrew Stewart was young and about to marry too. It seemed an adequate solution.

Randolph was to receive nothing, or as little as the laws of Scottish inheritance would allow – one half of a half of the moveable estate. This meant no property of any kind and as little capital as possible. This new will is the best evidence there is of the extent of Lord Galloway's bitterness. Even the servants were destined to receive more. His housekeeper, for instance, was bequeathed the late Lady Galloway's Morris 1000 and the sum of £5,000. There were other small legacies to those who had served him for ten years or more. He made payments to his gamekeeper and forester. Lady Antonia, as well as her legal rights, was to receive £10,000, his past first grand principal of the royal arch jewel, and his own Morris Minor. The Grand Lodge of Scotland was to receive his regalia as past grand master of Scotland. The Black Watch was to have his own father's letters written from the Crimea and during the Indian Mutiny. The vestry of his local church, All Saints', Challoch, was bequeathed £1,000.

Around this time Lily slipped and cracked her pelvis. The fall caused her much pain, but every morning she insisted on rising and making Randolph his breakfast. She refused to let him help her with the chores. She fussed and cared for him and did everything so that he might feel happy. In return he told her that she reminded him of Nan, the Cumloden laundry maid who had cuddled him to her bosom. Lily was proud of this and often repeated it to friends, who were horrified. 'But Lily! That's awful. She was a servant woman!' Her response was always the same. 'I did not see it as an insult at all. She was the only one who had ever given him any love.'

The one benefit of the feud was that it brought Lily and Randolph closer. Under attack from Lord Galloway and under the scrutiny of the press, each looked to the other for love and strength. A month after Lord Galloway sealed Randolph's disinheritance, as Lily was recovering from her injury, Randolph sent him one of the stiffest letters yet. Spurred on by Lily, Randolph was now standing up for himself. He no longer wanted to be hidden away, and he told his father this frankly. Of Lily he wrote, 'Each day our love grows stronger . . . She was willing to love my family too and what have you done to her, to try to break her spirit.' It was fighting talk. There was more:

> As I am now taking my rightful place in Society and attending social functions as Head of the House of Stewart I would be most grateful if you would let me know if there is a kilt and jacket available at Cumloden which would suit me . . . As I have to hire this dress for these occasions I find it rather expensive, and on my

income, impossible. As a future Earl I do not want to let the family down and I would appreciate your help without fuss. Whether you are interested or not, I am working every day, completely voluntary [*sic*] as my dear wife insists on this until she feels that I am completely recovered from my years of isolation from society.

The letter goes on to make clear that both he and Lily were 'distressed at the recent accounts in the press' and that 'neither of us had anything to do with the story that was in the *Express*', which must have tested Lord Galloway's patience since the story had quoted Lily so fully. But then, as Randolph, continues, 'All this is most distasteful to my dear wife and her wonderful family'.

You will have to accept that your son is no longer in need of psychiatrists or shunned from society. I intend taking my rightful place as from now.
Try loving a little instead of hating so much because enough damage has been done already. My dear wife loves me and will never let anyone hurt me in any way ... I consider it is my wife who is the Lady.
I would be grateful to know about the kilt. I trust your arthritis is better in this good weather and that one day you will stop being angry. Love Garlies.

Randolph did not get his kilt. Nevertheless Lily and Randolph's efforts for him to take his rightful place in society continued regardless.

The route to Lily and Randolph's problems with the press led directly to the door of 56 India Street, where lived the ageing Edinburgh socialite and society photographer Brodrick Haldane. If the perils, pleasures, and preoccupations of Edinburgh society as it was in the 1970s and 1980s could be encapsulated in one person, Brodrick Haldane of Gleneagles would do very well. Brodrick knew everybody. He was both snobbish and egalitarian. He liked a name and a title even more, but he was also happy to look beyond them. Someone listed in *Burke's* turned his head, but he was just as likely to befriend a man in leathers as a man in tweed (if they were pretty and rode a motorcycle, all the better). In fact, Brodrick was so open to new company that he was once cleaned out by a gang of international thieves, whom he had introduced to everybody as 'his interesting new friends'. 'I take as I find, I take as I find,' he twittered, looking mournfully at the gaps the theft left in his ornate drawing room. He came to know Lily very well, and even became her unlikely champion. But he also knew Peter McKay and Olga Maitland, and when there was Champagne to be bought and there were drawing rooms to be furnished, needs must.

Lounging on his chaise longue in his flat at 56 India Street, wearing soft slippers and a cravat, surrounded by his free-flying swifts, Haldane was a vision of vanity, refinement, and old-fashioned charm. When the journalist Lynn Barber interviewed him before his much-mourned death in 1996, she observed, 'He represents somewhat unfashionable virtues – keeping up a good front, eschewing self-pity, entertaining one's friends, honouring one's parents . . . one can see why his friends are so devoted to him.' And they were, particularly duchesses, exiled European queens, and homosexuals. 'All my men friends sooner or later got married,' he lamented to the writer, Roddy Martine, in his memoir *Time Exposure*. 'I think this might have been the reason why I turned to older women who showed an interest in my career.'

Cecil Beaton had called him 'the man who invented modern society photography'. Brodrick used a vest-pocket Kodak, held together with sticking plaster. Early on he had snapped his friends enjoying upper-class life – the London season, summers in the south of France, winters in Switzerland and Austria. 'From the moment he published a photograph of the Countess of Strathmore, the Queen Mother's mother, attending a fête at Glamis Castle, he never looked back,' reported the *Scotsman*. Because he was high-born (the first son, although his younger, heterosexual brother inherited Gleneagles) one connection always led to another, with the result that by the time he moved to Edinburgh in 1964 he knew, among others, the Mitford sisters; Margaret, Duchess of Argyll; the exiled Queen of Spain; Marlene Dietrich; Noël Coward; and Vladimir Nabokov.

On arriving in Edinburgh, even Brodrick with his impressive address book required a patron to ensure he made the right connections. His two close friends, Betty and Ursula Constable Maxwell ('cousins of Lord Lovat' he emphasises in *Time Exposure*) threw a series of dinners and drinks parties for him. Before long he began receiving invitations of his own accord. This kind of Edinburgh socialising – cliquey, private and based on introduction – still existed when Lily sought to 'bring out' Randolph. 'Bringing him out' could not be achieved simply by showing up in good restaurants (of which there was only one in the city anyway, L'Aperitif). It had to be done at private addresses, at the many drinks parties held in the New Town drawing rooms with their high windows and streams of light. Invitations were always extended on stiff card: the stiffer the card, the more promising the party. If the address of a party was Ainslie Place, this was very good, if Moray Place or Heriot Row, so much the better. At these parties, usually mid-week, guests moved around sipping wine or champagne and making small talk. Men were thought of in terms of the firm or chambers for which they worked, where they went to school, or the land they owned; the women by their husband's status, by their own titles, or by their fundraising. People preferred to socialise with familiar faces. They did not seek the variety of different social backgrounds. It was, broadly speaking, an inward looking and class-conscious world, the antithesis of cosmopolitan.

In only one respect Brodrick Haldane was different. Despite his distracted and effete persona, which gave the impression that he had stepped out of another century, his views on what made a good party were modern. He liked to burn black candles to create a bohemian atmosphere, and would shudder at the idea of an entire room packed only with the titled. He loved a duke, but particularly for the thrill of placing him next to a transsexual artist at supper, or for seeing him deep in conversation with a promising young male actor. For Brodrick, it was all about 'the mix', and of course, in Lily, he had 'the mix' incarnate.

He had heard much about the new Lord and Lady Garlies. He had seen their full-page picture in the *Edinburgh Tatler,* and had for years been a friend of Lady Antonia (although leaked gossip would not have come from her). He also shared friends in common with Lily. Michael Chinnery was often a guest at his parties as was Joseph Bonnar, now well on his way to becoming Edinburgh's premier society jeweller. It was, he had concluded before the stories had started to appear in the newspapers, time to have this odd couple over to 56 India Street so he could see them for himself.

Brodrick had a critical eye, one that craved beauty and refinement. He liked to see it in his reflection ('being considered unnaturally good looking, I did attract a lot of not entirely unwelcome attention from my own sex,' he told Roddy) and he liked it in his guests. Women invited the most comment. The Kennedy girls, for example, who he had met years before, were 'heavy-limbed' and the Duchess of Windsor was 'extremely ugly', with 'a nose that seemed to go on a long way' and 'no fingernails'. While Lily was stylish, she had a worn-out face free of all conventional beauty. Indeed, when Brodrick's friend, a former debutante and a beauty in her day, had seen Lily for the first time at a luncheon, she had thought that never in her entire life had she encountered such a dreadful face – 'all hard and knobbly – quite ugly!' Peering at Lily from the other end of the table, Lady Merioth had wanted to run for her oil paints. Setting this aside, however, she had been unbothered by Lily's roots when some of the other female guests had started to discuss Lily, saying once she had left, 'Quite dreadful!' and 'Common!', Lady Merioth, who had watched Lily spring from her seat to help Randolph cut up his food, piped up, 'Stop it! I think she loves him very much and frankly, he is very, very lucky to have her. Not the other way round.' 'What struck me was how much she cared for him,' she says, recalling the occasion.

Lily was an immediate hit with Brodrick. Protected by her title, she could be whoever she pleased – and she was simply her maverick self. Brodrick saw how much she loved Randolph and oddly, it was precisely because she had a queer face, a Borders accent, and a penchant for Nambarrie teabags that her passage into her new Edinburgh world was so smooth. It was an arresting combination. Soon she could be heard across a room hooting with laughter or mimicking guests. 'My dear,' Brodrick would relay to Michael Thornton, 'she is so wonderfully indiscreet.' In these early days Lily spoke openly and caustically about 'The earrrrl', which would be pronounced in a kind of deep Borders roll. Brodrick would always giggle and say with a sigh, 'Oh, Lily, dear, do say Lord Galloway or "my father-in-law". It is much more correct.' But Lily never did behave as though she cared what people thought of her. As a result she was adored, although much more by men than women, which, generally, was an accurate reflection of her own feelings towards the sexes. One stiff invitation card begot another.

Randolph was harder to accommodate. Although Lily was keen to put him into a dinner jacket at every available opportunity, he was disinclined towards large groups. They frightened him. During one soirée, for instance, he jumped up in the air and began to shout incomprehensibly. If Lily found this embarrassing she did not say so. She was unwilling to shuffle him home to save her hostess embarrassment. Randolph had had too many years of that, she thought. Instead she led him to a corner, whispering words of comfort until he calmed down. It was a curious spectacle for the other guests, but a moving one.

Brodrick Haldane's dealings with Peter McKay were never motivated by malice. Financial necessity was usually to blame. He was not as wealthy as he appeared (something of a theme among Lily's new friends). Often he stood on his head to arrest his balding – 'oh do try it!' he once said to Roddy Martine, getting into position, after noticing his friend's hair was on the thin side. He would often be left short by his extravagances – entertaining, for example, and surgery (he was once caught scuttling home with his face swathed in bandages following a hair transplant, the real reason behind his foppish mop). In the autumn of 1976 Brodrick's bank balance needed replenishing and once again Lily, Randolph, and Lord Galloway would fall victim. As usual, it started innocently enough.

There were only so many luncheon party conversations Broderick could leak to McKay, or photographs he could dispatch to the *Tatler*. With his latest plan, he really felt he had hit upon something original. So plentiful were the compliments of those who passed through 56 India Street that Brodrick decided he would throw open its doors to the general public. He called it his 'Sunday initiative'. For fifty pence a head, passers-by could enjoy the privilege of seeing how the other half lived, but in a more informal way than the usual stately home tours.

Brodrick's abode was not large – it was a flat – and he was very happy to include in the bargain a cup of tea and a chat, sometimes a sherry if he liked the look of the visitor. ('My dear', he would come to moan, 'the public is drinking me dry'.) His home was indeed beautiful. (Betty and Ursula Constable Maxwell owned Galloways, an upmarket interior decorating business in the city, and had given him some William Morris wallpaper and fabric.) 'Bedroom walls,' Brodrick opined later, 'must be papered and never painted', and 'One should always have something shabby in a room, to make it look lived in.' An oversized gilt-framed mirror dominated the inner wall of the drawing room, and in front of the windows stood two Coalbrookdale perfume urns borrowed from Gleneagles and originating from the home of Sir Walter Scott. At the very least, the Sunday initiative provided a good excuse for a party.

Financially, emotionally and artistically, Brodrick was advised by his dearest friend, Michael Thornton. Thornton thought the initiative a good idea and agreed to travel from London to Scotland to help with the party. Invitations (stiff card) were sent out for Wednesday 20 October 1976. Lily accepted immediately. When the day arrived, she found herself mingling with Edinburgh's A list: Sir Ian and Lady Moncreiffe of that ilk, and so on. Brodrick was in something of a dilemma. He had a room packed with society magazine favourites and yet it was unthinkable that he be seen photographing them himself, or that he would miss the chance to make some extra money. He took Michael Thornton aside. 'Look here. I rather think I'd like a whole page in the *Edinburgh Tatler*,' he whispered. 'Try and get a photograph of everybody, will you?'

Michael Thornton was not an expert in Scottish society and had no knowledge of how to use a camera, but Brodrick assured him that if he saw something interesting, he would tip him off. Meanwhile, out of the corner of her eye, Lily saw that Lady Antonia had arrived. By the end of the party, they found themselves quite happy, chatting over a glass of Champagne in the kitchen, a significant improvement considering the froideur that had existed between them in recent months. Had this been the end of the matter perhaps Lily's relationship with her sister-in-law might have grown. But Brodrick witnessed the exchange and beckoned Thornton to record it. 'Do get into the kitchen,' he whispered urgently. 'Lily is in there with Antonia. They seem to be patching up the most frightful row. It would make a wonderful picture for the paper.'

'And off I went, utterly under Brodrick's instruction,' Michael Thornton remembers, 'and as I took the picture I heard Lily say to Antonia, "Now we must do something to make things nicer for him." Antonia was surprised I wanted a photograph. "A picture of me?" she cried, rather like the Queen Mother. But I took it and fled.'

Thornton handed the films over to Brodrick, who delivered them to be processed the next day. He sent one batch to Camera Press, another to the *Edinburgh Tatler*. At the end of October, Lily opened the *Daily Express* to find herself and Lady Antonia staring out of the William Hickey gossip column under the caption 'All Smiles'. The headline read, 'Champagne evening ends the Galloway Family Feud'. Lily was described as 'Mrs Budge, an unaristocratic figure . . . an Edinburgh shopkeeper'. The story continued, rather overegging the issue of class difference:

> When Lady Garlies, who lives with her husband in a tiny flat in one of Edinburgh's poorest districts, spied her sister-in-law at the Haldane party an onlooker was heard to mutter 'Has Lily brought her gun?' But Haldane's effort at peacemaking eventually effected a reconcilation. After several glasses of champagne, the two ladies

Lily and Lady Antonia Dalrymple fall victim to Brodrick Haldane's desire to earn some Fleet Street pocket money.

were to be found close together in his kitchen, having a heart-to-heart over the family feud.

Once again Lord Galloway was 'fit to be tied'. Not only was Lily attending A-list functions – he had known the Haldanes for years – but she was also sipping Champagne with his own daughter. Lily accepted the incident with a shrug. She was becoming used to it. Lady Antonia wrote to Michael Thornton expressing her sorrow. When her father's attention had been drawn to the article in the *Daily Express*, she told him (adding that it was a very inaccurate account of what had passed between her and Lily), he had telephoned her and said that he was very angry with her for having spoken to Lily at all, considering the stories that had been published over the summer. Lady Antonia wanted nothing more than a satisfactory explanation as to how the story appeared, at which point she hoped for a reconciliation. The whole thing, she ended, had upset her very much and undermined her health. Brodrick vehemently denied he had been to blame and became quite offended. 'He was never really good about being put on the spot,' remembers Thornton: 'even when he was wrong he could become quite indignant.'

Lord Galloway, having received insufficient explanation, advised Lady Antonia to bring in a lawyer. Lady Antonia wrote to Thornton again saying that she had been quite prepared to drop the matter, feeling quite rightly that Lily had more cause to expect an apology than she. Surely Brodrick's common sense would have told him the problems such a photograph would cause? The chief trustee of Newhailes also dropped a letter to Brodrick requesting a formal apology. Brodrick in turn requested an apology for the request of an apology, quarrelled on the phone with Lady Antonia, and then threatened to speak to his cousin, a solicitor. As Lady Antonia told Thornton, the conversation left her feeling quite ill and unable to eat her supper. She went to bed with a sleeping pill.

In the middle of this, Lord Galloway telephoned Alex Haldane, Brodrick's brother and the 27th Laird of Gleneagles, in an attempt to get an answer. Alex Haldane was sympathetic. Brodrick was constantly making mischief and the only thing for it was for him to be driven to Cumloden to speak to Lord Galloway in person. Brodrick, sensing a storm awaiting him and desiring safety in numbers, once again roped in Thornton. Despite feeling as though he had been 'thrown into the lion's den', Thornton agreed to the trip, which they decided would provide an opportunity to visit the family graves of Margaret, Duchess of Arygll, a suitably depressing precursor to what was to follow.

No sooner had they arrived at Cumloden than Lord Galloway began his tirade. 'That woman is an adventuress! My son is quite unsuited to marriage and particularly to a woman of her character! He cannot be married. She will not get a penny of my money.' Michael Thornton had never been so terrified. 'Oh, he really went for her. Brodrick did not like that at all. He was really rather fond of Lily and he kept trying to pipe up with a defence but Lord Galloway insisted on shouting him down. Brodrick was not easily frightened but he was quite pale with fear. At one point, he said boldly, "I find her a most responsible woman," at which point Lord Galloway shouted, "Responsible! What kind of responsible woman would marry my son?" It was very unpleasant, and I gather a repeat of the scene Lily had encountered there.' The trip home was made in silence. Still, Brodrick refused to admit responsibility. Within three months Lady Antonia and Brodrick had patched up their quarrel. It was in many ways a ridiculous episode, but it provides a glimpse into a world that values discretion.

Lily continued to maintain that she had Randolph's best interests at heart. Only very occasionally did she allow herself to ponder whether it was she who was the problem, to wonder 'if I had indirectly brought a terrible strain on Randolph'. She *had* brought a terrible strain on him. The real question was whether or not it would be worth it in the end. She wrote later:

> A marvellous friend of his was able to reassure me in a letter: 'Lily, you mustn't blame yourself for all of this. I have never seen Randolph happier. He is a different person since he met you.' One night Randolph turned to me and said: 'Darling, you do know how much you mean to me. I started living on the day I met you.' And another night he started quoting a verse he'd heard – it was so apt for us as it talked about a past which we can

'forgive but not forget'. The tears began to choke me when he reached a line that said 'what would I be without your love?'

To their credit, Colonel Stewart and Lady Daphne refused to take sides, although the Colonel had been disappointed by the involvement of the press. The Christmas of 1976, Lily, Randolph, and A. J. Stewart once again travelled by bus to Middle Blainslie for the Christmas house party. As the bus pulled into Lauder they saw the Colonel pacing about. 'We've got trouble!' he called to them, 'Daphne's been stitched! It's been one hell of a day.' Lady Daphne had been attacked by her husband's bull mastiff while trying to prevent it from savaging her Boston terrier. Her arm was now in a sling and she could not cook. Lady Daphne's misfortune brought out the best in her guests. Lily, in evening dress, and A. J.,

A. J. Stewart in daywear in the grounds of Colonel
Stewart's house near the Borders town of Lauder, with
the excitable bull mastiff in the background.

in surcoat and sark, went straight to work in the kitchen. Lady Daphne took Lily aside. 'I can't get over Garlies,' she told her, 'I met him two years ago and thought he was a very sick man, now he is so well, and so happy and absolutely normal.' During the talk, Lady Daphne consoled Lily. She knew of the difficulties they were experiencing and suggested that they leave Edinburgh, away from the noise and the gossip, and start afresh in the Borders where they could live quietly and Randolph could work for himself on his own land. She would even provide them with two mares to get them going.

Lily's mind ran on the idea all the way home and on 2 January 1977, she wrote to Lord Galloway, full of fresh hope and Lady Daphne's plans: 'She made it all sound so easy just like a dream. I told her what I believed in and that our future was in Gods [*sic*] hands we would have to wait until he decided, we would soon get the message. But whatever he has in store for Garlies I will be behind him all the way.'

Lady Daphne's words of encouragement provided Lily with proof that she had been on the right path all along. She was eager to let Lord Galloway know:

> [Lady Daphne] said the more people see Garlies the more they talk, because he certainly was never treated as a normal person, its [*sic*] a miracle. I agree that after only one year of marriage its [*sic*] unbelievable the change in Garlies but I cant [*sic*] take all the credit. God has a plan for Garlies. I don't know what it is, but our marriage and our life today is a part of it. God only choose [*sic*] me to be an instrument in his work. Garlies is so kind and loving and is a marvelous [*sic*] husband, he takes his place very well indeed in Society I am very proud of him.

Was she trying to annoy Lord Galloway? It is doubtful since Lily did not possess the gift of subtlety. It was probably more the case that she had still not given up the idea of proving to Lord Galloway how good she was for his son. The letter goes on to discuss how Randolph was in the process of having a kilt made up in a random tartan, and that he was 'thrilled to bits he has to have his second fitting next week so he will have the whole outfit in time I hope for the clan gathering'. If this was a faux pas, she would make a worse one still by mentioning the late Lady Galloway.

> I suggested to Garlies today that we will have another Requim [*sic*] Mass like we did last year, for his mother, and my mother and father possible [*sic*] the 2nd March I will ask Fr Reid about it. We had it on the 10th March last year. I think the Countess would like that. Fr Reid really makes it special I know my parents will like it its [*sic*] nice to be remembered specially and its [*sic*] such a beautiful service.

Lily signs off, eventually, with condolence: 'We always have a candle burning for you and pray that your pain will not be too bad.'

I4

Will the Earl get a crumb of comfort?

Lord Galloway's pain was bad. As well as his mental anguish over the marriage, his arthritis was crippling him. He was often bedridden. Socialising was hardly worth the effort. Lady Antonia, who never ceased to be a loyal and obedient daughter, continued to visit him. The rest of the time, Lord Galloway was alone under the watchful eye of his long-serving housekeeper, Nessie Gorman. There was one new comfort, however. With the will now settled, Andrew and Sara Stewart had begun to visit Cumloden in order to get to know both their future second home and the man who had been kind enough – or troubled enough – to bequeath it to them. The delicate manner in which this was handled sits in stark contrast to Lily's efforts to ingratiate herself. Sara and Andrew were based in London, which made quick visits impossible. This posed a problem. Neither wanted to stay in the house. Lord Galloway was preparing for his own end. 'It was very important to us that it did not appear we were waiting for him to die,' explains Sara Stewart. It was decided that it would be more appropriate if they stayed elsewhere on the estate, in a little cottage in the grounds. At the end of 1976 and into 1977 there began a friendship. Lord Galloway had taken a gamble passing his estate on to Andrew Stewart, but he found that he liked him and his young wife. Sara Stewart was lively, from a good family, and interested in history. This fitted well with Lord Galloway's intellect and his own fascination with history (especially the Stewarts'). With time her quiet but confident deference put their relationship on an informal footing, sometimes even allowing for humour. 'One noticed he had rather a twinkle in his eye,' she remembers.

Most of us can be different things to different people. To Sara and Andrew Stewart, Lord Galloway was certainly not the tyrant Lily was painting in the press. He was a peer of the realm, emotionally shuttered, and even shy, but they saw all these characteristics as trappings of his vintage, of the life and era into which he had been born. They made adjustments accordingly, and Lord Galloway responded well. He occasionally threw small lunch parties in their honour, rustling up one or two of his ageing friends nearby. There were not armies of servants in starched aprons, nor were there opulent house parties of the kind immortalised by Julian Fellowes's *Gosford Park*. Cumloden was, in fact, in an atrocious state of repair, badly in need of renovation. The rooms were freezing and during lunch it was not uncommon for Lord Galloway – if his creaking limbs allowed it – to disappear under the tablecloth to crank up the electric heater. The couple had the good manners to refrain from asking for a tour of the house, but they could tell immediately that life there was not lived on a grand scale. Only later, after Lord Galloway's death, did they realise quite the extent of emotional and financial commitment that had been asked of them.

During these months of courtship nobody discussed Randolph's disinheritance and mental health. If anybody (and never Lord Galloway) spoke of him at all, it was always vaguely, in terms of him having been 'unwell' or a 'troubled soul'. Occasionally Lord Galloway would let slip the odd comment revealing his contempt for Lily, but Andrew and Sara Stewart were only mildly influenced. They had never met this unlikely Mrs Budge, and so had few feelings one way or the other, except, perhaps, to think that she sounded like a woman of whom one had to be wary.

It was only a question of time before news of the disinheritance leaked out. Lily and Randolph learnt of it by telephone in February 1977. 'You are to get nothing at all,' Lady Antonia reported to Randolph. Lily watched him return to his armchair, uncomprehending and broken. They could not do this to him, she told him, Cumloden was his home, his birthright. He was to be the 13th Earl of Galloway. At this moment Randolph's hatred and bitterness towards his father crystallised. He was to stress repeatedly over the next twenty years that it had always been there. Perhaps it had, although his letters to his father before his marriage are quite free of such negative sentiments. If hatred had been there from the start, it had remained buried. The disinheritance – and Lily – allowed it to flourish.

The highly emotional situation in which Lily and Randolph found themselves would test even the healthiest partnership. It is not at all surprising, then, that Randolph, completely free of medication, struggled to cope. His life had already undergone one transformation. There was Lily waiting for him in bed at the end of every day, and sitting there at the kitchen table every morning. Then there were the new skills that his changed milieu demanded of him. Where once, before he had met her, there had been the imposed order and routine of the brothers in their cassocks, there were now parties with people dressed in chiffon and tartan spinning round the drawing room to bagpipe music. There were Lily's poodles, too, which continued to unsettle him, and two cats. It was true that Randolph no longer drooped his head in shame, that he could hold a conversation. And as he weeded and hoed the flower borders of the charity hostel, clipped hedges, and made paths and tracks and cut lawns with a push or motor lawn mower, a sense of purpose was slowly entering his being. He had begun to write his memoirs, *Monosyllabic Autobiography*. And yet, like a shadow thrown across a brightly coloured painting, there was the fact that he was now cast out from the only world he knew. Despite the fortification Lily provided, he was as much a stranger in this new world of emotion as he had been in the privileged, colder world in which there had been none.

Lily began to see signs of Randolph's instability. With the additional stress of the prospect of losing Cumloden, he could no longer maintain self-control. On 27 February he had a fit of temper. That evening, he wrote her a letter and left it for her to read:

My Dear Lily, I must now apologise to you MOST DEEPLY for my GRIEVOUS misconduct to you this morning. My sudden outburst of ill temper was NOTHING to be laughed at. It was a DISGRACEFUL and WICKED perform-ance on my part to dare to have the audacity to behave in such a way. As far as housework is concerned I am UTTERLY incapable, and like the rest of my Family have the tendancy [*sic*] to either drop or spill things, through SHER [*sic*] clumsiness.

Carrying on a conversation follows a similar pattern. Sitting in a room talking as you have well discovered is not up my street. But when it comes to doing manual work such as digging in the garden, not necessarily digging, but any kind of garden work, the story differs. All this may sound as if I were currying favour, fishing for compliments or seeking excuses.

I do not care what the Earl of Galloway says, I have nursed this continued fear of him all my life, which latterly has developed into something far stranger than fear, arrogant and barbarous hatred, and I am not in no hurry [*sic*] at the present moment to either speak to him or look him in the face. As far as he is concerned I will merely send him a little letter from time to time, and furthermore it was HE who said that I should be locked up. Well, I am of the opinion that HE should be locked up, the way he has been carrying on of late. It seems REALLY AWFUL to be against one's own Father, but in this case both of us are partly to blame.

I must on NO account make any rash promises, especially during this present Season of Lent as regards my behaviour in the future, but I owe you my REPEATED and DEEPEST apologies to you for my GROSS lack of self-control towards you this morning.

Randolph Garlies
Or
Stick In The Mud.

Lily accepted the apology, as she would the many more that followed. It had been an unimportant quarrel. Nevertheless, at this point in the marriage, there was no limit to her forgiveness. Lord Galloway had repeatedly told her that Randolph was not fit for marriage. As he had asked Brodrick Haldane, 'What responsible woman would marry my son?' Lily's hope of victory lay in proving him wrong. This made her disinclined to give way to any feelings of doubt. It was a position that would bring her much pain and anguish.

A few days after their argument, Lily took a call from the William Hickey column. Would Lord Garlies care to comment on his disinheritance? Within days, the news hit the rest of the press. 'House of Stewart Set for Battle' read the headline in the *Daily Record.* 'Clan battle as son fights father's will' said the *Daily Mail.* This time it was Randolph who stepped to the telephone. 'I am absolutely sick and tired of my father', he told the journalist. 'I will be seeing my lawyer tomorrow. By Scottish law I am entitled to one third of everything at Cumloden. I am going to make sure I get it . . . I am partly to blame for my father's attitude towards me. I have punished him over the years with my insulting behaviour. We have never understood each other. I have suffered persecution for the last 25 years from the earl. He does not want me to be happy. He wants me to be on the scrounge all the time.'

With all communication now broken down, the press became the vehicle through which Lily and Randolph conducted the beginnings of their campaign to reclaim Randolph's birthright. 'My husband is naturally extremely angry about this,' Lily later told the *Daily Record.* 'He has consulted his solicitors and will fight his father. The 12th Earl seems to live in another century. There is no way he can take the title away from my husband, who will become the 13th Earl . . . My husband is a kind and gentle man and has done nothing to deserve this sort of treatment.' She did, during this interview, admit that as future chatelaine of Cumloden, she had hoped to set up a religious retreat and shrine. She conceded that 'perhaps this had annoyed the Earl'.

The following week, yet another story appeared in the *Sunday Express* in which Randolph, 'his voice shaking with rage', gave chapter and verse to Lady Olga: 'It is more than a big surprise, it is a very great shock to me. I am extremely upset. Cumloden is a very fine house with beautiful surroundings. I had always expected it would be mine. It is my right . . . I have great difficulty communicating with my father. He is one of the most awkward people I have ever known. He keeps me in the dark about all family matters.' Lord Galloway responded in three short sentences. 'I cannot talk about this. It is purely a private matter. Whatever happens is my own business.'

Lily and Randolph left Edinburgh for Walsingham to seek the

Partners in pilgrimage: Lily and Randolph in front of
Father Gordon Reid's charabanc on the way to
Walsingham seeking solace.

consoling presence of the Blessed Virgin. Miracle-maker though
Mary is, the situation did not alter – if anything, it deteriorated.
Randolph became increasingly obsessed with the notion of mortal
sin. Guilt dogged his every step. He regarded his 'Negative Attitude'
and the consequent 'Negative Impulses' as slights against God, as
well as against Lily. The following year he would seek guidance
from a priest and they would talk 'on the subject of Sin or Sins or
even Sinful Inclinations'. 'I still have the list of sins,' Randolph
wrote to Lily on 12 May, following another scene at Bernard
Terrace, 'which just now [I] am using as a book-marker, and will
show you when you have time to relax and forget the day to day
harassments.'

The day-to-day harassments could not be forgotten, though. They
increased. In 1977 Randolph's 'negative impulses' were getting
worse. He could not help it, poor love, she explained. But few of
her family – apart from Brebner and Dorothy – joined her in this
view. Paul Budge, for instance, who had read of the marriage in the
newspaper and turned up at Lily's doorstep out of the blue, had
thought Randolph 'crazy' from the start.

On 17 June 1977, and again on 2 September, Randolph was

admitted to the Royal Edinburgh following 'incidents' at home. He was placed in the care of a senior lecturer and honorary consultant who determined the cause of the violent eruptions to be 'increased stress concerning the possibility that he may be disinherited'. Three weeks after leaving the hospital, Randolph wrote to his father's lawyer informing him that he would be applying for his legal rights. He was, he told him, planning to take up a course in agriculture and forestry that would equip him to manage the estate to which he was entitled.

Lord Galloway was more determined than ever that Randolph and Lily would not end up walking the paths of Cumloden. Randolph's decision to fight the disinheritance had alerted him to the risk that perhaps his wishes would be overturned on his death. He consulted his lawyer. As a result on 7 December Lord Galloway signed a key codicil, one that was to cause much unsuccessful legal wrangling in the future. In it he evacuated himself of an entail of lands, legally freeing himself of any stipulations of primogeniture made in the past. It was an important legal technicality. The disinheritance Lord Galloway desired was now watertight.

That Christmas Marie-Laurence Maître, a student at the Sorbonne, arrived from Paris with Marie-Claude Garrison and their friend, Dominique. Lily and Randolph's distraction proved to be Father Reid's vexation. As Christmas Day approached Bernard Terrace was more a girls' boarding school than quiet refuge where a man in emotional turmoil might hope to regain emotional equilibrium. Breakfasts and suppers were regularly interrupted by Marie-Laurence's violent sobbing fits, brought about by her unrequited love for Lily's celibate priest. 'Oh isn't it sweet,' Lily would say to Randolph as he puffed his pipe in the corner, 'Marie-Laurence is in love for the first time.' Randolph sometimes found the hysteria challenging. As he had told Lily in his letter, 'sitting in a room talking as you have well discovered is not up my street'. Counselling a teenage girl with cobalt blue eyeshadow running down her plump cheeks was even less in the remit of his capabilities.

Lily's empathy with her young charge, for whom she was 'Mumsie', had a disquieting effect on Father Reid too. He was forced to take Lily aside. 'Now Lily, please try not to encourage her. It is all most awkward for me.' But Lily approached Marie-Laurence's

dilemma as she had approached her own life – with great emotion
and impulsiveness. 'It is your experience,' she told her, 'Tell him
how you feel and then you must grow from it. If you can't, only
then I will help you.'

The scene repeated itself the following Easter when Marie-
Laurence returned to Scotland determined to pursue her cause.
His Lordship, she noticed on the odd occasions she emerged from
the fog of her own despair, was more withdrawn and odd than
she remembered. Sometimes he shut himself in a room. 'Mumsie'
seemed fine although there were clearly tensions. Every evening
Marie-Laurence accompanied Lily while she trotted her poodles,
Ticus and Pepe, round The Meadows. The routine provided a break
for Lily and a crucial window of opportunity for Marie-Laurence,
whose eyes were trained on every path in the hope that she might
see a glimpse of Father Reid's cassock in the distance. (Marie-
Laurence laughs about this infatuation now, but says it cemented
her affection for both Lily and Scotland.)

On 13 June, after eighty-five admirable years of self-discipline and
service, Lord Galloway gave in to his pain and bitterness and died
at Cumloden. 'In the words of a Harrow song which epitomised
his strong sense of duty,' read a tribute in the *Stewart Magazine*, 'he
was always "Here sir" when he was really needed, whether in war
or peace. These words might do for his epitaph.'

There was a further flurry of obituaries in the national press, the
cleverer ones hinting delicately at the characteristics that had so
overawed his son. For it was acknowledged fondly that Lord Galloway, 'nicknamed "Beltie" like the breed of cattle whose territorial
title and sturdy physique he shared . . . applied a twinkling severity
to his Freemasonry', and 'as a former officer in the Scots Guards
things had to be right'.

The news of his death reached Lily and Randolph through the
local clergyman at All Saints', Challoch. 'When he died, I felt free,'
Randolph wrote later, 'but have had to try to overcome the feeling
of hate instead. This is not easy when he has disinherited me, and
has made things extremely difficult for my wife and myself.'

The funeral posed problems. 'My husband is now the Earl of
Galloway, and he will attend his father's funeral whether Lady

Antonia likes it or not,' Lily, now the 13th Countess of Galloway, told a newspaper reporter indignantly. On 16 July they travelled up to Newton Stewart with Brebner, Dorothy, Andrew and his wife, Linda, and checked into the Cree Bridge House Hotel using their new titles. It had been booked by the factor, who sent the £50.37 bill to Lord Galloway's trustees for settlement. The bill was swiftly batted back with the note, 'We should be glad to hear that Lord Galloway has paid this.'

Before his death, the 12th Earl of Galloway had been vexed by the idea that his son and daughter-in-law might be among the number gathered to send him off, and left instructions to the trustees and family members that they were to be prevented from placing themselves in the Galloway pew. In fact, to avoid a scene they were allowed to sit there. Newspaper photographers and reporters lurked about the front gate of the church, but the ceremony passed without confrontation. Ten days later the great and good of south-west Scotland attended Lord Galloway's memorial service at Penninghame St John's church, in Newton Stewart. The new Lord Galloway was not among them because, as Lady Olga Maitland made clear in her column, 'he could not afford the train fare'. The newspapers made merry work of the death. 'Will the earl get a crumb of comfort?' one asked.

When Lord Galloway's will was read there had been no change since he had signed the codicil at the end of 1977. Randolph was indeed to inherit the bare minimum – half of a half of the moveable estate. Following the funeral, the trustees sealed Cumloden in order to allow the Scottish arm of Phillips to move in and complete a full valuation of the moveable contents, which would determine how much Randolph received. By the second week in July, Lily and Randolph had appointed a lawyer, Mr Andrew Cubie of Fyfe, Ireland & Co. He was based in Melville Street and agreed to take them on after an imploring meeting with Father Reid. As it turned out Mr Cubie would come to regret this day. From the beginning he found Lily 'very strident about the fact that Garlies had the right to be walking at Cumloden', and realised immediately that she was on 'a journey to save him', 'that Garlies' horizons were being pushed out much further by his marriage to her', and that 'the nuances of Scots succession law didn't really get on to her screen'.

She dominated the meetings and as a result, Mr Cubie often found himself holding up a hand and issuing the order, 'Now look, can you just stop a moment. I want Randolph to tell me firstly if he understands all this and secondly if he agrees with what we are concluding because I am under instruction from him.'

'I had a lot of sympathy for him,' he remembers now.

> He was a man who had obviously been badly damaged by medical interventions. To what extent that struggle was made harder by Lily and her stridency I do not know. But I simply viewed it in the narrowness of Randolph and the whole thing was a harder exercise than I felt fair for him, which is why I stuck with trying to get some sort of remedy for him. Had he not met her, I am sure he would have continued to bump along the bottom in minimal care facilities, whether it be with the monks or some other closed order. I was absolutely confident that he knew exactly the steps that we were going to take. Sometimes he would sit before me and his fists would clench and I judged that as a mixture between a frustration about the issue and a frustration about not being able to articulate in quite the same way other people did.

Sara and Andrew Stewart, meanwhile, were expecting their first child, which Sara Stewart bitterly regretted not having told Lord Galloway before his death. When they heard that Randolph was to contest the will, they instructed their lawyers to make it absolutely clear that Lord Galloway's will was watertight. There was nothing Randolph could do. He would be far better not wasting what money was coming his way on legal fees. When it became clear that Lily and Randolph intended to continue with their fight, the young couple became more hostile towards Lily. 'Had she been a cosy old girl very happy to look after him, then of course we would have considered giving them a cottage in the grounds,' says Sara Stewart: 'nothing would have made us happier than bringing Randolph some happiness. But she absolutely was not that kind of person and one could not therefore act like that with her. We thought she was manipulative and out for what she could get.'

In a long interview Lily gave to *Woman's Own* later that year, she went to great efforts to escape the characterisation of a Lady Macbeth hovering in the background, pulling the strings. Instead she indicated that the fight was entirely of Randolph's doing. 'While I believe we will live useful lives if he loses his fight for Cumloden,' she told the journalist, 'I'm supporting him. He feels he must fight for his heritage and I feel a wife's place is backing her husband.' It was a manipulation of the truth, for as Mr Cubie had seen, Lily was especially 'strident' about the matter. But for all this 'stridency', it must be stressed that Randolph was obsessed with reclaiming Cumloden and remains so to this day. It was their shaved battle and they remained firm in their belief that they would win.

In the middle of July 1978 Randolph received a letter from the Edinburgh Centre of Rural Economy, a registered charity that looked after The Bush House, an estate in Midlothian where Randolph had applied for a job as a gardener. It was good news. He could begin on Monday, 24 July, 'on a three months casual basis to allow you time to get your own personal affairs in order and to make up your mind if the job suits you'. He was to work in a general capacity, 'principally connected with gardening, grounds maintenance, and occasionally forestry work and other duties'. Randolph and Lily thought it was the best way of preparing him for work on his own estate. In the meantime, he would be paid £1.10 an hour, and would work from 8 a.m. to 5 p.m. with a midday break of one hour from noon to 1 p.m. On the back of this letter Randolph scribbled some notes divided into two sections. The first is under the heading of Ross, one of his father's trustees:

1. Access to Cumloden Papers
2. Father's Annuity
3. 'Why have things been removed from Cumloden after my Father died?!'
4. What about the articles missing from Cumloden Inventory?!

The second is under the heading 'Cubie':

1. What the delay is over my Mother's Estate
2. I hope my wishes are being carried out with regard to Marriage Settlement

3. Robes, all things relating to the Heir, which is myself, and I will need them for the Parliamentary Opening
4. Baronet's Badge

The jottings give some idea of Lily and Randolph's preoccupations. The fight took over their lives. Their bond remained strong – in meetings with Mr Cubie they often disconcerted him by sitting like teenagers, clutching each other's hands – but their happiness was buckling under the strain, and Randolph was demonstrating increasing fits of 'filthy bad temper'. On 23 July, for instance, he attacked Lily's 'beloved poodle' and made 'an un-called for jumping gesture' just before tea. 'My general attitude and behaviour towards you during the last 24 hours, I am fully and utterly aware that you are heavily annoyed, vexed and aggrieved and thoroughly disgusted and sickened by it,' he wrote afterwards in yet another self-lacerating letter. 'With my deepest apologies to you my darling Cuddles, with a few tears, for my atrocious conduct.'

In the middle of August Mr Cubie sought a formal opinion of counsel from a barrister with whom he had worked in the past. The line of attack rested on whether or not Lord Galloway, in breaking with the tradition of primogeniture, had contravened a codicil made by his own father, the 11th Earl, following the death of the Hon. Keith Stewart. On 24 August the barrister made the preliminary and gloomy prediction that 'the thirteenth Earl may not have an enforceable right . . . to obtain the estate of Cumloden'. It was Lily to whom Mr Cubie delivered this news.

Throughout the rest of the month and into September, Lily and Randolph attended meetings at Melville Street, sometimes accompanied by Brebner. Correspondence they could ill afford flew back and forth daily. As well as the fight for Cumloden, they were concerned to pursue other points, as Randolph's lists show: the whereabouts of certain items in the house; the inaccuracy of the inventory; the speedy acquisition of the relevant paperwork which would enable Randolph to enter the House of Lords. This last quest – to see Randolph 'take his rightful seat' – was met by considerable, if petty, resistance, but as Mr Cubie pointed out, on that matter alone the trustees wielded no power. Whatever the ramifications for the British population, there remained only two sorts of people barred from the House of Lords. Randolph had many difficulties – more than enough to justify concern – but he was neither bankrupt nor an alien and as result he was, by law, entitled to vote on the legislature of the United Kingdom.

The barristers delivered his formal opinion at the end of September. It was in the negative. 'In short,' Mr Cubie reported back to them, 'the fact that your Grandfather provided by way of a Codicil of 12th February 1918 that the residue of his Estate including Cumloden was left absolutely to your late Father must mean that the Estate was left without attachment of conditions. Those conditions had of course been apparent in his earlier Will and would have given you some hope that the Estate would be bound to you in terms of that Will and in terms of entail. I think it is correct that the Codicil of 7th December 1977 of your late Father is competent to evacuate any destination to you under entailed provisions.'

The nub of his finding was that Lord Galloway had removed himself from any responsibility to the past. Mr Cubie offered one remaining possibility – that the all-important codicil of 7 December 1977 could be proved to be invalid – but he advised extreme caution:

> I think it is better to be realistic as to the prospects of upsetting the terms of your late Father's will at this stage than entering buoyantly into correspondence and possibly litigation only to be defeated in the end. The loss to you at that stage would be greater than an acceptance of an unjust position now . . . I am bound to say that I think the prospect of such matter being carried through successfully and to your advantage is limited. I see greater advantage in seeking to negotiate with the Trustees to obtain some improvement on the terms that have been provided for you.

His advice, which echoed the early message relayed to them by the young Stewarts, fell on stony ground. Lily's ears pricked, instead, at the suggestion of a new line of attack – to prove that Lord Galloway's signature on his codicil had been forged or 'assisted'. After all, Lord Galloway's signature did look rather shaky and Mr Cubie confirmed that such things did happen. Following an evening meeting on Tuesday, 17 October, Lily delivered to Mr Cubie a letter written by Lord Galloway in March 1976. This document was to be passed to a handwriting expert by the name of Campbell White, a gentleman 'accustomed to giving evidence in regard to disputed documents in the Court of Session'. He regarded one signature to be an insufficient template and at the beginning of November Lily and Randolph sent further letters – two sent by Lord Galloway to Randolph in 1976 and 1977 and a third, dated 10 March 1977, sent from Nessie Gorman, the housekeeper who had stood witness while Lord Galloway signed his codicil.

With each passing day they lost more legal ground, a decline matched by the state of their finances. They entered the New Year with low spirits and an even lower bank balance. Lily's overdraft with the Royal Bank of Scotland now stood at £7,495 and Randolph's at £2,859. Their bank manager, Mr Thexton, was a gentleman inclined toward seeing the broad picture, which is not always the case with those in his profession. But their monies out were sufficiently top-heavy to have drawn the attention of head office. Mr Thexton had been instructed by his superiors to provide answers and solutions. He got neither. It fell to Mr Cubie to plead their cause, not only to announce their inability to deliver back to the bank that which was due, but also to acquire for them further borrowing facilities. He had one weapon only – the final settlement of Lord Galloway's inheritance, which, while comparatively small, would be enough to settle their debts. He used this weapon well. At the beginning of January, the handwriting report now overdue, Mr Thexton visited them at 4 Bernard Terrace and such was his pity – or Lily and Randolph's ability at engaging it – that by the end of the meeting their debts had been frozen, a further joint account was to be established for all further transactions, and they would be allowed to draw up to £1,900 until 30 April. At that time all overdrafts would be settled by the inheritance, which Mr Cubie promised to transfer over to the Royal Bank of Scotland without delay. It was a supreme display of wishful thinking by all parties concerned, but for want of a better alternative, they all partook in the façade.

Mr Campbell White had spent quite some time peering into a

magnifying glass – indeed, his contemplation of Lord Galloway's scrawl lasted almost four months – but by the beginning of February he finally felt himself clear on the matter. There was, he said plainly, no sign whatsoever of foul play. 'The deterioration in the quality of the writing ... is in my opinion due to diminishing physical control of the writing instrument. This condition is regularly present in many elderly people.'

On receiving this heavy blow, Mr Cubie seized the opportunity to make things clear. Lily travelled to his office, where he spelt it out. They had no case. She returned home, leaving him concerned, not for the first time, that his counsel had made little impact on the course of her crusade. To be sure, he followed it through with a letter to Randolph – four pages of close type in which he reiterated the doom and expense that lay in wait should they proceed further:

> I have indicated to you at the meetings that I have had
> with you that it is not in my nature nor do I conceive it
> to be the role of a competent solicitor to encourage
> his clients into action as to which he has a substantial
> reservation without first the full implications of any
> particular line of action being considered in detail.

The finding of Mr Campbell White, 'the leading handwriting expert in Scotland', was not one they could disregard, nor was the £45 opinion they had purchased from counsel. At this point Mr Cubie was uncharacteristically blunt. Why, he asked Randolph, was it so very hard for him to believe that his father had disinherited him when during his lifetime he had expressed dislike followed by the intention to do so? But logic is little help to those feeling profound injustice. One avenue remained: 'The opinion of Senior Counsel taken to substantiate or refute the opinion already given by Mr Clark [the barrister].' Would they take this rocky, cliff-top path when all warning signs pointed in the opposite direction? Of course they would.

The weather in Scotland at this time was punishing – gloomy and grim. While Lily and Randolph were preoccupied with their legal affairs, a battle of national significance was raging around them. Pro- and anti-devolution campaigners were out on the streets in the blizzards and steely frosts in preparation for Referendum Day, set for 1 March, the Labour Government's first attempt to give Scotland self-government. One shudders to think what the Yes campaigners would have made of Randolph, a Conservative loboto-mised aristocrat eager to travel to Westminster to exercise his right to shape legislation that would affect the day-to-day running of their country. Lily, too, associated political power with Westminster, not Scotland. (Sir Alec Douglas-Home had made a rousing speech on television saying all Tories could vote No with a clear conscience and he implied that Mrs Thatcher, destined to be prime minister, had a Home Rule plan of her own.) If Lily and Randolph voted at all on the dank day that was 1 March, their votes would have been unequivocally in the negative, thus helping to secure the collapse of the campaign.

Lily and Randolph now faced greater trials than simply clawing back Randolph's inheritance. A few weeks after receiving Mr Cubie's opinion they attended their first meeting with the lawyers Mr Donald Stewart Ross and Mr Peter George Hugh Younie, two of Cumloden's three trustees. During this meeting it was made quite plain that funds would not be passed over until they were satisfied that Randolph was capable of managing his own affairs. They wanted testimonies from two independent medical prac-titioners saying Randolph was completely well. This fresh hurdle presented itself at a most inconvenient time. Lily and Randolph were busy preparing to move to London so that Randolph could take his seat in the Lords. April was drawing to a close and they were already more than £400 over the agreed £1,900 overdraft. Mr Thexton, showing the patience of a saint, had bumped up their facility to £2,700, £2,306 of which had already been spent. They had less than £400 on which to live until 31 May.

Any excitement Lily and Randolph felt in their preparation for the corridors of power was dampened by the looming medical test. They chose to return to the consultant at the Royal Edinburgh, who remembered Randolph from his earlier stays there. The date fell on 4 May. That morning, as the country went to the polls in what was to be a victorious election for Mrs Thatcher, Lily and Randolph cast their Conservative votes and then made their way over to the psychiatric hospital.

Randolph was headed for the Conservative benches anyway, but Lily's political leanings were not so much in the bloodlines. While liberal in an informal sense, she represented the working-class individual bent on self-improvement through the forces of capitalism that, ultimately, made Mrs Thatcher so successful. She admired Mrs Thatcher, and later she would offer herself up as a party worker. She even exchanged one or two letters with her, and in one, sent in 1983, showed much concern over Mrs Thatcher's troublesome eyeball and over the operation that ensued.

Randolph passed his psychiatric test, showing himself to be fully orientated, able to perform mathematical calculations, discuss current affairs, and to be quite free of false beliefs or unusual perceptions. It was a most satisfactory conclusion.

> Certainly there is no evidence of present mental illness which would lead me to think otherwise. Indeed I would think that the supportive relationship he has with his wife would be a further factor which should enable him to cope with any monies or administration which may come his way from his late father's estate.

Lily emerged in equally glowing terms. The consultant had found her 'concerned to give clear facts to me' and 'most concerned and supportive'. He was in no doubt that she genuinely loved and desired to help her husband. But the consultant delivered chilling words about Randolph's past medical care, now judged in a modern context. While acknowledging that in 1946 Randolph had been diagnosed as a schizophrenic at St Andrew's Hospital in Northampton and given insulin coma therapy, he wrote in his report that it was at a time 'when of course the diagnosis of schizophrenia was very uncertain'. Of the fifteen years Randolph then spent in the Crichton Royal Hospital, following his leucotomy, the consultant wrote, 'The psychiatric history at that stage reads more like a history of psychiatry rather than representing a high standard of psychiatric care.' He concluded:

> In my opinion, his somewhat shy personality together with his speech and occasional irritability is most likely to be secondary to the leucotomy. Indeed I should

point out that a leucotomy is virtually never given as a treatment for schizophrenia these days. Nevertheless following a leucotomy there can be some intellectual impairment or epilepsy.

Despite its obvious poignancy, Cubie was encouraged by the report and felt it sufficiently clear to eliminate the need for a second opinion. But he was wrong. It soon emerged that the consultant's comments – in particular his observation 'that the supportive relationship he [Randolph] has with his wife would be a further factor which should enable him to cope with any monies' – prompted the trustees to articulate an opinion that had, until then, remained unvoiced. 'I am afraid that it seems to me that [the] report confirms the impression one gets on seeing them together,' wrote Donald Ross, 'namely that he is capable of managing his affairs only with the assistance of his wife – so that she really has control.'

Mr Cubie met this with impatience. Mr Ross replied:

> It had of course occurred to me that there are supposed to be a great many hen-pecked husbands who are under their wife's thumbs and there are no doubt others who by reason of ill health depend on their spouses to deal with business affairs. There is probably nothing much which can be done about the former class but I am inclined to think that the latter should really have curators . . . However, as I remarked at our first meeting no one would be happier than I if it could be reasonably firmly established that the Thirteenth Earl is in fact a person to whom Trustees could safely transfer funds.

Lily had been cast as the villain long before Lord Galloway died. Now the legacy lived on. Concern over whether or not Randolph could manage his own funds was a polite way of expressing concern over whether or not those funds might end up in Lily's pocket.

15
Here, Sir!

So to-day – and oh! if ever
               Duty's voice is ringing clear
Bidding men to brave endeavour
               Be our answer 'We are here!'
               Come what will,
               Good or ill,
               We will answer We are here!
Here sir! Here sir! Here sir! Here sir!
               On the top of Harrow Hill,
Here sir! Here sir! Here sir! Here sir!
               In the windy yard at Bill.
'Here Sir!' *Harrow School Song Book*

The time had come for Randolph to fulfil his duty to Britain. As the day approached, Lily remained convinced that taking his seat in the House of Lords was the key to mending his moth-eaten spirit. It would raise Randolph up to the purpose for which he had been born and prove to Lord Galloway, posthumously, that she felt he had a son of whom he should have been proud, and whom he had severely underestimated. However, whenever she talked of such matters it was always with such passion and loyalty, like a tigress protecting her cub, thought Mr Cubie, that it was impossible not to notice the depth of her own excitement. Marie-Laurence Maître came the closest to working out why. 'It was revenge', she explained later, 'for the poverty and the hardship Lily had suffered through-out her life, and for how she had been treated by the Stewarts. I found that understandable.'

'I look back now and I still can't believe all we've been subjected to,' Lily wrote later. Lily associated the upper chamber with power, glory and the privilege of birth. If almost sixty years of her life had been spent at the lower end of the class spectrum, scrubbing floors for half a crown to give Brebner his lunch, here was the definitive moment at which she had reached the top.

She had acquired a taste for pomp and circumstance, too. As part of her efforts to rehabilitate Randolph, they had been sponsored and seconded to become members of the Scottish arm of the Military and Hospitaller Order of Saint Lazarus of Jerusalem, one of the oldest surviving orders, set up for Knights returning from the crusades with leprosy. The Order existed principally for socialising and fundraising, but Lily particularly enjoyed attending the ceremonies wearing a long, heavy black cloak, much like a church cape, pinned with a big green eight-pointed cross. On 7 May she had received confirmation from the Grand Chancellor in Malta that His Royal Highness the Grand Master, Prince Don Francisco Enrique de Borbon y de Borbon, had been graciously pleased to approve her promotion in the Order in the grade of 'Dame'. Nine months earlier Randolph had enjoyed a similar promotion to the grade of 'Knight of Justice'.

Lily's interest in the Order and her delight in dressing up attracted mirth from her family. They thought the idea of grown adults processing in cloaks and submitting to a strict hierarchy utterly absurd. Brebner took to calling the Grand Master 'Monsieur Bon-Bon' and heaven knows what Rose and Etta made of Lily's photographs. Rose, especially, had no time for Lily's newly acquired titles, the countess as well as the dame. Whenever they agreed to meet and Lily was characteristically late, while Rose was characteristically early (it had always been this way), Rose could now grumble crossly to her daughters, 'Who does she think she is? She might well be a Lady but she thinks she is the Queen of Sheba!'

The House of Lords, however, was not a joke, despite the dressing up. Its powers could shape the country. Because Lily's enthusiasm had been so great, Mr Cubie and Lord Lauderdale were keen to establish for themselves that Randolph wanted to take his seat as much as his wife wanted it for him. After some delicate questioning, Mr Cubie was satisfied that Randolph was not simply 'a pawn in [Lily's] hand', and that he would certainly 'enjoy elements of what he was being encouraged into'. Mr Cubie also saw that it was vital to Randolph that he 'get hold of the one thing that he could not be denied'. Lord Lauderdale, who had provided advice on how to complete the paperwork, says now that he 'lent an arm thinking everything would come all right, that it would provide some sense of purpose in life for the poor chap and help make their marriage successful.' Apart from the trustees, Lily and Randolph's relocation to London was generally regarded by friends and family to be a ray of fresh hope amid much gloom. One friend they met on a pilgrimage wrote to her, on hearing the news, 'It will give your husband some of the confidence he needs and he will meet some good and kind people. Keep on quietly but persistently and you will win through, never give up, but put your trust in God and Our Lord and His saints – your faith and prayers will see you through.'

It was fitting that two lifelong Conservatives from opposite ends of the class spectrum should be leaving Scotland now, a country which on 5 May had been shaded in red rather than blue, and which was quite unwilling to submit to the dawning of a new age. Faced with the prospect of Margaret Thatcher, Scottish Labour had emerged from the election stronger than ever before, but in England the party had suffered a huge defeat by the Conservatives. Scotland was a country divorced from elected power (and would remain so for eighteen years), and the battle for Scottish devolution, now carrying with it all the stigma of Callaghan's failed government, was officially dead. Power remained in Westminster; hope and optimism existed south of the border. Thatcher promised much and Lily and Randolph were keen to take part.

They travelled to London ten days after the general election. On 16 May, Randolph took his seat and Lily settled into her element. The stately surroundings, so perfect for the late Lord Galloway, were dark and daunting for Randolph. He had trouble holding a conversation at a lunch party. Now the expectation was that he would make speeches for his country. He would not. He remained silent. At the end of each long day, they travelled by bus to Victoria where their bed and breakfast bedroom awaited them, with its fraying blankets and the noise from the street below. Lily was exhilarated. She had never felt so alive as she did now. It was

Lily and Randolph, fresh from Scotland, outside
St Matthew's, Westminster.

a new world filled with interesting people and she grasped it with
both hands.

Although the Scottish peers and peeresses formed a tight-knit
group, before long two in particular took Lily under their wing.
Lady Kinloss and the countess of Loudoun, both hereditary peeresses, befriended her after seeing her sitting knitting in the tearoom. Lady Kinloss, a crossbencher and a Swahili-speaking goat
breeder who had worked for the Foreign Office during the war,
cannot remember the exact moment she made Lily's acquaintance,
but the acquaintance itself was never forgotten. Within the Lords,
the social differences between them evaporated. Everybody was
equal, and besides, the peeresses found their new friend hugely
entertaining and a great bonus to tearoom life. Those who witnessed their conversations marvelled at their ability to fly at each
other with corrections and contradictions. It was all quite harmless,
and despite the unspoken competition (it secretly pleased the peeresses that Lily had no public voice), Lady Loudoun and Lady Kinloss
were kind and loyal. Lady Kinloss loved to hear Lily's stories and
thought her 'very amusing, but prone to a great imagination'.

'Sometimes she would get into an awful muddle with a story,' she recalls, 'and halfway through would say "No, No, that's not right!" and then we'd start all over again.' Often Lady Kinloss noticed that Lily spoke of subjects not usually broached in the House, like her miscarriage, for instance. 'She would talk endlessly of The One I Lost,' Lady Kinloss remembers, 'in fact, she loved talking about children, her grandchildren, her own children, until in the end I would have to say "Lily, please! Enough talk of babies for today."' Lord Lauderdale would sometimes overhear such conversations and, as usual, try to slip off unnoticed. 'Her voice was so loud!' he remembers, shaking his head, 'and she would say the most outrageous and indiscreet things which were not always to her credit, and certainly to nobody else's credit. Talkative wives are hell you know, and I was always rather grateful when she'd gone.'

The peeresses provided Lily with a sense of belonging and Lady Kinloss, in particular, was touched by how much her new friend seemed to value this. Kindness and generosity came naturally to Lily and they did not go unnoticed. Once, when she and Lady Kinloss were taking some air, Lady Kinloss stepped into the road and got her legs entangled with a tow-rope attached to a car. Lady Kinloss's legs were badly lacerated by the accident. Lily carried her into a cab and took her to hospital, remaining with her past midnight until she could be taken back home.

It is unclear exactly when life at the Lords began to affect Randolph. It is most likely to have started after the summer recess, although almost from the start, Lady Kinloss was terrified of him, and as her husband says by way of providing context, 'Nobody scares my wife – but he did!' Lily had told her of various violent episodes, one on Victoria Bridge when he had assaulted her and been pulled off by workmen. As a result, Lily had begun to wear occasional bruises. Being a crossbencher Lady Kinloss often sat directly opposite Randolph, which gave her full view of the violent expression on his face. Lily came to refer to this as his 'black look', usually a precursor to a fit of temper or violence. On one occasion, during the following winter when Lily was in bed with flu, Lady Loudoun and Lady Kinloss approached Randolph with a flask of soup for their friend, but fixed with the 'black look', that they ran away down the corridor, terrified.

By the end of June Randolph's struggle to inherit Cumloden was over. As Mr Cubie had warned, Senior Counsel agreed that they had no case to pursue. This came as a devastating blow to Randolph, at once inconceivable and horribly real. He would not accept the news, and the stress of hearing it confirmed made his looks all the blacker. Lily wrote to Mr Cubie informing him that they would travel to Edinburgh immediately to talk with the barrister. Mr Cubie deterred her from taking this path. During the summer recess, save for a trip to Lourdes with the Society of Mary at the beginning of June, Lily and Randolph remained in London. They visited Harrow School – odd considering Randolph had been so unhappy there – travelled down the Thames on a boat, and generally behaved like tourists. There exists a photograph of Lily swamped by pigeons in Trafalgar Square, and in these pictures Randolph appears happy too. It was a pleasant diversion, but the question over his mental health remained.

The trustees continued in their demands that Randolph undergo more medical tests. In July Mr Cubie finally saw of the medical opinion from the Crichton Royal Hospital provided to Lord Galloway's trustees in 1974. Randolph was, Mr Cubie argued, a different man now, no longer subjected to heavy drug therapy and certainly fit enough to be in the House of Lords. Precisely what was it that he did there? the trustees replied.

Mr Ross, acting on behalf of all the trustees, approached counsel, the first step in lodging a petition with the Court of Session for the appointment of a *curator bonis*. This angered and panicked Randolph even more. His and Lily's overdraft, at £5,130, was deemed to be out of control. On 24 October, when Randolph and Lily were in Edinburgh for an appointment with Mr Ross, Randolph snapped. While out for a walk in Hope Park Terrace, he saw an elderly woman walking her two dogs. As she passed, he punched her on the nose and smashed her spectacles. 'Within minutes I was picked up by the police, and taken to the station and searched,' Randolph later wrote. Following the attack, the police took him to George IV Bridge Police Headquarters and put him in a cell, where he remained for twenty-four hours.

Lily was immediately protective. The following day she went to Edinburgh Sheriff Court and watched Randolph plead guilty to assault. His lawyer presented a strong case of his acute emotional stress. It was quite true that he had smashed his victim's spectacles. As the Deputy Fiscal told the court, 'she received a few cuts from the glass'. When the police asked Randolph to explain his outburst, he replied, 'The woman was a complete stranger. I do not know why I did it.' Randolph was fined £30 – 'justfiabl[e]', he wrote later, and was permitted to return home. The next day, the case appeared in the *Scotsman* under the headline 'Earl admits punching "stranger"'.

While there had been violent outbursts before leaving for Scotland, this attack was serious, for the violence and for the fact that it was so random. Lily blamed the shock of their case collapsing and took Randolph home. Both Brebner and Marie-Laurence Maître, who continued to visit Scotland throughout 1978 and 1979, noticed Randolph's decline around this time. 'He wasn't at all well,' Marie-Laurence recalls. 'Clearly very sick. And I used to ask Lily about the bruises and how she coped and "Why? Why did you marry him?" And she would say, "There is this connection between us. I cannot explain it, but of course I never dreamt it would turn out like this. Never."'

Lily continued to excuse his violence, telling all those who expressed concern for her that Randolph could not help it, that it was entirely due to the stress of their situation. He was now back on a small daily dose of Librium. As a precaution, however, while they remained in Edinburgh, Brebner visited daily to ensure Lily was not at risk. It now appeared that the late Lord Galloway's prophecy – that Randolph was not fit to be married – might be coming true.

The attack, or the 'exceptional outburst', as Mr Cubie called it, had put him in a fix. On 30 October he wrote to Randolph saying '[It] has done little to aid the attempts that I have been making to represent you as a person who has both feet very solidly on the ground.' It felt to Lily and Randolph as though they were being attacked from all sides. The bank wanted answers and the trustees more medical tests. Randolph went back to the consultant at the Royal Edinburgh, who remained firm in his original opinion: there

existed no signs of mental illness and no psychiatric reasons why
Randolph could not answer for himself. The assault was attributed
to the stress of the legal fight. Randolph was also tested for epilepsy
(of which no evidence was found) and his GP provided yet another
full account of his recent medical history, stating that Randolph was
now living a normal life on only a very small daily dose of Librium.

Was it an error of judgment for Lily to return Randolph to the
Lords? She did not even ask the question. She was convinced Scotland was the problem and that Randolph needed to get away from
all reminders of his disinheritance. The following March she would
tell the William Hickey column, in response to yet another story
about them, 'In Scotland he doesn't seem to have the same confidence . . . he gets the feeling of being persecuted. I see such a
difference down in London. The breeding was there. It just needed
bringing out. It's because of the society he's now moving in . . . If
I had my way we would live in London permanently. In fact we are
hoping to buy a flat here.' Apart from anything else, they needed
his attendance fees.

By the beginning of 1980 they were more than £9,000 in debt.
By the middle of February there was still no sign of the inheritance.
Yet another medical test – a psychometric assessment – had been
recommended by a neurologist to determine the degree of significant brain damage caused by the lobotomy. All this was becoming
very confusing for Lily and was deeply upsetting for Randolph. The
doctors' names were piling up, each one responsible for examining
different functions of his brain, and it meant constant travelling
back and forth from Scotland.

On 10 April, they travelled back to Edinburgh for the psychometric tests, which included speech, hearing, non-verbal reasoning,
formal verbal tasks, rote verbal memorising, and imaginative tasks.
Randolph passed them all and in some categories his responses
were above average. It was concluded that he had a good level of
general cognitive function. The problem, as the specialist saw it,
lay in what he called Randolph's abnormal personality development
and lack of 'normal social experience'. The 13th Earl, he wrote,
was 'notably immature, docile, and lacking in spontaneity', which
in turn had created prejudice ('as may well have occurred with his
father') or at least an impression that was not wholly accurate.

Randolph's intellect was not below average, but he did have difficulties with social interaction. It was yet another affirmation of Lily's opinion of her husband: a poor love whose life had been ruined through circumstances, but who, with help, could lead a fuller life. He was not 'mad' or 'insane' or even 'schizophrenic'. He was damaged, but not severely intellectually impaired. In the final, heartbreaking paragraph of the consultant's report, he concluded that it was very probably far too late to be able to correct the abnormalities of Randolph's personality, but with sympathetic help and guidance he would be able to continue to live a more normal life and deal with his impulses in a more rational way. Lily saw the words as a reminder of her duty. The quality of her husband's future depended entirely on the strength of her love.

It was a breakthrough, and yet the stalling continued. In the second week of May, Mr Cubie caught a whiff of imminent victory. 'I am satisfied in his own mind that [Mr Ross] is now prepared to accept the situation,' he wrote to Randolph on 16 May. 'I am confident that . . . the matter will be resolved next week.' Mr Cubie was about to receive another setback. Events in London had overtaken his small victory in Scotland.

16

I would have hated to commit murder

On 12 May 1980, Randolph attacked Lily in their small room in The Hansel and Gretel Hotel in Belgrave Road, SW1. This attack was not like the others. It was much more brutal and uncontrolled. She felt it would never end. It was as if Randolph had become somebody else, not her husband at all. She later said he had become 'possessed' and as a consequence, he did not know what he was doing, or to whom he was doing it. He tried to strangle her; he hit her in the face and tore her nightdress. If the Blessed Virgin had had a hand in Lily's decision to marry Randolph, it was she to whom Lily turned again, this time praying to her to save her life. Eventually she fell off the bed and scrambled for the telephone.

Lily did not summon the police. She did not want Randolph arrested, nor did she want to alert the press. She called Lord Lauderdale instead. It was late – past midnight – but he rose from his bed in Ovington Square, contacted his private doctor, and drove over to Belgrave Road. When he arrived he found Lily and Randolph in their room in a state of profound shock. Randolph had emerged from his trance and was sitting docile and childlike on the bed. Shortly after Lord Lauderdale's GP arrived and attempted to console Randolph. Lord Lauderdale has a clear memory of the physician's approach. 'Old chap, you are very unwell. We must take you to hospital. I do not want to say to you that you are mad, but you . . . well, it's too often and too much.'

The stress of the legal fight, identified by the first consultant as being the cause of Randolph's attack on the stranger, had become intolerable. Lily and Randolph's marriage had not been in good health, not for the fact that they were falling out of love, but because Randolph's loss of Cumloden had placed such a burden on them. Did he blame her? He did not say he did. But Lily's nature was not the kind to restore a sense of calm to a situation. If anything, she would probably have made it worse, by being highly emotional herself, or by fussing over him, offering words that provided no consolation because none existed. Trapped together in a small, ragged room in a noisy, dirty city, it was only a matter of time before Randolph snapped.

Randolph did not want to leave the hotel for hospital. He repeated over and over that he was needed for a vote in the Lords. Eventually, however, the doctor managed to coax him up and guide him into the car. They travelled to All Saints Hospital, [it is unclear where exactly this was] where he was admitted. A doctor saw Lily and told her to return the following day. A slip in her medical notes records the meeting:

> The Countess of Galloway will be coming in the emergency clinic this morning. She got beaten up by her husband, the Earl of Galloway, last night. He is safe in All Saints Hospital. She has facial, neck (she was nearly strangled) and chest injuries ... there could be legal implications.
>
> Please ask her to complete a night visit form for her husband and an emergency treatment form for her husband and herself.

There were to be no legal implications. It was unthinkable that Lily would set the police on Randolph. Even so, the attack had devastated her. Lily would come to speak of it as an attempt on her life, an explanation Lord Lauderdale thought something of an exaggeration. Whether it was or not, the medical note taken that night proves it was serious. She had, she told Brebner later, genuinely felt it might end in her death and this feeling of fright was so excessive that it had changed her view of Randolph's future almost instantly. If she had been ignoring the signs of his ill health, pretending to herself that she could make him well and restore him to normality, this was the moment when she allowed herself to see things for what they were. Perhaps Lord Galloway had been right all along.

The following morning she was treated for her injuries. 'I felt very, very sad for them,' recalls Lord Lauderdale. 'I was quite sure that she had to get him back to Scotland and into care as soon as possible. I'd hoped that the House of Lords might have helped him, but its effect had been to completely overwhelm him. He did not know anything about public life or the constitution, and he was very nervy and frightened of the surroundings.'

When Randolph was considered strong enough he was released. Lily took him back to Edinburgh where he was readmitted to the Royal Edinburgh. A period of intense assessment began. Lily stayed away. Randolph wrote to her instead, a somewhat wild and, at times, incoherent document.

> A poisonous feeling once ignited could give rise to cor-
> ruption and violation on an expensive and large scale,
> causing infliction of injury, damage to property or both,
> it would have been more in keeping, if when I had these
> awful feelings within to have thrown myself on the
> ground, battered my head on the bedroom floor rather
> than having hurt and pulverised you with such brutal
> infinitism, even viciously tearing your nighty to ribbons,
> for which is part and parcel of a punishment I ought
> jolly well be made to pay for in damages.
>
> A disgraceful, disgusting, dishonourable and down-
> grading performance on my part, needless to say diaboli-
> cal, barbarous and wicked, but this may sound like
> cushioning myself behind the excuse of what one of the
> psychiatric examiners said, that there was very little hope
> that my disorderly and disorientated behaviour could
> ever be rectified. Excuses, unless deeply founded, are
> utterly useless, leading merely and justifiably to invitation
> from the party who suffered the violation from such a
> person whose frenetic and or psycho-pathic inclinations
> had caused irreparable damage. But I must not and can-
> not finish on a defeatist's note, because you are as much
> entitled to benign kindness and in response to what

goodness and kindness you have shown on me. I have hardly kept my eyes dry each night since, my pillow and cushions in a sodden and soaking mass, myself but for the grevious, excrutiating bodily harm I inflicted on you.

My late father was a crank, an old crook and as well as quite mad was the meanest of skinflints in carpet slippers or boots. I had you severely agitated, and in a state of utmost shock, and your poor nerves badly jangled.

A little more reason from my part to satisfy what is aimed for. Bad feelings, poisonous and vicious feelings terminating in multiple and open demonstrations as in the hotel. I would have hated to commit murder, but fiendish, frantic mad corruptions on you, and letting rip. No way to let steam from an over-filled safety valve. Both of us would hate to separate.

'My poor darling,' she wrote to her old school friend, Alice, now Mrs McCormick, with whom she had remained in contact, despite Alice travelling the world as a nurse in the Forces. 'It is just so sad. He just couldn't take any more . . . it has been a terrible shock to me . . . He always lived in hope he would get it [Cumloden] the lawyers fought it on every issue. But I knew it was hopeless and tried to tell him that it didn't matter all that much as long as we had our health and we were happy.'

Randolph was in no fit state to think clearly, but he was sure about one thing. He did not want to lose Lily. He did not realise that he already had. She had closed off the possibility of ever living with him again. Just as she had instinctively accepted him into her life, now she instinctively knew that he must leave it. Lily did not view this as 'the end', nor did she think in terms of leaving him. She loved him still – her behaviour towards him while he was in hospital proves this – it was more that she had decided that they had no domestic future. He would always be her husband – 'Pity, Lily, there's nothing wrong with that,' as Father Reid had told her – but now they would have to live apart. She could not risk another attack, nor could she live with a man she feared.

At the beginning of June Lily fled to Paris to stay with Marie-Laurence Maître. It was the first time Marie-Laurence had seen Lily notably reduced by her circumstances. She was low and sad and covered with bruises. 'I never dreamt it would be like this, never,' she said. Her trip coincided with Pope John Paul II's visit to Paris and, in the crowd gathered at Sacré Coeur, she prayed for strength. When she eventually returned to Edinburgh, she was still too weak to face Randolph in hospital. It was Mr Cubie, now brought up to speed, and Michael Chinnery who provided the lifeline between them. Chinnery, who was working as a psychiatric nurse at the Royal Edinburgh, acted as postman, delivering letters and Lily's gifts of money, clothes, and fresh laundry. Randolph remained ever hopeful.

'A voice tells me how wrong I was to have ill treated you to such an extent earlier this summer and back in the spring,' he wrote to her in one letter of this time. 'It may be a longish time before we reunite but do please note, my love for you exists still, to some extent, if I had means of showing such love. But it would be nice to meet if and when you feel better and stronger, by which time I hope I may have a little something for you.' His closing remark, however, shows that even he was starting to suspect that perhaps he would not be returning to Bernard Terrace: 'In the event of my going elsewhere on leaving here the roller wheeled bag would be very handy, not to mention the Galloway kilt.'

At the end of July Lily, no clearer about how to face the future, asked Mr Cubie to approach the hospital for a full account of Randolph's mental health. The following week Mr Cubie spoke to the doctor and on 5 August reported back to her that there was no question of Randolph being released at the moment. He would have to undergo a further period of assessment before any decision could be made about his medium- and long-term future. Lily was at sea. Mr Cubie attempted to reassure her, saying that they would have a firmer idea within ten days, during which time there would be another assessment of Randolph's capabilities.

In the third week of August, Mr Cubie travelled to the Royal Edinburgh himself. 'I found your husband quiet but not apparently disturbed about speaking to me concerning the estate of his late father,' he wrote to her. It was left to Mr Cubie to spell out to Randolph that because of what he called 'the change in his circumstances', matters could only proceed with the estate if a *curator bonis* was appointed. 'He did not demur to such a step being taken,' Mr Cubie told Lily, 'and indeed in answer to direct questions . . . indicated that he had no objection to such a course being taken. His only response was that he wished to be satisfied about the moveable estate.' Mr Cubie made the position clear. Randolph was not, at present, capable of judging whether a *curator* should or should not be appointed. That responsibility rested with next of kin – Lily and Lady Antonia – and the relevant medical evidence. There was no conflict now. Lily and Lady Antonia were in full agreement.

In a letter to Alice McCormick some months later, Lily wrote, 'God certainly works in mysterious ways.' It is the one comment that reveals how the incident challenged her faith. It withstood the force. Lily remained as devout as ever, finding solace in surrender. God was determining that she should once again be alone. It was His sign to her that Randolph needed proper medical care. In spite of this Randolph continued to dominate her life. She washed his clothes and did his shopping, and in return, he sent her love letters: 'Please note that I love you, but the incinerated heat of these last incidents caused me to explode in riotous tyranny without due provocation . . . I can appreciate your feeling nervous and scared after the demonic assault of mine on you, my darling.'

At 4 p.m. on Monday, 8 September Lily went to Mr Cubie's office and gave her permission for the appointment of a *curator bonis*. The following day Mr Cubie received five items of silver from Randolph's childhood, which had been handed over to the trustees by Andrew Stewart. One was Randolph's christening mug, inscribed 'Randolph Keith Reginal Lord Garlies given to him on his baptism on 21 November 1928 by his godfather Percy Marlborough Stewart.' When Randolph heard that the silver had been returned, he wrote to Lily, pending its valuation, 'It seems as though you made a good job of polishing that silver'.

Amid her unhappiness, Lily received an offer she could not refuse, a 'holiday in the sun . . . to build up my strength to face the future.' Her destination was to be Las Palmas in Gran Canaria and her hostess the eccentric Countess of Mayo, who in 1975 had moved out of her duplex apartment in Princes Street. 'Recuperation will be what you most need,' Randolph advised from his hospital bed, 'after all the earlier affront, shame and disgrace showered upon you by one person, diagnosed by many of unsound mind.'

PART THREE

He was part of my dream, of course – but then I was part of his dream, too!

LEWIS CARROLL, *Through the Looking-Glass*

17

We have the name darling, but alas, we do not have the game

The Countess of Mayo, a month off her ninetieth birthday, could not easily walk or see. It made her so furious that sometimes she hurled her false teeth across a room. A stiff gin always restored her to good humour, though, and in Las Palmas, where she lived, there was always a flotilla of attentive if resentful Spanish waiters at the colonial-style British Club on hand to serve her one. Lady Mayo liked having people at her beck and call. She liked it even more if this made them cross. Her home helps regularly threw down their dishcloths declaring they'd had enough, but for Lady Mayo, it was almost a sport.

Las Palmas, with its steady flow of tourists, its sea of sun umbrellas and its boutiques selling garish holiday wear, seems an unlikely place for a woman such as Lady Mayo to live out her final years. One would imagine her more in a draughty castle north of Inverness, but in leaving Scotland for the sun, Lady Mayo had followed a well-trodden path. To venture into the British Club, a large house with French windows, shutters, and palm trees, tucked away from the main thoroughfare, one might well think, palm trees aside, that one was at a New Town garden party. Every afternoon with-out fail Lady Mayo and her fellow Scottish expats would be on the lawn among the palm trees, looking and behaving as though it were the Raj. Sometimes they might attend the music club or the drama club, but usually the attraction was the bar and the drinks it served – gin or Dubonnet. They held luncheon parties on the balconies of their flats and washed down huge prawn salads with carafes of wine, so that when they finally appeared at the

British Club, the Spanish staff might well have had reason to sigh.

They were an imposing group, accustomed to good service and grand living. Among their number was Lady Laura Finley, once heard to cry, 'Money is like confetti to me!' (This attitude would come to be useful to Lily during her trip.) There were also Viscount Harberton, otherwise known as Lieutenant-Colonel Tom Pomeroy, a tall, heel-clicking fellow in his sixties and his companion, Lady Wilma Butt (they later upgraded to Monte Carlo); Veronica Pavillard, who came from a shipping family; Rear Admiral Robert Oliver and his wife Joyce, who visited from Lochside, their large house in the Borders; and a couple of honorary European aristocrats – Violet, the Baroness von Gegern (Austrian) and Count Nicholas Bruskolowski (Russian).

While Joyce Oliver wore the best jewellery, Lady Mayo was the most arresting presence of the lot. Lady Mayo's features bore traces of an earlier beauty, although photographs of her in the 1920s reveal a nose considerably larger than was the case now. But eyes, nose, cheekbones, all floured with face powder, were eclipsed by the two pieces of elastic that travelled from ear to ear to catch the droop of her many chins. It is puzzling that she thought such a bizarre measure masked rather than highlighted the effect of gravity. It meant there was a touch of the over-fed cockerel about her. But this was Lady Mayo's cross to bear. Her money had run out. There could be no more surgery, and she had quite an appetite, never for wholesome dishes.

Still, Lady Mayo went to great efforts to contain the ravaging effects of age. She was grandly groomed with long silver hair swept back in a chignon. Her hands were tiny, with long fingers slightly turned up at the tips. In maintenance of what she called her aura, she dressed only in purple, although she conceded to varying the shade. If clothes in other colours took her fancy, such as furs, she would place instructions for them to be dyed mauve. She liked to wear hats, sometimes two at once, always adorned with plastic orchids and swathes of gold toile. One of her favourites had such a wide brim and so many ostrich feathers upon it that in photographs she appeared as if under a sun parasol. She had three indulgences: diamonds, headgear, and gin, although there would always be the facade of requesting straight tonic before she added,

The Countess of Mayo shielding from the sun under a
feather hat on the balcony of her Las Palmas apartment.

'Tuck a little gin in there, will you, darling?' She would combine
the first two indulgences in the form of tiaras, repaired clumsily,
and myopically, with fuse wire.

Lady Mayo had not been run out of Edinburgh exactly, but
around the time of Lily's marriage to Randolph it had been made
clear to her by American Express, her long-suffering landlord, that
the moment had come for her to vacate her duplex apartment on
Princes Street, for which she had continually refused to pay a proper
rent. She was suffering badly from arthritis and so, with the handsome pay-off she managed to extract from American Express by
way of compensation, she saw her chance to leave Edinburgh for
a warmer clime. She bought two conjoined flats at 5 Graciliano
Afonso, Las Palmas.

With Mayo unwilling to apply herself to matters of hygiene – her
lavatory and fridge were barely in working order – it is a wonder
that the dirt cultivated in her apartments did not kill her. She simply
could not hold on to her staff. They were unwilling to tolerate

her Edwardian grandeur, the Spanish temperament being wholly ill-suited to such condescension. Lady Mayo had made little alteration to her lifestyle since leaving Edinburgh. Some of her furniture and belongings were stored in a repository in the basement of Jenners department store, but much had followed her, so that the apartments appeared cluttered. There were ageing pink corsets that looked like chandeliers; hats; old pieces of cloth; and fairy lights. She'd even insisted on bringing her 'wobble belt', a lethal looking contraption intended for weight loss. Lady Mayo saw in Lily's distress a chance for company, but also the chance to make life easier for herself. She had proposed 'a holiday' for her troubled friend, although what she had in mind for her – companionship and 'a little bit of help' – was anything but.

On 18 November 1980 Lily boarded her plane laden with items from Lady Mayo's shopping list: crumpets, TCP, Polyfilla, and OMO, the only cleaning product capable of lifting the stains on her revolting pans. She had little inkling of the fetid domestic scene that awaited her. After the trauma of Randolph's attack she saw the stay abroad as a chance to recuperate, to get away from Scotland and clear her mind. When her taxi pulled up outside Lady Mayo's apartment block – a large white building overlooking the harbour – she noticed her friend had raised a Union Jack to full mast. How very like her, she thought. It was only once inside that Lily realised the flag was not a flag at all, but a dishcloth: Lady Mayo's idea of a joke.

It was fitting that two old ladies partial to the twin distractions of men and dance had met through William Mowat Thomson. From the beginning a complicated dynamic existed between them. Although Lady Mayo and Lily shared a similar sense of humour and delight in the absurd, Lady Mayo could never quite look beyond what she judged to be Lily's 'low birth'. 'She has such terrible legs, darling,' she'd sigh to William, 'no doubt the result of a lifetime behind the plough.' (In fact, Lily's legs were rather shapely for her years.) And yet at the same time, such was Lady Mayo's immense respect for the workings of the aristocracy that she saw, with considerable annoyance, that Lily's title, in all that it stood for, was superior to her own. As a result, Lily often noted that her friend liked to put her down as a way of establishing a state of unchallenged superiority. Lady Mayo's attitude was, of course, quite ridiculous and only very occasionally did Lily allow herself to rise to the bait and protest, 'Now stop it! You have gone too far! That is quite enough.'

That Lily accepted Lady Mayo's offer of a 'holiday' is a sign of her desperation to get away. Lady Mayo was not an easy woman to live with. For one thing, she was a kleptomaniac, and for another, she was allergic to housework. Lily's first reaction to the apartment was dismay. Her second was that she should get to work cleaning it up. Lily had been promised rest but rest was impossible amid filth. Lily was keen to earn her keep, but even she saw that scrubbing floors and cleaning lavatories was asking rather a lot. It was a big job, and as she pressed on each day the weather gradually cooled and became cold. Her single pleasure was attending a church she had found nearby. A month after arriving, she wrote to Alice, 'I was really bad with my nerves as it has been a terrible shock to me the doctor advised me to get away a while . . . The place was in a bit of a muddle I cleaned it all up . . . I'll try and get some one to live in with her before I leave . . . It's a nice church here and I've met some nice people it's very low of course . . . but I think one always finds peace in Church, especially when you are away from home.'

When Alice finished the letter she burst into tears. There was something about its sad, quiet tone that struck her heart. She was right to have been upset by it. Lily was very, very unhappy and her situation with Randolph was made all the more poignant for the fact that she seemed to be trying so hard to remain optimistic while being taken advantage of, domestically at least, by Lady Mayo, who sat on her balcony wearing an ironic, amused smile. 'She's treating her like a servant woman,' Alice cried to her husband (she had remained as extreme in emotion as she had been in the play-ground). 'How dare that woman take advantage of her like that!'

Although separated by the sea, Lily's thoughts returned constantly to Randolph and his future. She turned it over and over in her mind, but whichever way she viewed it she always came out with the same answer. She could not take him back to live with her in Bernard Terrace, however much she loved him. Later, in *No*

Silver Spoon she was to recall how she felt, sitting on the beach among the tourists, watching the surf. 'One little boat was tossed about helplessly as the wind caught its sail, that's rather like me I thought, at the moment I am being tossed about on the Ocean of life, I often wonder if I will ever reach the safety of the Harbour.' Lady Mayo was uncomprehending. 'Darling, for heaven's sakes,' she'd say, 'get yourself a new lawyer. Take it from me. These things can always be sorted out to one's advantage.' Mayo was wrong on this occasion, but in general, she was wily and wise and usually got her way. This was the result of the events of her life, a life even more rackety than Lily's, and that, everybody agreed, was saying something.

The Countess of Mayo was not Scottish, or even Irish, as her title suggests, but from Rigmaden, near Kendal in the north of England. Luckily for one of such lavish tastes and social aspirations, she spent her childhood in Edwardian splendour in High Park, their large family mansion. But the north of England could not contain her. She charmed her father's gentlemen friends, who were greatly amused that she could high-kick their top hats from their heads. In the 1920s she went to London as a debutante and stayed there until 1941, when she returned north, this time staying on the train as it rattled across the Berwickshire border toward Edinburgh, the next city she set out to conquer.

The years between the relatively innocent state in which she left High Park and the rather more experienced, frayed state in which she returned north were given over to London society and international travel. She had enjoyed many privileges, such as meeting Sir Winston Churchill, with whom she was photographed looking divine in diamonds and a mink tippet, 'having a little chat', and she knew many European royals – or so she said. She had been canny in her choice of connections. Sometimes she lurked outside the side entrance of Claridges, dressed in full fig, so she could genuflect as those of truly noble birth stepped toward their awaiting motorcars.

Miss Noel Haliburton Wilson of Kendal, Westmorland, 'a direct descendant of Sir Walter Scott', as the society pages called her, spent those early years in the bedrooms of many men, not always bachelors. As she later wrote in her unpublished memoirs, *Ginger for*

A younger but bigger-nosed Lady Mayo, then Lady Naas, in conversation
with Sir Winston Churchill.

Sport, 'I could fill the rest of this book with anidotes [*sic*], jealousies,
slandering, accusations I received . . . Why even Lord X's [*sic*] friend
came in to say that he nearly fought a dwell [*sic*] for me.' Of another
suitor, she wrote, 'His letter of invitation was that I reminded him
of the bursting buds of spring and that as Spring had arrived he
hoped that I would lunch with him at the smartest hotel in London.
He had blue eyes and bushy eyebrows and danced like a dream.'

'I adored parties and garden parties – and they were parties in
those days,' Mayo wrote of her time as a hostess in London. 'It is
very trying to get a name for giving the most original parties, for
one has to keep one's brain up to scratch.' At one such gathering,
where guests had been instructed to 'Come dressed representing
the letter A', Mayo gave the following prizes:

1. A weekend in a country cottage no questions asked
2. A 100-mile drive in a Rolls-Royce

3. An autographed picture of the Duke of Windsor, by the artist Hynes
4. 6 bottles of white Hungarian wine presented by the Archduke
5. [she seems to have forgotten prize five]
6. two bottles of port presented to me by His Royal Highness
7. A kiss from the hostess
8. A night with the hostess

In notching up her impressive sexual record, she acquired an illegitimate child, a boy who called her Auntie instead of Mama, so that when she married Ulick Henry Bourke, Lord Naas, destined to become the 9th Earl of Mayo, she was not as pure as she might have been, but he was grateful. 'A married man is the easiest fry to win,' she recalled later, '. . . there is no flattering attainment need be coupled to that woman who wins over a married man. To win an old batchelor [*sic*] and one with a title after one has sowed ones wild oats, when one is over 40 is an achievement – and that was my case.'

Their sexual incompatibility eventually separated them – they remained childless – and she continued to enjoy her title, taking it with her into the heart of Edinburgh society. Her arrival there was intended to mark the beginning of a new period of her life, a quieter, more spiritual time. 'Royalty cut her wedding cake. Ambassadors have sat at her table,' read a Scottish newspaper report headlined 'The Countess Gives Up The Social Round'. 'With the highest in the land she has been on friendly intimacy,' it continued. 'But the "social merry-go-round" makes no appeal to the Countess of Mayo.' She had, by then, been to an ashram in India, learnt about yoga and meditation, adopted vegetarianism and gained a PhD in America in 'spiritual enlightenment', a rather spurious sounding qualification that she used to great effect.

Lady Mayo became known in Edinburgh for her 'academy', which she called Truth in Action, set up in the chaos of her top floor flat in Princes Street: Truth in Action was one ring; Lady Mayo, three rings. 'We had some wonderful healings there,' she later wrote in her self-published book, *Celestial Visions for the New Age*. The exact principles of Lady Mayo's 'teaching' remain hazy. 'It isn't a new dogma, a new creed, or a new teaching,' she explained to a confused reporter at the time. 'It's YOU. It's a means of enabling every man, as the repository of all the wisdom in the world, to find the tutor in himself.' This was the sort of fighting talk she preached to the disciples who flocked to her twice-weekly meetings – an hour and a half of praise and rejoicing followed by a lecture 'delivered by the Countess herself'.

'Talk about the things you want to happen. Have implicit faith, and they will happen,' she urged her disciples. It was a philosophy she employed when throwing a dinner party: 'Only one ration book, my own, was available for the provision of food, but on four successive days we succeeded in organising a sit-down meal for parties of 57, 15, 87 and 48 people respectively. Whenever I went into my lobby I found it attacked with small or large parcels of food. I hadn't asked for these donations. I merely trusted that they would be forthcoming.'

It was not long before Lady Mayo's academy resembled more a Parisian salon than a centre for learning: 'I am ashamed to say I cut short, or even forgot, my meditations,' she wrote in *Celestial Visions*. 'Life was full of fun and gaity [*sic*], so I gave excuse to myself that I had no time to spare.' She pulled herself together, however, and the miracles resumed. In one chapter in her book, titled 'There Is Nothing Lost in Spirit', she gives an account of losing her pink, half-rimmed spectacles while dozing on the sands at North Berwick. On returning home and finding herself, bizarrely, in need of them for 'a radio programme and Epilogue', she asks, 'Where are my specs, dear?' What happened next is best told in her words: 'We "encircled" my spectacles together in God's Light ... and we agreed that God's circle of light protected everything and anything, and that my pink-rimmed spectacles were being taken care of.' The next day she hopped on a bus and, led by the Father, began in prayer aimlessly wandering the length of the beach. Her sign was a sweetwrapper lying in the sand. 'I bent down to pick it up – I nearly fell over. It was as if a hand pushed me over and I stumbled too far, but my hand which was groping for the sweet saved me, although it dug further down into the sand. I steadied and finally lifted myself up, regained my balance, and Lo and

Behold, the sweet and the spectacles were in my hand. Thank you Father!'

As Christmas Day approached, which was also Lady Mayo's ninetieth birthday, Lily began to wonder what they were going to eat for lunch. Lady Mayo could not cook and had resolutely refused to embrace the local cuisine. She seemed to exist on ready-roasted chickens and crumpets, and she did not mind if the crumpets were mouldy. More than once Lily had caught her reaching for packets at the back of a cupboard and giving them a wipe on the side of her dress. Unwilling to join her in this, Lily had often met the housekeeping bills and as a result her non-existent funds were running even lower. Time had not alleviated Lady Mayo's mischief-making. If anything, she was becoming more outrageous.

'Galloway! We'll have some tea now, shall we,' was a common cry, and sometimes she would purposefully drop her napkin for the pleasure of seeing Lily bend to retrieve it. Lily's undergarments had gone missing from the washing line strung up on the balcony. 'She's six sizes larger than I am and she can't even wear them!' Lily had complained to Joseph on the telephone. And one night Lady Mayo had attempted to climb into bed with her. If Lily's nerves had not been so frayed, she would have relished such antics but, much like her bank account, she was running on empty and was less inclined towards laughter. Even in his morose and somewhat incoherent state, Randolph detected Lily's disappointment at the nature of her 'holiday'. 'You appear to have had an awful drudge of a holiday with continued housework,' he wrote in one of his many letters. 'How wonderful Lady Mayo being 90 on Christmas Day. You both appear to be under the dark hand of woe in the household situation. Try and take things easier over the festive season ... I am afraid my darling that I have been a great strain on your nerves, a grief and worry to you, but I love you dearly all the same.'

Why did Lily not call it a day and board the first flight home to spend Christmas with her family? Put bluntly, she was stuck there. The bank would release no further funds. On 12 December, Mr Cubie forwarded a letter in which he included her bank statement, two bounced cheques, and a copy of a letter from Mr Thexton spelling out that the bank would no longer honour any cheques drawn on the joint account. 'I suggest that on your return from abroad, you contact me immediately,' he advised. 'I anticipate that by the time you do return matters in regard to the appointment of a *curator* will be well advanced and therefore although the communication from the bank is difficult and depressing, it may not be as significant as it might first appear.'

Relief arrived with news from Edinburgh. William and Joseph were coming to Las Palmas for a birthday celebration. The dinner party was to be at the Reina Isabel, the grandest hotel on the Playa de las Canteras, and William was picking up the bill. When the men arrived, Lily noticed William's suitcase was half-empty – 'So he can snatch back all the things she's stolen from him,' Joseph whispered. The party was to be nothing like as lavish as those Mayo had held in her heyday, but the sense of occasion and the misbehaviour that preceded it was much along the lines of Lady Mayo's alphabet party.

Joseph Bonnar has never forgotten the trip. 'We had a lunch one day with a few of Mayo's ex-pat friends. There was a vast crystal ashtray on the table. Mayo, looking like a pantomime dame, waited until William was out of view and I saw this thing being edged nearer and nearer her lap. It was crammed full of cigarette stubs. She suddenly snatched it, tipped them all out on the linen and put it into her handbag. William caught the end of this and cried, "Noel, what are you doing?" "Darling, I liked it," she said.' He went and pulled it out of her bag, scooped the butts back into and put it back on the table. 'Please don't do that,' he said. 'The waiters are watching.'

The photographs of the party itself show Lily in the cream evening dress she wore for the blessing of her marriage to Randolph. She has a tiny tiara, probably borrowed from Lady Mayo ('half the stones missing and fake,' observed Joseph Bonnar), three rows of large pearls, and a Knights of Lazarus Grand Dame of Justice Cross with ribbon pinned on her left shoulder. Next to Mayo's largesse, accentuated by her jewels and an embroidered fuchsia and mauve kaftan, Lily looks fragile, almost girlish. 'When we approached the hotel,' recalls Joseph Bonnar, 'Mayo said, "Right Jo, you first please with Lady Galloway." I said, "No, no, it's your birthday." To which she said, "It may well be, darling, but her title takes precedence." So there it was, I had to lead in with Lily, followed by Lady Mayo on William's arm. It was fantasy stuff. Lily knew her shortcomings and certainly wasn't fooled by her, but she enjoyed her company and for all the arguing, they were pals.'

That night Lily dined properly for the first time in a while. She ate poached salmon, drank a glass of champagne, and even danced on the terrace. The high point of the birthday was the presentation of Lady Mayo's gift from William, a delicate hair ornament in the shape of a crown, pearls on each of its five points, set on a tortoiseshell comb, before the party set off to dine.

'We walked in and there she was setting at it with a hacksaw,' remembers Joseph Bonnar. 'She had absolutely no intention of wearing that ornament as it was intended. She wanted rid of the comb.' When Mayo emerged dressed for dinner, the hair ornament did indeed bear a resemblance to a miniature crown, perched at the front of her head and secured into her hairline with fuse wire.

Once Christmas had passed and their visitors returned to Scotland, Lily's life with Lady Mayo returned to what Randolph accurately described as 'an awful drudge'. The housework continued, punctuated by churchgoing and spells at the British Club where Lily held her own, no doubt because of respect for her title. She had since made two more friends whom she nicknamed 'the Bananas Boys', two homosexual Spaniards who ran Bananas, Veronica Pavillard's seafront boutique, and wore open shirts exposing large medallions. Despite the fun of the Bananas Boys, her worry for Randolph was ever present. By the early New Year, the Royal Edinburgh's revolving door policy meant that after another spell there, Randolph had been moved back into a bed and breakfast paid for by social security. Despite Lily's impoverished state and the fact that Randolph was, in some ways, better off – Mr Cubie was providing him with an allowance – she continued to send him all she could, small presents and the odd £10 here and there.

'I love you still,' he told her in a letter, 'but can not explain fully my reasons for barbarism, even murderousness toward you dear. I hate to think of the nightmarish experiences you had since 1975, being near a devilish husband with embedded spells of wickedness cum madness.' By mid-January he wrote to her with the news that he was living in a boarding house in Hartington Gardens, which he said 'suits me fine . . . my pocket allowance is very reasonable . . . Please keep it in mind that I love you, and I only grieve for having corrupted and abused you so,' he continued. 'You are my darling and always will be even though we are at present far apart, but let us hope for an eventual reconciliation, though the bulk of that rests with me.'

The letters they exchanged began to take on a familiar pattern. She would inform him of her woe – in one she told him she was stranded, short of cash, with no traveller's passport and 'on the verge of prison' – and he would respond with sympathy, browbeating, and further protestations of love. On 9 February 1981 he wrote:

> I feel quite responsible for this long tale of woe you are experiencing through my atrocious enormitites [*sic*] last year, further it is a breach of oath on my part so that will await me when I appear before the Judgement Seat of Our Lord . . . I hope for your sake that you will get out of the awful conundrum you have been through, you must have worked the round of the clock for Lady Mayo . . .
>
> Darling I love you and hope that your journey home will be satisfactory and without undue hitch or detrimental happenings.

Lily was penniless. By spring she was desperate to return to Scotland. Eventually Lady Finley, she to whom money was confetti, stumped up for the fare. As Lily flew back to everything she had left behind before Christmas, as exhausted and frayed as when she had boarded the plane out, something Lady Mayo had said came flooding back: 'You and I are exactly the same. We have the name darling, but alas, we do not have the game.'

18

Poor Margot is ghastly

Once she was back in Edinburgh Lily's immediate future lay in reverting to the past. Yet again she was penniless and in need of a job. The only work she knew was cleaning or antique dealing and since the latter required money, energy, and application, not to mention furniture and china, the easiest option was to fall back into domestic service.

By now, she had learned to use the press to her own advantage. She had no intention of claiming benefit, and under the headline 'Countess is told: "Get state aid"', she spoke openly of her plight to the William Hickey column, more as a plea for help than a means of revenge:

> We need somebody's help. Our situation is so desperate. My husband had a nervous breakdown a year ago, and has since had to be taken care of in a small private home here in Edinburgh. But he cannot stay there because no one can cope with him. The trouble is I cannot afford anything better for him. I must get a job. The only thing I can do is find a nice family where I can be a house-keeper. I am willing to turn my hand to anything. At the moment we are dependent on whatever my two sons by my former marriage can give us.
>
> I have tried to get help from my husband's family, but the only reaction has been to suggest that I go on social security. I have never been on that in all my life and I am damned if I'd do that whatever happens.

Lily's fragile state required rest rather than toil. 'Trust in your sons, Dr X [their GP] and people like the Earl of Lauderdale and

Mr Cubie,' Randolph consoled her. At the end of April Randolph wrote to Lord Lauderdale pleading that Lily did not deserve her 'nervous and mental torture'. Lord Lauderdale remained their most influential friend, and while he was powerless to remedy the couple's personal problems he did write to Randolph's GP for a detailed summary of his illness. On 30 April the GP replied, with a copy sent to Lily. It provides the clearest summary of Randolph's baffling condition:

> Apart from the fact that psychiatry is a young and necessarily inexact department of medicine, Lord Galloway's mental condition simply does not fall into any of the well known categories of mental illness e.g. it is not possible to say that he is 'schizophrenic' or 'depressed' or even that he is 'mentally unbalanced' . . .
>
> The difficulty of exact diagnosis is emphasised by the different attitudes of the psychiatric specialists who have had him under their charge. In the early days he was obviously considered to be a schizophrenic. More recently when he was admitted to the Royal Edinburgh Hospital, the specialist after exhaustive investigations, discharged him with the diagnosis of 'transient situational crisis'. Still later, he has been under grave suspicion of 'temporal lobe epilepsy' but on detailed examination it was concluded that the evidence was not clear. Detailed examination and report dated 13.5.80 concluded that he has a 'frontal lobe syndrome associated with poor impulse control as a sequel to his leucotomy. There is no clear evidence that his present episodes of violence stem from an active psychotic process, but possibly from tension caused by present marital problems. On this, I would only comment that the tension the psychiatrist rightly associates with the presence of his wife is not so much due to what are called marital problems in everyday parlance, but to the continued frustration he feels because of his being for practical purposes disinherited, while the estates are managed by his cousin; while his wife, who previously thought it best to

help him by being with him, is now convinced that it is
in his interest as well as hers, that they remain separate.

The letter posed as many questions as it answered. Randolph
had suffered a 'transient situational crisis' (a 'don't know' diagnosis
which indicates the confusion over Randolph's symptoms), possibly
temporal lobe epilepsy (which mimics schizophrenia), and had
'Frontal lobe syndrome associated with poor impulse control' (his
frontal lobes, controlling functions such as patience, judgment,
balance, restraint, and abstract thinking, had been damaged by the
lobotomy). None of these conditions appeared to have come from
a psychotic process such as schizophrenia. What is interesting about
the letter, too, is the ambivalence of the medical opinion relating
to Lily's role in Randolph's life. The psychiatrist who had examined
Randolph following his attack on Lily had thought that it had
stemmed from marital problems. And yet, as their GP, who knew
the history, made clear, they did not have marital problems – at
least not in the normal sense. He was of the opinion that the
breakdown was a mixture of everything that had happened. This
feels nearer the mark. To be poor and living in one room would
drive a wedge between the most stable of couples. The fact was that
Randolph still loved Lily and wanted to live with her again.

Lily could not yet bring herself to see him. She had to move
away again, away from Edinburgh and the bad memories it held
for her. If she could find a job in London with accommodation
she would even be able to visit her friends in the House of Lords
tearoom. She bought the *Lady*. Two housekeeping posts caught her
eye, the first with an aristocratic family in Mayfair and the second
with Margot Grahame, an ageing Hollywood actress of whom Lily
had never heard. Fatigued by the trials and demands of the Countess of Mayo, Lily should, perhaps, have sought the steadier
employer. But it was not her way to pursue the quiet life and
sidestep the histrionics of a former star. So, with Joseph Bonnar's
encouragement – 'Oh for heavens sakes Lily, take the actress!' –
she accepted the post with Miss Grahame at 26 Barrie House, an
art deco mansion block on Lancaster Gate.

If Lily felt uneasy about the distance she intended to place
between herself and Randolph, this was alleviated when she came

across a volume of his memoirs, still at Bernard Terrace, in which he seems to have criticised her and blamed her. This volume has gone missing. Perhaps it has been destroyed, but whatever Randolph wrote it upset her greatly. Uncharacteristically she wrote to him in hospital saying that she knew he hated her and that all the present unhappiness was his 'just deserts'. Randolph responded to this with a letter in which he expressed again a lifetime of sorrow and bitterness, with the leitmotif of his father:

To My Supposed Wife, Lady Lily May Galloway

Perhaps it would have been better had we never known one another, for it appears that I have caused you not only grief, but no count of anger and disgust by what I said in my memoirs, not only about my family but about you especially, who are of greater importance by far than my family.

You and your own family differ extensively from my family, who could not have held a candle to any member of your family, yourself included. A weakness held the reins in my family, needless to say a father so mean, sadistic and cruel, as ill luck would have its way I contracted these uncharitable genes. My late father although an awful fool was not ever violent physically, he had a violent mind which was simultaneously very weak. As you well know I hated him as much as he hated me. Please get this clear, I do not hate you, far from it, I love you, and as far as the hurtful things I said about you I am sorry, this having added insult to injury. As you know I have lived a life of sin on the negative side, bad temper, violence and crotchetiness. I may be an ego-centric and an introvert, a prig and a snob, but none of these tot up to the enormity of violence, and violence in my speech as well as in my actions.

Before you go to another place I had better turn a clean sheet and begin anew, for seemingly I have taken the distasteful traits of my late father, having become persecutor, with all the punishment I have inflicted upon you during these last six years, more especially the last two.

You said on good grounds that what has been happening to me and what is happening is my just deserts, the woes I have deserved through my long continued and cruel punishment to all who have been specially kind to me. Returning bad and evil for good, ungratefulness to an exaggerated extreme on my part. Do not think that I am boasting and bragging about my shortcoming, I am not . . .

The letter was too much. Lily did not respond. She was suffering from her nerves. She had never been a good sleeper or enjoyed a healthy appetite. Now she looked like a frail bird.

Randolph's long-term housing had still not been resolved. Lily was not willing to take him and nor was Lady Antonia Dalrymple. In the spring of 1981 he was moved to Leather Cottage in Colinton Road, a series of rooms supervised by a Mr Bob Harris, for whom Randolph did not care and with whom he clashed. It was an echo of how he had been at Harrow. He was hardly civil to the other inhabitants, he would not pull his weight in the house, and he felt offended by Mr Harris, whom he found 'hard to please no matter whether in the right or wrong'. Around the same time Lily heard that she had landed the job with Margot Grahame (Margot had been delighted by the idea of having a countess-cum-housekeeper and had not given the appointment a second thought). Because of their argument over the memoirs Lily was not communicating with Randolph. Whenever this happened – as it would sporadically over the years – Brebner would step into the breach and act as mediator. He became adept at it. On this occasion it fell to him to tell Randolph the news of Lily's departure for London. On 28 May Randolph replied to him, apologising for hurting Lily and him, too:

Things have not been going well with your own family. Your poor mother is distraught and ready to leave for London . . . she is obviously aghast and aggrieved that she would and on good account not want to see me after how shabbily I have treated her in more ways than one. I wrote last week to her, but not my best letter as I have given her the impression by what I wrote that I was suffering from a persecution complex and split personality.

Some of the things I said in my memoirs had distressed her most bitterly. I feel that I have abused and punished you too, thus upsetting your mother.

Things cannot continue as they have been and are doing at the present time. I feel and know that I should not be living on other people and off other people. Mr Harris has more than sufficient which he has to cope with other than an awkward person such as myself. At this stage I should be getting on with some garden work of some kind, forestry or agriculture instead of skidding along on an unknown route, so it is not surprising that your dear mother is ill and sick at heart and mind and is going to another area ... For yourself and Dorothy and the rest of your family this must be a great source of worry, not only to myself, but to your dear mother.

On 20 June he wrote another letter to Brebner in which he expressed his affection for Lily and the Millar family. 'Poor dear,' he wrote, 'she is now leading a thoroughly shattered and disordered life, all due to my abominable treatment of her ... Time used to pass with me extra quickly but the present year so far has dragged ... I do love her, whether I write to her or not, I am ever dearly fond of her ... I am very fond of you and am only too sorry that I had not treated you better than you deserve.'

Brebner was the only one of Lily's sons sympathetic to Randolph's difficulties. Andrew, still in Duns, was distanced from the situation, and Benjamin was hostile because of the violence. But Brebner felt much as Lily did about Randolph: he pitied him and cared about him. He tried to cheer him up by sending him copies of the *Galloway Gazette*. Randolph continued to receive visits from his sister, who would pick him up in her motorcar and drive him back to Newhailes for short stays. She met with social workers too, and occasionally took Randolph to see his old friends, the monks in Roslin. On Mondays, Wednesdays, and Fridays, Randolph returned to the

Royal Edinburgh where his therapy included working in the
gardens.

Barrie House is a portered apartment block on Lancaster Gate,
overlooking Hyde Park. When Lily arrived there in a black cab in
May 1981 she was directed up to Margot's flat and led through to
her bedroom. Miss Grahame was sitting in her antique French bed,
a lumpy silhouette in the dark room. She wore lipstick and owlish
sunglasses. Lily addressed her from the beginning as Miss Grahame,
to which Margot roared her disapproval. Lily was not dissuaded.
She approved of such formality. 'Then I shall call you . . . how
about Lady Di!' the actress cried (Lady Diana Spencer was about
to marry the Prince of Wales).

There were photographs in gilt frames dotted about the walls.
Lily could not see them clearly, but the following morning, when
she took Margot her breakfast (which she did not eat), she saw
they showed a beautiful young woman with a fine figure and porcelain skin. In some she was in repose on the beach; in others she
was looking sultry for a Hollywood studio photographer. Surely this
drink-raddled, potato-shaped woman before her could not be the
woman in the pictures? As Lily looked from one to the other, it
became clear that she was.

Margot had been famous both on the American screen and the
British stage. In her Hollywood days she looked and acted every
bit the American starlet, although she was entirely English. Then
she had platinum blonde hair and the kind of large, exotic features
that pant for paint: rouge for her cheeks; kohl for her brows and
her beauty spot; and dark Chanel for her rosebud lips. On celluloid,
at least, she could be found glued to a gangster's side, trailing
cigarette smoke and fox fur across the floor of his drinking den.
Margot had been under no illusions. She'd understood perfectly
well that her reputation in British pictures was based on the fact
that she excelled at playing streamlined hussies, an honour she
owed to Jean Harlow, the original Platinum Blonde. Margot's
studio, International Pictures, keen to repeat the Harlow success,
branded her their very own Aluminium Blonde and by 1932 she
was reportedly the highest paid actress in Britain. But a nice girl

only wishes to play a nasty tart for so long. So she fixed on the notion of broadening her horizons. It was her first husband, the actor Francis Lister, who took her to Hollywood. He had gained a part in MGM'S *Mutiny on the Bounty* and she went along, she recalled later, purely for the ride. Nevertheless she found time 'to call at several studios'.

The reception she received was not worthy of an English lady. 'The way they looked me over! Talked about me to my face,' she would remember. ' "Look at the dame – she's got all it takes." "Rather cute, ain't she?" – remarks like that. Somebody said, "See lady, you're all right – you're fine, you're wonderful. But you ain't what we think of when we want an English star, see?" I asked politely what they were thinking of when they wanted an English girl. "Well, Miss Grahame, it's like this over here. When we want something English, see – no offence please – well then, we want an English *lady*." '

This exchange deterred her and she gave up until the last day, when the director John Ford called her in for a casting. 'I didn't in the least feel like seeing more of the studio people. I looked like nothing on earth and felt worse and wore my oldest rags. I got the customary scrutinising. "Kinda cute," they said. And "nice legs." Then John Ford barked, "Can you act?" Well, I wasn't going to be the shy down-and-out little girl. After all, I was the first English glamour screen blonde. I said "Yes, I act very well." "Ever spoken Irish?" "All my life!" ' Thirty minutes later she was made up and tested on set for the part of the harlot Katie Madden in *The Informer* (which went on to win four Oscars including best actor for Victor McLagen and best adapted screenplay). By 4 p.m. she'd signed – she was a harlot once more, but a *Hollywood* harlot – and agreed a seven-year contract with RKO at $500 a week. The publicity department immediately released a statement announcing choice details about their new star.

> She is five feet four and a half inches tall, has aluminium hair, and green-blue eyes. She is very clothes conscious and is extravagant when choosing her wardrobe. She loves good jewellery, especially diamonds. She weighs 121 pounds. She never has to diet.

Her response to the issue of dieting is prescient: 'No wonder I don't when all who live in Hollywood eat only salads.' Some fifty years later Miss Grahame's interests were much the same – clothes and diamonds. There were big differences, though. Her hair was now red – 'red as flaming fires of hell' was how she directed her stylist – and her body was so bloated that her peignoirs strained at their buttons. She needed not only a diet, but also the best rehab clinic her ex-husbands' money could buy.

When Lily encountered Margot, over made up, overweight, and overwrought in her bed, it seemed impossible that she could have ever lived any other way. The decline had in fact been relatively recent. It had begun in 1973, following the death of her long-term companion, the literary agent, A. D. Peters, with whom she had lived in the Barrie House apartment for twenty-five years. (Between him and Lister there had been a second husband, a Canadian goldmine millionaire). They had met in 1948, when Margot was in Rome filming *Black Magic*, co-directed by Orson Welles, who also starred. As well as making her name in Hollywood by then Margot was also a respected figure on the London stage. At the time A. D. Peters was an impresario – he produced several J. B. Priestley plays at the Duchess Theatre. He was already a distinguished literary agent, too. His clients included Evelyn, Alec and Auberon Waugh, V. S. Pritchett, Arthur Koestler, Nancy Mitford, C. S. Forester, Norman Collins, Rebecca West, and Elizabeth Jane Howard. He told the *Daily Telegraph* in 1953, 'If I get a good book by an unknown author I can place it in a week.'

It was a meeting of minds if not types. A. D. Peters was an emotionally uptight intellectual while Margot was prone to hysteria. Still, there existed a deep connection, which began in the bedroom, and was secured by a mutual love of the stage. They knew the same people and talked the same language. Peters brought intellectual and literary credibility to the relationship, while Margot provided Hollywood glamour and adoration laced with a considerable amount of sexual jealousy (particularly regarding Elizabeth Jane Howard, to whom Peters was, according to his protégé and successor Michael Sissons, 'very attracted'). They would throw magnificent parties at Barrie House. The Christmas party, held in the drawing room, was legendary. Peters was an avid art collector and had an eye for painters before they became too fashionable and unaffordable. The drawing room walls were hung with Sickerts and Nicholsons and Nashes. Krug was the drink of choice and the guests flocked: Hugh 'Binkie' Beaumont, the legendary theatrical impresario who more or less controlled British theatre at the time; Noel Coward; J. B. Priestley; Terence Rattigan and Rebecca West; and the theatre producer Charles Russell. As London's finest talked over the finer points of literature and playwriting, Margot drifted in and out of rooms looking and behaving every inch the Hollywood diva.

Michael Sissons had recently come down from Oxford and been taken under A. D. Peters's wing as a potential successor to his

Margot Grahame captured in full diva glory in 1950. 'Lipstick, mascara and eye-brow pencil only used. NO powder, rouge or shading', the studio's note states.

literary agency (now merged and called PFD, overseen by Michael Sissons and Pat Kavanagh). Quite reasonably, he found Margot 'rather amazing'. 'Margot really could not stop talking about sex,' he remembers. 'She had put herself about in spectacular fashion in the 1930s and had slept with some of the great names. "Darling", she'd say, "did I ever tell you how I had Clark Gable?" and I'd say, no Margot, but I'm sure you're going to now.' She was also, he noticed, a woman prone to wearing 'superstructures around her bosoms'. 'She was extremely self-obsessed in that way that actresses are and she saw herself as a slice of Hollywood. She'd sweep into the literary agency, all done up, her bosom literally under her chin, and shout, "Oh darling, you haven't got such a thing as a bottle of whisky round here, have you? Fix me a whisky and soda." And she'd knock back this tumbler full and it was only 11 a.m. She was a boozer even then. There was always the green Rolls waiting outside for her. Peters managed to get it when an American film producer reneged on a big deal. It may even have been an Evelyn Waugh project. He gave it to Peters to offer to the disgruntled client. The client said, "I have no use for a green Rolls." So Margot and Peters got to keep it. A villainous chauffeur drove it and he used to flatter Margot rotten. "Oh gor, m'ludy, if I were a younger man." We used to go out in the Rolls to performances. I remember sitting in the back with Peters and Alan Clark going to *Oh! What a Lovely War!*

For all Margot's furs and front she was a respected actress with a good heart. Noël Coward adored her and roped her into his work as President of the Actors' Orphanage, a charity dedicated to the destitute young of the acting profession. (During the war he had been instrumental in evacuating many of its children to North America.) Showing characteristic wit, at fun-fair days at Regent's Park, Coward would place her on the coconut stands and she'd work there for hours, flirting and charming the public. This sort of work was not always easy. On Thursday, 22 September 1949, for instance, Coward records in his diary, 'Stormy Actors' Orphanage meeting when I flew at everyone, myself included, and I think I galvanized them into some sort of awareness of their responsibilities.'

Charles Russell, who produced a revival of Coward's *Blithe Spirit* in 1954, in which Margot was cast as the second wife, Ruth, remembers thinking her 'a dynamic actress, forceful and when on the screen you did not look at anybody else'. Noël Coward wrote of this revival in his diaries. Margot was playing alongside Kay Kendall, Dennis Price and Irene Handl. They had quite an act to follow. (The last performance of the play, the 1,997th performance since opening in July 1941, had been held at the Duchess Theatre on 9 March 1946. It had been a full house.) A revival had worried Coward and he was right. The performances did not meet with his approval, including Margot's. On 7 October 1954, he wrote, 'Poor Margot is ghastly. She is just a large, breasty, good-hearted hunk of tangerine meat.'

Poor Margot indeed. Despite Coward's withering comment, Russell vouches for her. 'By comparison to Irene Handl, Margot was a real professional,' he says.

> She was always on time and keen to get on with the cast. Irene was marvellous casting but couldn't remember the lines so she made them up, and so couldn't give the other actors their cues. We couldn't go to the West End with Irene Handl so we had to sack the whole lot of them. We couldn't go back to Shaftesbury Avenue when it was not as good as when it had been done originally.
>
> Margot existed in a time when actresses loved to be famous but had to earn that fame from proper hard work. They liked their work to be acknowledged and they gave up everything for it. Their idea of themselves was inextricably bound up with that fame. Margot was just like Joan Crawford in that respect.

Whether or not Margot's acting skills were on the decline, A. D. Peters needed his 'large, breasty, good-hearted hunk of tangerine meat' and she needed him. They depended on each other – both Charles Russell and Michael Sissons noted it every time they saw the couple together. All the while Peters was alive, Margot could cope with anything, including her fading fame. At the age of eighty, though, with characteristic clarity of thought, A. D. Peters decided that he had quite simply had enough. He was ready to die. Understandably Margot became hysterical. 'She phoned me,' recalls Sissons, 'saying, "Darling, you have to come to the flat immediately.

Peters is being quite ridiculous. He says he is ready to die. You *have* to do something. Please tell him how ridiculous he is being.'' ' But Peters's mind was made up and he did exactly as intended, dying 'a contented and much-loved man' in the antique French bed he had shared with Margot for twenty-five years.

Margot never pulled herself out of her grief. Lily found her full of bitter regret and resentment, not only because Peters had never married her, but also because she had lost her fame, her beauty and her friends. Her solace was brandy and prescription drugs. If Coward's comment in 1954 had been a little unkind, Margot Grahame had certainly proved capable of growing into the insult. She could barely stand she was so swollen with drink. Help had to be on hand at all times.

Lily was installed in a small *chambre de bonne*, close to Margot's dark boudoir. She wore a white, starched housecoat. For one who rarely rose from her bed, Margot was at the centre of a surprising amount of activity. She stirred just before noon, but the house woke early with the comings and goings of staff and aides, most of whom were superfluous but whom Margot retained anyway for the company. Of these, the most absurd was her theatrical agent. She would

Margot Grahame, with a touch of Elizabeth Taylor about her, in owlish sunglasses with her friend and fan Esme, photographed by Lily in Barrie House.

perch on the side of Margot's bed once a week and run through a list of forthcoming parts that might once have suited her client. She gave an Oscar-worthy performance every time.

Of all the retainers the three most important were Margot's hairdresser, a young Australian called Keith Hancock Banks who travelled from his base at Selfridges; her fey, gay, and adored Coutts banker, Dominic Scott Frost, keeper of her jewellery; and her doctor, Lord Hunt of Fawley. It is difficult to decide which of these men had the most trying time, although Lord Hunt was the oldest. He was also almost blind and had an arthritic hip. Like the agent and, for that matter, the van driver from the vintners who delivered the supply of cognac, Lord Hunt came weekly. He arrived in a Bentley driven by his chauffeuse, who was trained to spring from her seat and assist as he tottered into the lift. Lord Hunt was president of the Royal College of Practitioners, for which he was given his peerage. He could no longer see his patient properly – perhaps just as well considering her decline – but he was fond of her and listened to her worries with the attention and dedication of a physician just starting his career. Having cared for Peters until his death, Hunt was a link to the past, and his role in Margot's life was now more unofficial counsellor than practising doctor. Whenever there was a genuine health concern, his son Jonathan, who was in the process of taking over his practice, would be called in to administer care.

'Shall we just say,' remembers Dr Jonathan Hunt, 'that there was an input–output imbalance.'

> She did not get her calories in the usual way and was completely sedentary. She was over fourteen stone and a very difficult patient to manage, both for who she was and the nature of her many complaints. She studiously ignored all our advice. If she hadn't things would have been very different, but it was vital that we took her complaints seriously as one never knew what might happen. Certain aspects of her care had to be put through the legal process, so that we could protect ourselves professionally.
>
> One chose the timing of one's visits very carefully. Midday was usually a good time as this was when she rose.

Early evening would always be a disaster but whatever the
time of day, it was always dark in there as she remained
in bed and never drew the curtains. But one could not
help noticing that she could certainly put on the make-up.

It is a testimony to Lily's personality that the obstinate, querulous,
and often drunk Miss Grahame, so used to the methods of Daisy
Bannister, her previous long-serving housekeeper, swung herself
round to accommodate – even be guided by – a replacement. Lily's
impact on the household was immediate. She reduced Margot's
daily brandy consumption from three bottles to one, and though
Margot continued to drink, Lily's good humour did much to revive
her. Joseph Bonnar, too, was a huge asset. Lily introduced them
and once Margot realised that he was homosexual and one of
Edinburgh's most reputable jewellers, she threw open the doors of
her apartment and insisted he stay whenever he could. Her high
regard for him was richly returned. Here was a man with exactly
the right frames of reference. Joseph Bonnar recalls of his visits:

> She would say things like, 'Oh darling, you see when I
> was in Jamaica, Noël said to me . . .' and I would be bang
> on cue saying, 'Margot darling, you don't mean Noël
> Coward?' She loved that. Once, to try and help Lily, I
> said, 'Now Margot, I'm not going to come until I know
> that you are out of bed.' When I arrived, there she was
> in her wheelchair, deck shoes, slacks, a blazer that just
> about met in the middle. It was cruise gear of the most
> fabulous kind. She changed three times that day – once
> into a cocktail dress and then evening dress for dinner
> which Lily prepared but of course ended up down the
> sink because Margot refused to eat solids. That's when
> we first saw the full extent of her jewels. She got on the
> phone to Dominic Scott Frost at Coutts, who Lily adored.
> 'Dominic, it's Margot, darling. Can we bring in the box?'
> He said, 'Margot, can't we do it next week? It really is
> quite difficult to open a strong room on a Friday after-
> noon.' To which she said, 'Well, darling, that's exactly
> why I'm phoning you. We want them right now.' And
> do you know, a van arrived and these big men brought

in the box and Lily and I and Margot tipped it out over
the bed. It was all Van Cleef and Cartier, diamond
brooches the size of Margot's bosoms that she was riffling
through and chucking about the place. I said, 'Margot,
for heavens sake, be careful', and she'd say, 'Oh darling,
it's all right, nobody will steal that, it's got a curse on it.
Get out your eyeglass and read the inscription on that
one, "*To the lovely Miss Grahame from the Maharajah of
Jaipur.*"'

Despite Margot's abuse of her body, she still liked to have her
hair styled. Often she lost track of her own appointments, so that
Lily would answer the door to Keith the hairdresser. 'He'd fling
her into her wheelchair and run her down the hall to a deep sink
and then fling the wheelchair over, practically breaking her neck,'
remembers Joseph Bonnar, 'and she would bawl instructions at
him about the deeper hue she wanted for her hair.'

He'd always refuse at first, saying it was perfectly fine the
way it was, but she would scream 'I want it dyed as red
as the fires of hell, you bastard.' And he would laugh
and say, 'okay, okay', and there would be Lily in the
background saying, 'Behave yourself, Miss Grahame.
That's shocking!' Often he would lead Margot onto the
subject of sex. Once he admired the portrait of her hanging over the fireplace [Margot left it to him in her will],
allegedly painted by an aristocratic lady friend from her
heyday. 'Well, darling,' she said, 'you know why it's so
good? I fucked her once!' and she burst out laughing.
She was always saying things like this to which Lily would
snap, 'Enough of that dirty talk, Miss Grahame! Enough!'
but I knew that Lily loved it really. It's why she stayed
with her.

If nothing else, Margot helped take Lily's mind off her own
problems. Life with her might have been difficult but it was never
boring and there was little time during the day for brooding or
self-pity. Sometimes it was even fun. On one occasion, for example,
Margot decided to amuse them all at Lord Hunt's expense. She

announced she was to play a trick on the doctor and that they were to wait outside the door until she let out a small cry at which point they were to look in. They agreed. The distinguished old man was led into her boudoir, tottering slowly with the aid of a stick and a guide dog. He asked her how she was and she replied that her chest was restricted. She gave them their cue and when Lily and Joseph Bonnar peered round, they saw that Margot had opened her peignoir and was shaking her oversized, exposed bosoms at her elderly doctor, quite unaware in his sightlessness of the vision before him. Lily remained outside, rocking with laughter.

While Margot invited certain informalities, her head was turned by a title and she took great efforts to inform visitors that she had both a Lord and a Lady on her payroll. This was interpreted as 'reflected glamour'. Lily still insisted on calling Margot Miss Grahame, and Margot insisted on calling Lily 'Lady Di'. 'Dear Di,' reads one of Margot's dog-eared messages, penned on 9 August in a drunken, green scrawl, 'Love and Welcome Home, Margot G'. With it is the accompanying message, 'So much happiness to have you home, Margot Grahame.'

For all her hysterics, Margot adored Lily. Dr Jonathan Hunt had observed immediately that Lily was a blessing – 'A very caring person, a sensible, pragmatic individual who behaved only as a loyal housekeeper and at no time exuded the demeanour that other of one's patients who were countesses exuded.'

That Lily was a countess was accepted without question by the rest of the staff. They considered it 'such an extraordinary thing' that it simply had to be true. As Dr Hunt says, 'to have made that up would have been quite ridiculous'. She was popular and not at all stiff or starchy. Whenever Margot became too much – even for her – she would telephone the doctor or the lawyer for support. On other occasions Lily telephoned Joseph, who attempted to raise her out of her exhaustion by making her laugh.

Lily's chief concerns were Margot's drinking and her refusal to eat or rise from her bed. This worry, made worse by exhaustion from being called upon throughout the night, was by now beginning to damage her health. In October, Mr Nigel Bulmer, Margot's long-suffering lawyer at Farrer & Co (the Queen's lawyers), wrote the following memorandum to her, as was his custom:

Attended Dr Hunt on his telephoning. He mentioned
your housekeeper Lady Galloway had gone to hospital
with chest pains which he thought might be a mild coronary. The question might arise of obtaining for you a new
housekeeper/companion. There had also been some
excitement over the alleged loss of some of your jewellery
and the police had been called in. The jewellery had
been found. Dr Hunt then advised that this jewellery
should be logged at the bank. Said we agreed and would
speak to you about this.

Lily had not had a coronary. It was more that the incident of the
lost jewels, which had been a storm in a teacup, had placed a huge
strain on her. The jewels were eventually found under Margot's
bed, but by then Lily was in Westminster Hospital. On another
occasion, she was taken in for swelling in her abdomen and ankles.
Her consultant wrote back to her doctor in Scotland, 'I think that
the episodes of extensive drinking (of tea, not alcohol) and swelling
of the ankles etc are related to anxiety. She feels anxious, her
mouth gets dry and she drinks. I am sure you know about all her
family problems and the fact that Lady Galloway is looking after a
very demanding lady, and all this, I am sure, is the basis of her
problems.'

A month or so after her arrival Lily had received word from
Andrew Cubie that on 30 June the Court of Session had appointed
him as Randolph's *curator bonis*. The business of the late Lord
Galloway's estate had still not been settled, and in the interim
period Randolph's living expenses were coming out of money left
to him in the estate of his late mother. The appointment of the
curator bonis was a sad end to their struggle. Randolph's money now
had to pass through Mr Cubie's hands first.

While Lily was in London, Randolph went in and out of the
Royal Edinburgh. He wrote constantly, each letter containing fresh
accounts of the bad state of their finances – 'there seems to be no
end to this awful tomb' – and affirmations of undying love: 'Please
remember and do not forget I love you dearly, my darling, in spite
of everything that has crossed our paths.'

He continued to receive small payments – from the DHSS, from his mother's estate, and two insignificant family trust funds that had been established for him – but this did nothing to quell his bitterness. Although they were no longer living as man and wife, Lily continued to view him as her husband, and she sent him gifts whenever she could. Sometimes these would be cheques from her wages, and sometimes small presents such as a pair of new pyjamas. 'I only regret there is nothing forthcoming to relieve your financial embarrassment,' Randolph wrote back. 'I do love you all the same and only wish I could send you something as a lift.'

On 27 November 1981, Lily received a letter from him that provided an unwanted confirmation that they should live apart. During his temporary release from hospital, he had assaulted another stranger, this time in Morningside. Randolph's violence had been provoked by frustration at finding himself short of cash while in a shop. The consequences were even more serious. His victim, an old man, was taken to hospital with a fractured skull. When the police arrived Randolph did all he could to resist arrest. 'On the law's arrival I tried to shrug them off, so I had to be put on a charge of wilful and grievous assault to the aged, a breach of the peace, and unruly conduct, a triplefold sentence.'

Randolph was taken to the police station, charged and released pending his court case. In a letter to Lily three days later, he returned to the familiar theme of his father, who he felt 'would leer and gloat with delight that things were going wrong, ever wishing us ill and out of luck'.

There was one positive outcome of this hopeless and depressing episode. The trustees, perhaps now finally aware that Randolph's suffering was more than any man deserved, agreed to transfer funds in lieu of the settlement of the 12th Earl's estate. On 23 December £10,000 landed in the curatory and this was repeated at the end of March the following year. Of the first £10,000, £8,750 was made over immediately to the Royal Bank of Scotland and Mr Cubie kept the rest, to cover eighteen months' worth of legal work.

Lily was worried Randolph would end up in jail. Mr Cubie tried to reassure her: 'So far as the proposed prosecution against your husband is concerned, I have heard nothing further and I only hope that as and when charged documents are received by your

husband that he will forward them to me immediately to permit
me to take some action for him.'

How did Lily view the attack? 'Oh, he's a poor love,' she would
repeat, over and over, although she refrained from talking about
it to Miss Grahame, realising how the actress would seize upon it
and dramatise it for all that it was worth. It was as if each fresh
cruelty strengthened her bond with Randolph. By normal standards, it was not a real relationship – it could not be, Randolph
was too unwell – but even during this period, when she was not
seeing him at all, Lily remained loyal and preoccupied by his wellbeing.

The marriage provided her with something private and cherished, a constant force incomprehensible to the outside world and
operating totally outside any laws of reason. Separation was their
future. Divorce was not. The word did not even so much as pass
her lips – especially not when she considered that he needed her
more than ever. That Christmas Randolph advised her, 'Let the
great day float by as a drifting spectre.' They were to spend it apart,
she with Margot and he with Lady Antonia at Newhailes. Lily sent
him socks in black and grey, scents, body talcs, aftershave, and
floral and fruit flavoured teas. He sent her some of the paintings
he had begun to create, tableaux of birds and creatures like those
one sees at a nursery school. Lily spent New Year's Eve with Margot
too, each jolting the other out of loneliness.

Margot was not in good health. She still ignored Lord Hunt's
advice and was cross at the idea of having to get up from bed, but
she was drinking less brandy. There was nothing to tell Lily that
Margot was any worse than normal that night. Lily left her in bed
a little after midnight. Ten minutes later, or thereabouts, a nurse
was summoned to bring her some Campbell's tomato soup, which
Margot drank unassisted and alone, as she had requested. At
around 12.30 a.m. the nurse, thinking Margot strangely unde-
manding and sensing that this was not a good sign, looked in and
found her lying quite still, an unsightly red river of soup trickling
over her chin and chest.

The nurse rushed into Lily's room. Lily, struggling to get Margot
out of her peignoir, assumed she was lolling in a drunken stupor.
It was only when she felt the body was growing cold that she realised

Margot was dead. She rushed for the telephone and summoned an ambulance. She also phoned for Dr Jonathan Hunt, who was on holiday in Salzburg. A locum struggled across town. He declared Margot dead.

Margot Grahame had choked on her soup, which had ignited her bronchial problems. Had she had her way, she would have been properly made up and waited on in her final hour of glory. But the drama lay only in the timing. 'That was typical of Margot,' Jonathan Hunt observes, 'Nobody else could have pulled it off so close to midnight.'

Lily was deeply saddened by Margot's death. It was yet another trauma for her to cope with. She telephoned Brebner in Scotland and begged him, 'Please come to London. Please. Margot is dead.' He told her calmly that it was the middle of the night, New Year's Day, and that he could not possibly board a train.

Less than two hours before Margot's death, Lily had taken a polaroid of her. It shows her flat on her back in bed, sunglasses on, nails painted, already looking more than a little worse for wear. Her address book is beside her and she appears to be holding up a photograph. Above her head, mounted on the wall, is a gilt-framed picture of her in the Hollywood days.

In the days that followed Coutts Bank, the official executors of Margot's will, moved in and sealed the house. Lily was allowed to remain in residence and given an important role as on-site caretaker, particularly considering that the apartment was crammed with Peters's art collection. 'It was in our interests to pay Lady Galloway to stay on as housekeeper,' remembers Bob Cammiade of Coutts. 'We found her to be an excellent custodian of the assets. During one of my visits with a representative from Christies Lady Galloway said, "Margot always wore a large diamond cross on a black velvet band. I have dusted everywhere and can't find it." As a result, I went straight to the undertakers. Margot was still wearing it. It was later valued between £10,000 and £12,000, and had Lady Galloway not remembered, it would have been cremated with Margot and spread over the grounds of Golders Green Crematorium.'

In Lily's role as official guard dog she encountered a stream of strangers who arrived to claim informal bequests. There had been much will-dangling during Margot's later life, which Nigel Bulmer, her lawyer, recognised to be 'very much the pattern of a manipulative individual'. Lily received £5,000, which would have been twice that amount had Margot roused herself to sign a prepared codicil.

The content of Margot's will is a testimony to the trajectory of her life. By the end there was nobody left to whom she could leave the sum she had amassed over the years through marriages and movies. All she had was her staff. As Nigel Bulmer recognises 'Business with Margot was always small and incidental, but she greatly enjoyed the chat.'

Lily; Daisy Bannister, 'my adored former housekeeper who served me so well and faithfully for many years'; Nigel Bulmer; Dr Hunt; her bankers; her hairdresser; the Battersea Dogs Home; and the Royal National Institute for the Deaf were all left generous bequests. But it made little dent in her £322,000 estate, the bulk of which she gave to the Royal National Lifeboat Institution and the Guide Dogs for the Blind.

On 3 February Lily attended Margot's inquest and heard the pathologist's report. The official cause of death was given as respiratory failure caused by chronic bronchitis and heavy drinking. A broken heart leaves no physical trace. The coroner, Dr Paul Knapman, recorded a verdict of death due to natural causes, and concluded that Margot 'looked back on the old days and could not come to terms with her new life'.

Margot received a three-paragraph obituary in *Variety*, but the biggest splash was in the *Daily Express*, following the inquest: 'One-time star Margot dies sad and so lonely.' Margot's distant friend, the eighty-one-year-old comedian Arthur Askey commented: 'What Margot suffered is unfortunately part and parcel of show business. One year your name is in lights and everyone wants to know you. The next year you are forgotten.'

Following the inquest Margot was cremated, her ashes mingled and sprinkled with those of her mother and father, and 'with those of Augustus Dudley Peters with whom I enjoyed so many happy years and whose ashes are held by J. H. Kenyon Limited at 81 Westbourne Grove London, W2 awaiting my demise.' She had chosen three tunes for the occasion: 'None but the Lonely Heart', 'Because', and 'You are My Heart's Delight', music which recalled happier days.

19

Never judge a person until you've walked a mile in their shoes

As the shock of Margot's death subsided, its consequences came into focus. Lily was once again jobless and had nowhere to stay in London. She remained sanguine, however. The natural course for her was to return to Edinburgh. Bernard Terrace had periodically been let out to student boarders, although she had always kept a room for herself. But Edinburgh made her feel claustrophobic. It reminded her of crushed dreams. London provided anonymity. There she could be who she wanted to be, which was the Countess of Galloway, without all the baggage that Scotland was so keen to remember.

She spent many of those early days of 1982 travelling across the city, mostly by foot or train, occasionally by taxi, registering with countless employment agencies in the hope of taking on any kind of work on which she could survive. Her lack of success was not for want of good references, which she had secured when helping to wind up Margot's estate. 'She is a kindly and affectionate person who has brought much solace to those for whom she has needed to care,' wrote Lord Lauderdale. 'Lady Galloway looked after Miss Grahame's household with a great deal of capability and it is my opinion that she is most honest and trustworthy,' testified Dr Jonathan Hunt. Dominic Scott Frost, who opened up a Coutts account for her – a marvel considering her financial affairs – wrote that she 'can be relied upon to fulfil efficiently any task she undertakes'. But Lily was past retirement age and one imagines she posed a rather curious prospect to those who sought to place her.

During this period she moved three times. She stayed first in a small travellers' hotel in Kensington before ending up, via lodgings in Dollis Hill, in a rented flat in Palace Road, SW1. In March and then in April she received two pieces of news about Randolph's future. On 11 March he appeared in court facing charges relating to his assault on the old man in Morningside. The case was adjourned until 25 March, when he was found guilty and placed on a year's probation with the condition that he remained under the supervision of the Royal Edinburgh. A month later Mr Cubie informed her of the final figure of Randolph's inheritance. The net moveable estate – to which he was entitled a half of a half – had come in at £215,168.29. More than half of this had been lost to capital transfer tax, and 'expenses of realisation' amounted to £10,009.34. The final lump sum owed to Randolph was £24,502.26 rising to £28,032.04 on account of the interest accrued over the years. After the two prior payments of £10,000, what he actually received now was £8,030. This money was given over to Mr Cubie on 13 April 1982 and with that, nearly four years of fighting and wrangling was brought to an official end.

Throughout this peripatetic period Lily kept a diary, although it is more a record of her daily spending habits than an insight into her emotions regarding the events that were going on around her. It is full of lists: '*Express* 17p, potatoes 52p, chicken £2, tomatoes 48p, oranges 30p, Turkish Delight 16p, nuts for birds 18p, plants for Brebner 42p, milk 17½p.' Some days her expenditure was as low as 76p. Her luxuries were the *Daily Express, Woman's Own*, and cigarettes, with the occasional 'chocolate treat'.

Apart from one or two mournful entries, such as that of Tuesday, 29 June: 'Phoned Brebner from the HoL – I feel very lonely and upset, Brebner not at all well' – there is a lack of introspection and self-pity. 'Finished pants for Clare (large doll),' she writes one day following a trip to the Portobello Road. Another entry shows similar spirit: 'Went to Kensington to have my hair permed – light perm rinse and shampoo £30 (What a disgrace!)' The diary is full of such small self-admonishments. Thursday, 22 July: 'Dressed up in new suit – from now on its [*sic*] important I get a job and income from Bernard Terrace to survive.'

Despite the overall instability of Lily's life, there remained one or two constants. She took mass at St Matthew's and tea and toast with the peeresses at the House of Lords. During the summer months, her seventeen-year-old granddaughter, Brebner's daughter Susan, travelled down to London looking for part-time work and asked to stay for a few days. This delighted Lily. Susan played an important role during this time. She kept loneliness at bay and ignited Lily's optimism, which at times bordered on effervescence, despite all that had happened.

A contributing factor to this optimism was the prospect of a trip to America. A year before, on her return to Edinburgh from Las Palmas, Lily had found a letter addressed to 'Lord Randolph'. Its sender was Mrs Merry Jayne McMichael Fischbach, convenor of the North American Gathering of the Stewarts of Galloway, who requested that Randolph 'as our chieftan [*sic*]' and his 'Lady' might wish to preside over the Ohio Scottish Games on 27 June at the College of Wooster Ohio. 'If you are unable to attend,' she wrote, 'would you send a representative, or, if this is not possible, send a message which could be read to clansmen and clanswomen as well as other persons attending the Games?' It had been a cheering letter for Lily to receive on Randolph's behalf, both for the opportunity to travel outside Europe, and for what it signified. Lily had responded immediately, indicating that she would dearly love to attend, but being short of cash, could only do so if the Clan Stewart Society in America was inclined to raise the funds for her fare. It was not. But Lily had seized on this first overture and the exchange had blossomed into an endearing pen-pal relationship. Mrs McMichael Fischbach, delighted to have struck upon such a forthcoming and warm Scottish countess, remained determined to bring Lily into the fold. On 1 June 1982 Donald Macleay, President of the Clan Stewart Society in America, wrote to Lily extending an invitation for her to be the Society's guest in America for three or four days at the Stone Mountain Gathering, during which the Society would be holding its annual meeting. He said that the invitation rested upon the understanding that she would be representing Randolph 'Chief of the Stewarts of Gallaway [*sic*]'.

With Mrs McMichael Fischbach's help, Lily was to fly first to Cleveland, Ohio, where perhaps she might like to be piped into the arrivals lounge and filmed by a crew from the local television station? She would travel on to Atlanta for the meeting and then to Florida, possibly returning to England via Cleveland and New York.

Lily was thrilled. It was the role she had longed to fulfil the year before. Her sense of pride and anticipation could be matched only by the enthusiasm of her pen pal, for whom Lily was now all but royal.

Mrs Fischbach had begun, the year before, with a tone of utmost deference – 'If it is agreeable with you Madam, I would enjoy corresponding with you.' Later she wrote, 'Madam, if at any time I commit an error in etiquette in our correspondence, please bear in mind that as an American, I am unaccustomed to corresponding with a Peeress.' But with time Lily had put her at ease. She still considered herself Lily's 'obedient servant', but she was ready with advice.

> My heart aches to learn that the Earl is suffering from severe mental trauma. Clan members, like myself, always hold the hope that their chief is amenable and able to assume to position of clan leadership; to lend support to recruiting efforts of the clan society and for other clan orientated projects. However, you and I both know that it is often the women, whether the chief's wife or clans-women, who are the ones who step into the breach and pull things together. It is to your credit that you are willing to do so and to the Earl who made a wise choice when he married you. I sense that you will do what you can to keep your husband's birthright intact despite the obstacles created by his father.

Mrs Fischbach enlisted Miss Emily Hunter Boyd into the friend-ship. 'The minute one of your letters arrive, I call her and read it to her. We laughingly call ourselves the Bobbsey Twins.' (Their affinity with the lengthy series of Bobbsey Twins books is touching but it is unclear whether they identified more with the older pair, Bert and Nan, or the younger two, Flossie and Freddie.) During their correspondence, in which Mrs Fischbach, a self-declared aficionado of bagpipe music and all things Stewart, was adoring and deferential, Lily began to contemplate the idea of moving to

America. The fantasy reveals her eagerness to flee the past and build a fresh future, in a place where she could make new friends and receive a warmer welcome. Lord Galloway's rejection of her had damaged her more than she cared to admit to herself. Once again, she felt she did not fit.

Her American correspondents were full of ideas about what she might do in the US, some of which were not altogether sound propositions. 'As attractive as you are,' Mrs Fischbach wrote her, 'I am sure that you could obtain a position as a spokesperson for an airline or travel bureau or something similar. Betty has told me about the lovely gardens belonging to your late father-in-law, perhaps they could be used as a background for an advertising photo?'

Another idea was that Lily become a companion to a wealthy American lady. 'I regret to say it, but there are Americans who would be delighted to be able to show off their titled "pet".' Another was that she move to the south-west – 'preferably Texas' – and set up a school teaching etiquette and manners. And if she did not fancy posing in the Cumloden flowerbeds or establishing herself as a Miss Manners for Texan heiresses, there was always debt collection – 'an area which has boomed with the depressed economy' – or writing lurid magazine stories. 'Look at Her Highness, The Princess of Wales' grandmother,' Mrs Fischbach advised of the oeuvre of Barbara Cartland. 'She's making a bloody fortune writing romances!' The Bobbseys came up with many other ideas, including a mail-order business specialising in Scottish products; genealogical research; importing and exporting tartans; and bed and breakfast – 'I am sure, My Lady, that you would be a most charming and gracious hostess.'

Randolph spent the summer of 1982 moving around the Lowlands. Part of his time was spent at Lothlorien, a compassionate community between Dumfries and Castle Douglas that soothed troubled souls with agricultural pursuits and domestic animals. Here each inhabitant had a basic but private log cabin. Lothlorien's simplicity and horticultural bent suited Randolph perfectly. It was also relatively near to Cumloden. But there was not a full-time vacancy, and he had to join a list. In the meantime he rested with his sister at Newhailes. She was widowed and without children and she took him with her to buffet lunches hosted by friends, some in the grand houses they had known from childhood. The trips had a jollying effect, but it was only a matter of time before these enforced periods of cohabitation took their toll on both parties. Randolph did not like Edinburgh. It was noisy and it contained too much traffic. Once he was even tipped off his bicycle by a double-decker bus – 'A reimbursement for my foolishness through the year,' he wrote.

From Newhailes, he moved on to a bed and breakfast in Blacket Place – 'From manor to rathole,' he observed. The negative attitude with which he entered the house did not bode well, and it took a week for news about what happened next to reach Lily in London.

> Blacket Place was an utter washout. I had just been there for 48 hours, the manager demanded some payment for lodging, on this they insist, I hadn't no [*sic*] money so the big noise ordered me off his premises. So from just before 5pm until midnight on Tuesday evening I was wheeling my luggage in random directions. I went first to Royal Edinburgh, where I was told that they had no accommodation, they sent me to the Salvation Army Camp in Victoria Street? [*sic*], and in desperation as the hour of midnight was fast approaching, I came across a nice English couple who helped me no end. I was put up for the rest of the night in this camp place, sleeping on the floor with a whole lot of other poor wanderers and vagrants. Come 6.20am the awakening to a dryish crust on Wednesday morning. Then from just after 7 to just after 9 I was helped by a nice Canadian lady wheeling my bag out to Morningside.

Although Lily did not see much of Randolph during this time, he was constantly on her mind. She was as protective of him as she had ever been, and she became preoccupied with the quest to secure for him a permanent address. Throughout August she repeatedly telephoned Mr Cubie pleading that he might do something to help them (she always referred to it as a joint problem). The situation caused Mr Cubie some angst. Randolph had two living relatives, neither of whom felt they could take him on. Equally, Randolph could not stay in hospital indefinitely. On

31 August Mr Cubie wrote to Lily trying to explain the problem: 'I must stress that I share with you your frustration as to the inability of the society in which we live to find a proper home for your husband given that both you and Lady Antonia Dalrymple find it impossible to have Lord Galloway reside with you.'

He went on to point out that not for a moment did he criticise the hospital: 'I do well appreciate their major difficulty in finding suitable accommodation for a man like your husband given that your home and that of your sister-in-law are closed to him.' He had, he said, pointed out on several occasions to the hospital authorities his 'considerable concern about the wellbeing not only of your husband but also of the risk to the community'. However, at the end of the day, it was not a matter under his jurisdiction. His role in Randolph's life was purely as protector of his funds and he could not, he stated plainly, 'be the arbiter of matters relating to his medical welfare'.

Lily was scheduled to fly to America in October. 'She was over the moon about that trip,' remembers Brebner: 'she could not stop talking about it. It was one thing she really had to look forward to.' In the third week of September Lily received a letter from Mr Macleay. She opened the envelope with excitement, assuming it to contain finalisation of her itinerary. It did not:

> Recent publicity, considered by the Board to be most unfortunate, indicates that actually, at the very least, there exists between yourself and the Gallaways [*sic*] a discord which has assumed serious proportions. Under such circumstances, the Board has concluded that it would be inappropriate for this Society to appear to be taking sides in that situation, which could be inferred from sponsorship by it of your visit to Stone Mountain. It is my duty, therefore, to advise you that by action of the Board the invitation is withdrawn.

Had the society seen the newspaper articles, or had somebody made a point of telling it? Lily thought the latter. She did not know who; only that it was clear old grudges lived on. The late Lord Galloway was six years dead and his estate wound up. The only family members intimately connected with past events were Sara and

Andrew Stewart at Cumloden and Lady Antonia at Newhailes. But Scotland is a small country and Edinburgh even smaller. Gossip continued to travel fast. It was the work of a blind assassin and the bullet wounded her. She had invested so much hope in the trip. Her distress was in equal measure to the excitement it replaced. It was one of the few moments in her life when she allowed herself the release of tears. She was, Brebner saw, not only crying for the missed opportunity, but for yet another rejection and all the rejections of the past. How could she be held in such low regard?

She informed Randolph immediately, who referred to it as 'this business of the Stewarts . . . a mirrored echo of the past'. Shortly afterwards, in another letter, he wrote:

> It is a known fact that you and I love each other to high extent, that we are the supposed Lord and Lady Galloway . . . yet where are we? Standing on our heads in the middle of nowhere with an upturned begging bowl containing nothing more than a tattered shoestring or two from the sodden gutters.

The indignation of the Bobssey Twins can not be overstated. 'We have always found you to be a very gentile [*sic*] lady and that nothing in your letters gave us any reason to believe otherwise, and our conversations with you confirmed our beliefs,' Mrs Fischbach wrote as soon as she found out. It was a decision that was to have wider ramifications than just hurting Lily's feelings. It caused internal division within the society itself. During this period her friends sent her a membership form offering to be her sponsors, 'our gift to you'. When Lily opened it she found her name had been entered as Lily Brown Stewart. 'Please do not question the way it has been filled in,' her American friends told her. 'It is politic that it be done this way. With a membership, there is not a way in the world that you can be denied entrance to our clan meeting.'

Their loyalty was touching but Lily understood very well that her presence was undesirable, and consequently she did not board her flight. Sometime later in the year, when the meeting she had longed to attend had passed, Lily learned that many of the American members had been horrified by her treatment, and had expressed the view that 'since the invitation had been extended, it should be honoured'.

Mrs Fischbach was more robust in her opinion, and in the autumn she expressed her wisest view to date:

> Have you had any success in tracking down the woman who told Don Macleay all those malicious tales about you? Whoever she is, someone should put a muzzle on her mouth! My philosophy is to never judge a person 'until I have walked a mile in their shoes' (it is an American Indian phrase) and I am astounded that some people will go about willy, nilly, making cruel and vicious comments without any foundation in fact about other people!

On top of the recent upset, Lily was also having 'a god-forsaken time' answering Mr Cubie's professional inquiries about her spending habits. Now that he was Randolph's *curator bonis*, she was subjected to belittling exchanges. On 27 September, for example, Mr Cubie wrote her a letter about three entries on the joint account. What were the Bank Giro credit on 13 July 1981 for £35, and the cheque for £25 cashed on the same day? And what of the cheque for £56.23 cashed on 19 August 1981? He needed a reply urgently. The transactions were over a year old. Of course, she had no idea.

Worse, the matter of finding Randolph permanent accommodation had still not been resolved. In October, near his birthday, he wrote, 'It is simply TOO AWFUL the fact that I am 54 years old and live like a rabbit.' Incapable as Lily appeared to be of steering her own straight passage through life, she remained determined to settle Randolph. She now understood only too well that he was not suited to life in Edinburgh, although it had been her home, and so it was that when she finally returned to Edinburgh from London, he left. By November she had managed to have him installed, once and for all, in the caravan site at Lothlorien, where he would remain in relative contentment for some years. The tone of despair that had marked his correspondence vanished almost overnight and in its place was his childlike recall of the simple things that brought him pleasure. That Christmas, she sent him a basketful of new clothes, a pair of new boots for working on the soil, and £20 to buy a pair of thick warm socks. He added the following to his thank-you letter:

> Late in the morning I set out with a party to get a hold of a poor old black sheep in one of the fields, four of us carried the poor thing to the open air larder, stretched out on sacks, and in ghastly conditions of driving snow, freezing hard as it fell. The local butcher came in the afternoon to inoculate the animal, and strip it of its coat.

Against all medical opinion, Lily became convinced that she was ill. She had a history of high blood pressure, but new symptoms appeared in 1983. She complained that her legs felt 'heavily weighted' and that when she took her new standard poodle, Paris, for a daily walk across The Meadows, she found it difficult to get back. There were 'thumping headaches' as well as a feeling of fear that struck her whenever she left the house alone. She was taking heavy medication for hypertension, but it was having little impact. Medical tests were either negative or inconclusive, and as a result everybody concluded – behind her back – that she was turning into a hypochondriac.

In August she went to see a consultant attached to wards twenty-eight and thirty-one of the Royal Infirmary. He could find nothing wrong with her – her urine was fine, her blood pressure was acceptable, and there were no new physical symptoms. By contrast he saw that her private life was far from problem-free. In a letter to Lily's GP he reported how he had 'allowed her to expose the story of her relationship with her husband during the past few years, including his physical attacks on her'. It was his opinion that Lily's worry for Randolph and the recent events were at the root of her ill health:

> She has a genuine affection for him and still visits him in Dumfries . . . She has considerable worries about finance, both in relation to the bills for her own home and money for his care, which passes through a *Curator Bonis* . . . I think she understood that the stresses of her life contribute greatly to the physical symptoms. I explained that although she had hypertension and that the drugs used

in the treatment of it may have contributed a little to
her symptoms, this was not the main problem.

It was not the first time that Lily's emotional state had undermined
her health. Exactly thirty years had passed since the consultant at
the Bruntsfield Hospital had identified Sis as the cause of Lily's
crushing headaches. The same thing was happening again.

Lily was preoccupied by money and anxious about the future,
and with good reason. Apart from the odd sale of a doll, she had
no income of her own except her state pension. A housekeeping job
was out of the question. She was too weak. Since the appointment of
a *curator bonis*, her and Randolph's financial affairs were considered
to be quite separate. She could no longer pay her mortgage from
their joint account – forbidden because he was no longer living
there – and there was no question of any lump sum being used to
repay her debt. Any money that came to Randolph would not be
used to alleviate her financial situation. What was Lily to do if it
fell to her to pay off their entire debt? She could never hope to
clear it. She pestered Mr Cubie constantly for reassurance. He
pointed out to her as plainly as he could that should she be left
with a debt – which she was to be – he would argue with the bank
that such a liability should be written off. 'I must, however, make
it quite clear that there can be no question in the circumstances
of your husband's financial position of his being in a position either
to make sums of capital or allowance available to you ... That I
believe you now accept although, of course, at an earlier time it
did appear that his inheritance would have proved more substantial
than it now will be in total.'

She was also preoccupied with the payment of Randolph's housing bill. Would it continue? Would he be looked after? He was so
unwell and she could not help him, she complained to Mr Cubie.
She was thousands of pounds in debt, and quite apart from food,
there were other bills to meet, such as her rates, and then there
was a horrifying legal letter from the council threatening action.

Randolph sensed Lily's hysteria from afar. He resumed writing
to Mr Cubie, but the response was always the same. There was no
question that Lily could have access to his inheritance. 'Sadly your
wife is well aware of this,' Mr Cubie replied in one letter, 'and

although I sympathise with her in her predicament there is nothing that I can do in the way of letting her have additional funds.' It was around this time that Lily received an offer of financial help from Lady Antonia, the sister-in-law of whom she had once been so wary. She accepted without guilt and was thankful for such a kind gesture.

Nevertheless poverty and ill health continued to dominate Lily's life throughout 1984. By 1985 she began complaining of having 'funny turns' while out with Paris. She felt as if she was 'lifting in the air and spinning'. It occurred three or four times a week, she said. On one occasion she blacked out. Other times she would feel a painful heaviness in both hands, which travelled to the top of her chest and neck and to her jaw. It was a crushing pain and it lasted from twenty minutes to an hour, although there were no palpitations. The symptoms sounded serious enough, and after an examination at the Royal Infirmary, Lily was wired up to a twenty-four-hour ECG tape. It confirmed that she had angina, which was exacerbated by her fear and anxiety. She was locked in a vicious circle. She could not stop worrying while the problem remained and all the while she worried, her health deteriorated.

It would be quite possible to list every detail of Lily's financial affairs. For all her inability to manage her money, she kept an accurate record of the correspondence, a sign of how much it confused and frightened her. On 30 May 1986, for example, Lily owed the bank precisely £26,952.42 and as of 29 May, the interest was accruing at a daily rate of £7.57. It could not be allowed to continue. Brebner stepped in. Randolph's debt had been cleared, but Lily's had not because Bernard Terrace was considered an asset. Mr Cubie suggested that the flat could be made over to the bank in the event of her death. The bank agreed and arranged for a standard security to be held over the property. Although all letters relating to the bank's claim on Bernard Terrace were phrased delicately, they forced Lily to confront her own death. What had been intended as a measure to soothe her nerves now excited her more. The attacks of angina became more frequent and she began contracting chest infections, many requiring hospitalisation.

Lily's lungs were not the problem. Considering the extent of her emotional suffering – her past guilt over her feelings for Sis; the anguish of her failed marriages to Jock and then Jimmy; the disappointment of Paul Budge; the distrust of the Stewarts; and now, still, the peculiar kind of love as well as the sense of loss she felt in being married to Randolph – it is fitting that it was her heart that became sick. At the end of 1986 it was finally identified as being severely diseased. A quadruple heart bypass was scheduled for the beginning of 1987. Despite the seriousness of the operation, Lily felt vindicated. She had been ill all along.

She made up her mind that she must leave Bernard Terrace. She could no longer afford the upkeep or easily climb the stairs. By the end of the year, just before her operation, she moved to a ground floor flat in Dalkeith Road. She loathed it almost from the start. The French windows at the back, which had seemed such a good idea at the time, were now viewed as an invitation to burglars and she felt unsafe and unsteady in such an unfamiliar environment. Much of this was to do with the worry of the pending operation, but she was also seventy years old and she was developing the nerviness often seen in the elderly. It was as if, after a decade of surprising youth and modernity, her age had finally caught up with her.

In the New Year, Brebner was taken aside by the consultant and told that it was unlikely Lily would live to see the year out. The news came as a deep shock. Quietly, he relayed the conversation to the family members and they began to deal with it in their own way, mentioning nothing to Lily.

The operation was carried out and Lily regained consciousness. She began to slowly recuperate, taking it in turns to stay with Brebner, Andrew, and Benjamin. Lily was a difficult, demanding patient, and at times she acted quite unreasonably, flicking over the television channel while somebody was watching a programme or pretending she was frailer than was really the case so that she could be waited on throughout the day. All this placed her three sons and, in particular, their wives, under considerable stress, made worse for the fact that Lily, either consciously or subconsciously, seemed to enjoy causing friction within their marriages. It was written off as a product of Lily's jealousy, and while she was often successful in causing rifts and rows, she never managed to cause long-term damage. The operation had not restored her to good health – her angina continued to afflict her even at rest – but she was better than she had been. It came as some relief to all when Lily finally allowed herself to believe that she was well enough to live alone.

In June 1987 Lily had a lunch engagement with Michael Thornton. They met in the reception of the Caledonian Hotel and she got tipsy on a glass of champagne. Much to Michael Thornton's delight, towards the end of the lunch, after he had written her a cheque for £400 – 'I didn't get the money back, of course I didn't, nor did she ask for it in the first place, but one felt so sorry for her' – Lily began singing in a loud voice 'Why Did You Call Me Lily?', the show-stealing first song sung by Dora Bryan in *The Water Gypsies*. As heads began to turn, he smiled to himself. This was the Lily he knew and loved. There was life in the old girl yet.

20

New places to wear diamonds

By the 1990s everybody wanted Lily at their party. Her presence provided diarists with copy and photographers with a picture, and now, after all these years – fifteen since her marriage to Randolph – there need not be a scandal attached. In one diary column from that time, she is pictured surrounded by men half her age. She appears most relaxed in such company, languid even, in front of the drapes. The text reads:

> There was an imposing congregation of *le tout* Edinburgh at the party given for Lady Edith Foxwell, former doyenne of London's Embassy Club, by Clifford Brake Kirkpatrick at Arthur Lodge, a Greek Revival mansion on the outskirts of the city, last Sunday evening.
>
> The 200 guests included such trend-setters as Lily, Countess of Galloway; Lady Sorrel Bentinck; Jacqueline, Lady Killearn, who had been chauffeur-driven from London for the occasion; and Comte Pierre de Fresne, of Mon Tresor.

She would turn up in a cloud of Givenchy Shalimar, her feet and ankles laced into a pair of Kurt Geiger boots, a Versace jacket (from Jenners, during the sale) hanging off her tiny frame, with a sable coat thrown over the top. In cold weather she wore a large matching sable hat. Lily's fur collection was a source of pride. She had inherited Margot's mink, but she also had two or three others of her own, always bought from charity shops. Whenever she saw a fox stole, she would buy it and make it into a pillbox hat. She held a stick and sometimes wore a silver hip flask, containing brandy, monogrammed with the letter G. Beside her one would always find a handsome young man, loyally holding her handbag or topping up her brandy cocktail. If this picture of Lily creates the impression that she and Randolph miraculously came into the money for which they had fought so hard, then that is exactly as Lily would have liked it. The truth was rather different. Lily was as poor as ever, she had just grown adept at covering it up, with a little help from her friends.

Even before the devolution that followed Labour's massive victory in the 1997 election, and the triumphant opening of the Scottish Parliament in the summer of 1999, Edinburgh was becoming a city that people flocked to rather than fled from. In *Stone Voices*, Neal Ascherson's meditation on Scotland, he identifies an explosion of creativity during the 1980s. He calls it 'much the most remarkable period in culture since the "Scottish Renaissance"'. He also confirms the English migration to his country, interpreted as an escape northwards from the social turmoil of Thatcherism. Allan Massie connects the change with the architectural rejuvenation of the city. In his book, *Edinburgh*, he writes that in 1975 it was the repairs and the renewal of the New Town that had earned it an international reputation for excellence in architectural conservation. But as the New Town had grown, the Old Town had continued to suffer. It had been crumbling away. Buildings fell or remained derelict; commerce was fizzling out. The office boom predicted for the high street had failed to materialise. And then, quite suddenly, around the 1980s – leading up to Lily's own rejuvenation – a team of young enthusiasts had appeared with the hope of breathing life into it once more. Within only a few years the change to the Old Town was remarkable. Gaps along the Cowgate were filled with houses and student flats, there was a new sheriff-court, old buildings began to be rehabilitated, and fashionable wine bars began appearing down once forbidden alleys.

There is no doubt that Lily's renaissance was dependent on some wider social change having occurred. The social forces that had for so long governed the city were also modernising. '*Le tout*' Edinburgh was now considered to be more than the county set or the landed gentry down from their estates. Democracy was in the air, in every way. Edinburgh, a city that for forty years had come alive only once a year, during the International Edinburgh Festival, was now opening up to the world. The media began to talk about good restaurants, art galleries and small businesses. Property prices started to soar. It was a city in the process of becoming properly fashionable. Now the key to Edinburgh society was 'a cosmopolitan mix', something Brodrick Haldane had recognised a decade earlier. Placed at the centre of the 'mix' were the Boys, a new breed of party guest, mostly without trust funds but adequately compensated by the possession of various talents and the drive to use them. They were young, good-looking, homosexual and, in one way or another, helping to invigorate the city just as they were helping to invigorate Lily.

It started at a party held by Joseph Bonnar, who was now a highly successful society jeweller with a double-fronted shop on Thistle Street. Lily had been introduced to a blonde, floppy-haired boy called Arthur Allen, a civil servant and the boyfriend of a fashionable interior designer called Mark Rowley. Each took the other to their hearts and, within weeks, the net widened so that her fans included a painter, a fashionable restaurateur, and so on. The mechanics of the attraction were simple. Lily seemed to incorporate what Edinburgh now was; the coexistence of the old and the new. Her title made her seem grand and yet her personality, despite her years, was refreshing and accessible. They loved her because she was good fun, modern, grandmotherly, and, if truth be told, titled. Would the Countess care to borrow diamonds for the gala opening at the National Gallery of Scotland? She very much would. Might the Countess be presented to the Queen Mother? She might well indeed. Had she, per chance, dyed her roots with the juice of her Nambarrie teabags? Of course she had.

She loved them because they were adoring, kind, pleasing to the eye, and generous. They treated her like porcelain, lavished her with gifts, took her out for dinner, and sent her on all-expenses-paid trips to Claridges. It was, they felt, the lifestyle she deserved and after all that had happened, she could not help but agree. Very soon Arthur Allen, considered her principal walker, became known as 'handbag carrier to the House of Stewart', a sobriquet he relished.

What would old Lord Galloway have made of it, peering up from his grave? We can be sure that he would have viewed Lily's social ascent as confirmation of all he had suspected: that it was the title that had glittered above all else. But Lily's life with the Boys, lived as it was in the mould of the grand countess, was not the whole picture, or even half of it. It was a role she played to keep herself in friends and party invitations, and she played it very well. 'I got the impression that she, like the rest of us back then, wasn't sure who she was,' recalls Roland Wallis, the painter for whom she would later sit and one of the Boys. 'We created a very unreal world. We'd gather lilac in the spring and hold soirees in these grand drawing rooms. And yet if you looked closely you'd see the drapes were held together by safety pins, that the wood on the fire had been collected from skips and that the wine was so bad, the kind vagrants drink, but decanted out of its bottle so that it had the appearance of being respectable. We all of us really wanted to be in *Brideshead* and so her role for us was to play the grand countess. She did her research, she learned the protocol, the family history, the relevance of the Stewarts and so, socially speaking, that developed as her anchor.'

Lily might have sent thank-you bouquets from Flowers by Maxwell, the most prestigious florist in the city (she always paid by account using House of Lords stationery) but she chose for herself the cheapest carnations. In truth her life was a paradox. Very few people knew the true extent of her poverty. She had moved from Dalkeith Road to Home Royal House, a sheltered housing complex in Marchmont. It was a tiny flat, crammed with every antique she had collected over the years and rather dominated by a large statue of the Blessed Virgin. Her sources of income were the buying and selling of her antique dolls, which gazed down on her from various shelves and ledges, her pension, her disability allowance (a result of her weakening health), and a bi-annual hand-out from the Royal United Kingdom Beneficent Association (Rukba), a charity set up to help genteel ladies fallen on hard times. The donations had been Mr Cubie's idea, but they so offended Lily's pride that she told nobody. Still, the manner in which she spent them was not wholly orthodox (since the arrival of the Boys in her life, she had developed such a taste for Claridges that sometimes even they could not satisfy it). All items of clothing contained in the Rukba parcels were given to Etta or occasionally dispatched to the local charity shops, save for the vests, which she found to her liking.

Despite such new and exciting acquaintances, old friendships lived on. Joseph Bonnar, William Mowat Thomson, Brodrick Haldane, A. J. Stewart, all continued to play a part in Lily's life. Even Lady Mayo was back in Edinburgh. She had left Las Palmas in 1985 to live out her final days with William in St Bernard's Crescent, which meant that Lily now saw much more of her. They often took tea together, in Edinburgh or London at Lady Mayo's club. One such outing made the newspaper. 'Hilarious scenes at London's Victoria station,' reported the diarist. Lady Mayo had been spotted 'sailing across the platform on a luggage trolley . . . propelling this fine ancient was a fellow countess . . . Lady Galloway.' 'It's lucky Lady Mayo has lost a lot of weight recently,' Lily told the reporter. 'She was much heavier when I first knew her.' The article concluded, 'A talent for conveying the titled must run in the family. Lady Galloway's father was a chauffeur.'

At Lady Mayo's one-hundredth birthday luncheon on Boxing Day, 1990, thrown by William in all his characteristic generosity, Lily, wearing diamonds (borrowed) and sable (Margot's), was considered one of the most important guests wedged in among the Irish crystal, the eighteenth-century nankin blue china, the silver tea urns and the empire claret jug that adorned his antique dining table.

Much like 56 India Street, William's home had become well-known beyond Edinburgh society so that film crews hired it out and art experts wrote of it as a 'virtuoso Georgian collection'. The drawing room, it was noted in a glossy magazine, 'seems to shimmer with gold capturing all the opulence and grace of a Klimt painting'. One gentleman, quite overwhelmed, wrote the following:

> Countless looking-glasses adorn the walls in elaborately-carved filigreed frames. When William organises musical evenings – as the proprieter [*sic*] of the Theatre School of Dance and Drama for forty years, his is an accomplished hand at the Blüthner grand piano – he lights the room with candles in gilt wall brackets. Mirrors

reflect objects of equal quality such as 19th century gilt
fauteuils covered in Beauvais tapestry, an Italian Blacka-
moor pedestal table and a Japanese medicine cabinet
inlaid with ivory and precious stones. Other cabinets,
two inlaid with mother-of-pearl and ivory, accommodate
collections of Gold Anchor Chelsea porcelain, Coalport,
Meissen and Davenport.

And there was more. Those so inclined could find collections of
antiquarian books; glass; lace; costumes; silver; French custard cups;
Wedgwood chestnut baskets; and one hundred ladies visiting-card
cases in mother-of-pearl. There was, of course, the attraction of
Lady Mayo herself, often found peeping from the bed hangings of
her four-poster bed on the ground floor, the view through which,
it was remarked in the press, was 'unbelievably pretty'. Today on the
same Blüthner piano there is a handsome collection of gilt-framed
photographs which serve as a handy compression of *Debretts*. There
is a photograph of Margaret, Duchess of Argylle, for instance, and
the Countess of Mayo, who sits among other such ladies with less
pronounceable titles. Among them, too, is Lily, in floor-length
cream lace, clutching a strip of Stewart tartan, bearing not a trace
of the Mrs Budge she once was. It is, in fact, a photograph taken
for the portrait she commissioned from Roland Wallis in 1994.
The portrait is at the centre of quite a separate tale but for now it
provides good evidence of the grand company she kept.

It is ironic, considering Lily was in her social prime, that it was now
she needed Randolph most. It was he to whom her thoughts would
turn at the end of a party, and she became increasingly in need of
signs of his love. Many of those in her new world assumed they
were divorced. Only Arthur Allen understood the role Randolph
continued to play in Lily's life. 'Sometimes I would go round there
and she would spread his letters out and ask me to read them.
"You see," she would say, "We do love each other, but it just
couldn't be." I found it very touching. Sometimes she would regret
that she couldn't live with him and she would torture herself, but
I would always say, "But Lily, you couldn't, you just couldn't."'
Lothlorian had closed and Randolph had been moved to Senwick

House, a residential home in Brighouse Bay, Borgue, Kircudbright-shire, primarily for the old. Once again, he was desperately unhappy. Lily became preoccupied with getting him re-housed so that they might spend more time together. Randolph's bitterness had returned. In his letters he talked again of 'beggarly and mean pittances' – 'I have too often been treated as a labourer, this I look down upon as a personal insult' – and was full of loathing for those who had always been against him, as he saw it. Now he spoke of how he thought their phones had been tapped. 'Flashing back to the early months when we were at Bernard Terrace,' he wrote to Lily on 12 November 1990, six weeks before Mayo's hundredth-birthday luncheon, 'our enemies were hard at work eavesdropping on us, tapping phone lines and trying to blow up an occasional exaggerated story in the paper. They are still at it, wishing us permanent want and hardship, keeping good money and fine jewellery stored away mouldering in a vault. They have no right treating us like dirt, they want us off the face of civilisation, certainly living apart.'

In another letter, he wrote to her, 'I have nothing, you have nothing and we were left without a single penny. In such a case living with nothing would render my making a will null and void ... sorry to be so depressing but it is one of the hardest facts of existence that is quite intolerable and without reason to be chained permanently without a leg to walk on.'

It seemed like a lifetime had passed since Randolph was sitting on the Conservative benches in the upper chamber. But Lily continued to receive *Hansard*, the last remnant of their days in Westminster, which she sent him so he could keep up with affairs (the Conservatives were in for a fourth term now under John Major). She also sent photographs of herself, which he put on his ledge, 'where I can see them'.

On 17 November 1992 Mr Cubie was discharged as *curator bonis*, having made a case to the court of 'exhaustion of funds in the Ward's Estate'. Brebner Millar, who has remained a loyal friend to his stepfather, was given power of attorney. Around the same time, Lady Mayo died, approaching her 102nd birthday. When William Mowat Thomson broke the news to Lily, she sighed and said, 'Oh well, William, she's had a good kick of the ball.'

At the end of that eventful year, at the finale of the summit meeting of the European Community, which had brought world leaders to Edinburgh for the first time and attracted international television crews, there was a huge demonstration on Lily's doorstep. On The Meadows, where she had had her epiphany and where for years she had walked her poodles, 30,000 people gathered in a march for Scottish democracy. 'Scottishness is not some pedigree lineage,' the novelist William McIlvanney told the cheering crowds, 'This is a mongrel tradition!'

If there was no sighting of Lily at a party, it was often the case that she was in her favourite hospital bed in the Royal Infirmary. Were proof needed of the proficiency and saintliness of the doctors and nurses propping up the NHS, one need look no further than Lily's medical records. In 1989 she was admitted into hospital three times. In 1990 this shot up to six admissions; in 1991 she had three spells on the ward; in 1992 three spells; and in 1993 six spells. In between she was diagnosed as having neuropathy and mild diabetes, cataracts, chest pains, and further frequent attacks of angina.

The house calls, the admissions, and the investigations were great in number and often appear to have been quite unnecessary. Her sons, having recovered from the shock that Lily might die, quickly got the measure of the matter. They saw that many of their mother's 'episodes' since the bypass occurred at crucial moments in the calendar. She had been known to have 'a turn' at a party where she was not receiving quite as much attention as she might have expected, and there was always some episode or other in the days running up to any planned holidays, which eventually resulted in Lily being informed of long-planned holidays at the last minute. Lily's new GP, Dr Fiona MacLaren, thought her 'very theatrical and lively', and as a result 'a pleasure to see, but always easily distracted from her problem'. As a result of this, it was concluded that Lily's health concerns now came from her fear of growing old, her loneliness, and her need to know people cared.

Whenever she was admitted to hospital there was a drama, but once she had been installed in her bed and attended by her usual physician, Dr Watson, this subsided and yielded to a degree of contentment, particularly if she anticipated the arrival of flowers and visitors. 'From Royal House to Royal Hospital,' her dancer friend Alan Alexander wrote to her during one stay. His attitude towards her hospitalisations is a measure of how they rarely caused people concern: 'Can't imagine ward 24 [*sic*] was too regale [*sic*], until, of course, you arrived! You are full of surprises but calls from the sick bed one can do without. You sounded your usual buoyant self. And no doubt that self same stuff will propel you out of there at the double – that could be an excuse for another soiree.'

Following the six admissions in 1993 Dr MacLaren and Dr Watson concluded that Lily's demands were no longer acceptable. They saw clearly and correctly that hospitalisation was something she sought rather than feared. It steadied her and made her feel safe, particularly safe from death. In January 1994 Lily was referred to a consultant psychiatrist. He assessed her and reported back:

> It may not be coincidental that the worsening of her condition over the past 6 months coincided with her younger son moving out of town and her oldest son being unable to visit her because of a ruptured Achilles tendon . . . At interview Lady Galloway was pleasant, but obviously used to dealing with doctors and 'holding court'! I found no evidence of mental illness in her thinking, mood or outlook nor was she cognitively impaired. There was nothing in her account or presentation that would be indicative of abnormal illness behaviour.

Lily was pronounced 'lonely and isolated' due to 'the dislocation from her sons of whom she is obviously very fond'. The psychiatrist concluded: 'I think it is not improbable that Lady Galloway is going to "react" no matter what is prescribed.'

But Lily could not free herself of her obsession with death, particularly at night when she was alone. She approached her friend, the solicitor James Stewart Taylor, and made out a will (about which she would constantly change her mind, much like Margot Grahame had). It was also during this period that she commissioned a self-portrait, almost as if she were desperate to have her life recorded in some tangible and lasting way. Roland Wallis (another Boy), part-time artist, part-time art tutor at Fettes school, was a natural choice. Conscious of appearing vain, she presented the idea to him as if it had come from Brebner, his filial tribute to her in her old age. Lily did not articulate her chief concern, at least not in a straightforward way, but Roland Wallis understood immediately. Lily wanted a portrait that made her look distinguished and attractive, a portrait grand in tone, exactly the kind that might have hung in the picture gallery at Cumloden had she been its chatelaine.

It was a difficult commission. Although the overall effect of Lily's appearance was one of grandness, at close quarters she possessed none of the privileged softness captured in photographs of her late mother-in-law. The combination of old age, cigarettes and the legacy of the teenage lipodystrophy had rendered the skin on Lily's face as tough as a leather slipper. Curled round its edges was hair far too inky in hue for a woman of her years, something her stylist at Jenners department store was constantly trying to change with no success. Dupuytren's Contracture, a hereditary complaint, had drawn forward the fingers on her right hand so that they were locked in a permanent claw-like curl. Her life had made her even less of a beauty than she had been in her youth. But Lily did not want reminding of her hardships or her heartbreaks. She was happy to pay the £1,000 fee, but in so doing she wanted a positive gloss applied to her likeness. Wallis had two choices: to cast her in her own image, or to refrain from painting her altogether. He chose the former, and chased away thoughts of artistic compromise by mounting the argument to himself that this was to be an exercise in interpretation rather than an analytical, physical study.

Lily chose for the occasion her usual floor length dress in cream lace, onto which she pinned a rosette and swag in the Galloway tartan and her emerald green Grand Dame of Justice decoration awarded by the Order of Lazarus. Wallis thought this too obvious and attempted to steer her towards a more subtle display of what she felt should be celebrated about her life. She half acquiesced. She agreed to pin the decoration less prominently and hold the tartan loosely in her right hand, which had the advantage of covering up her fingers. There were three sittings in Roland Wallis's studio in Bellevue Crescent. Lily could not manage the stairs, so the painting was completed using photographs. Within two months the portrait was finished. In retrospect, Wallis agrees that it 'was far too traditional' and that it 'lacked confidence'. He cites as his defence his willingness to please Lily, to provide her with the version of herself that she so wanted. She gazes out of the picture with an imperious air. There is no hint of her exuberance or her humour, but as an exercise in evoking the virtues of dignity, self-control and confidence, it works very well. What Wallis recognised as her 'inherent lightness', her faith, is conveyed through the paling and smoothing of her physical aspect. Her hair is brown instead of black, her skin is smooth and creamy, and her lips and rouge a soft pink. The fingers of her left hand are long and fine and on the third she wears a large ring, not the Galloway diamonds, because they were in the bank, but a mid-nineteenth-century blue enamelled plaque set with split pearls and rose-cut diamonds.

The unveiling was celebrated by a champagne launch attended by the Boys, Brebner and Dorothy, and written up in the *Scotsman*: 'Last Monday evening saw a small, select gathering assembled in Edinburgh for the unveiling of a portrait of the Countess of Gallo-way (whose family shares common antecedents with the royal house of Stuart), painted by Roland Wallis.' After a brief spell above the fireplace in Joseph Bonnar's drawing room, the painting became part of an exhibition in Musselborough and was then eventually moved on to a wall in the main room of Lily's flat in Home Royal House, where it dominated the room and set about haunting her.

Lily first voiced her fears about the painting to Brebner. She told him that a shadow was creeping up the lower part of her skirt and was travelling slowly into the centre of the canvas. She became convinced that her right hand, the one holding the Galloway tartan, was melting and worse still, that blood was dripping from her fingers. With each passing day she felt the shadow was growing ever stronger, mocking her and overwhelming her confidence at every turn. She talked of it incessantly: to Dr MacLaren, to Joseph Bonnar, to Brebner, to anybody who cared to listen. The painting was moved to another wall with no effect.

She called for Wallis. He had since left Edinburgh for Bristol but he came immediately, bemused, intrigued, and at first not grasping the seriousness of the situation. On seeing it again, he declared it quite as it was before, but offered to return Lily her £1,000. She did not accept. She did not want a refund, nor did she want to sit for another portrait. She wanted her painting as it had been when first finished. Wallis did not know how to respond to this. The

Lily poses with her curious portrait and the artist Roland Wallis on the evening of its Champagne launch.

painting was as it had been when first finished. The atmosphere between them became tense. Wallis could not sleep for anxiety and he felt perpetually 'trapped and churned up'. 'I was convinced she had suffered some kind of serious psychological breakdown,' he remembers.

If she had, it passed. Lily eventually stopped talking about her portrait although her feelings for it never recovered. Sometime after the unhappy affair, she had a cataract removed and it was generally concluded that her eyesight had been to blame for her bizarre obsession. Lily refused to accept this and maintained to the end that her vision then had not been in any way impaired or blurred at that stage. It had been the painting. It had a life of its own.

Since neither Lily nor Randolph could drive a car, their marriage – now resembling much more an old-fashioned courtship – depended on the goodwill of a succession of minder drivers prepared to ferry them across the many miles of Scottish countryside that separated Edinburgh and the south-west where Randolph lived. Around the time that Lily began to feel 'dislocated', she experienced one piece of good luck. Miss Elsie Duff entered her life.

Duff (never Elsie) was an obliging chauffeuse, always ready with the offer of her little car. She was a silver-haired spinster, and consequently could always be relied upon to put to use her sensible driving shoes, footwear that did nothing for the stoutness of her limbs, which protruded like piano legs from beneath her tweed skirt. Her hair was razored into the nape of her neck and she spoke at a pitch more masculine than feminine. During the Second World War she had driven ambulances and joined the Land Army, barking orders at the girls based on her extensive knowledge of animal husbandry, particularly chickens and pigs. Such memories featured heavily in her conversation. Lily's friendship with her was more than likely sealed during Duff's visits to Home Royal House, where Duff had kept up with another Land Girl spinster until she died.

Miss Duff possessed a terrifying manner but she also possessed a Morris Minor, which was the most important consideration. Very quickly she became the glue that bound Lily and Randolph back together. Darling, I'm thinking of you and wish you were nearer

Edinburgh so that we could be in touch more often,' Lily had written to Randolph. 'If when you come [*sic*],' Randolph responded to her in June 1995, 'it might be a good thing if Miss Duff resumed her seat behind the car steering wheel.'

Duff would pick Lily up from Home Royal House, drive across to the south-west, pick Randolph up, and take them out for the day, often to Newton Stewart so Randolph could be close to Cumloden. He had remained obsessed with the estate and liked to view it whenever he could. 'We glimpsed Cumloden through the trees. The castle and its wooded surroundings, much the same as when they belonged to us,' he had written to Lily, following an earlier trip there with his sister.

Lily and Randolph stop for lunch in 1992 at Glen Trool during one of their outings, chauffeured by Miss Duff.

The excursions with Duff were not without their dramas. Sometimes there would be heated exchanges between Duff and Lily, who were constantly 'nipping at each other', as Brebner puts it. Randolph remained silent during their explosions. On one or two occasions Duff lost control of the Morris. Often they would visit All Saints Church, Challoch, the burial ground of Randolph's forebears, and the Reverend Father Campbell Danskin would conduct a private mass and then take them to the rectory for sherry. Once Lily reported back to Randolph following an outing without him,

'Miss Duff is out of the hospital. She took me to church a week last Sunday but I really don't think she is fit to drive the car. I didn't feel safe she was going through red lights and everything.'

After another trip, Lily wrote to Randolph, 'Duff has gone AWOL.' A week or so later, Duff resurfaced and appeared to be quite well. When Lily inquired after her absence, she heard, with surprise, that Duff had been in a mental institution. 'Fancy it!' she told Lily, shaking her head, 'I cannot imagine any Duff ever being locked up in a lunatic asylum!'

Duff provided Lily with company. They holidayed together, mostly driving tours around England and Scotland visiting convents and monasteries, leaving as they went a trail of odd shoes, stray bracelets and sunglasses. During one trip, Lily sent a postcard to Arthur Allen and Mark Rowley which sets the tone:

> Darling Boys,
>
> Miss Duff is still suffering from shingles and is a bit off colour but it doesn't stop her ... The hotel is lovely – not a patch on Claridges!!! But very nice the food splendid. The company well, all old ladies very snobbish, a little in awe of a countess in their midst in fact can't cope so I'm slightly ignored but the young men of the staff are happy. See you soon.
>
> tons of love

While Duff's spirit remained strong, age was robbing her of steam and stamina, which in time made her a less reliable chauffeuse. 'Miss Duff is out of hospital and is able to do short journeys by car,' Lily wrote to Randolph hopefully on 28 May 1996. But soon after Miss Duff was not able to travel anywhere. She died. Her death robbed Lily of a friend and a driver. She lost Brodrick Haldane that year, too. On Christmas Eve, in 1995, he had slipped on the ice-bound pavement of Drummond Place while on his way to a lunch party. He was taken into the Royal Infirmary and treated for a broken leg, but while recuperating he contracted pneumonia and in early February he died of heart failure. Lily was already preoccupied by death, and the losses unsettled her even more. Brebner provided her with emotional support and company, although he was less available for tours than Miss Duff had been. 'I wish [he] would bring me down to Galloway to see you dear,' Lily wrote to Randolph, 'It's not easy for me now without Miss Duff. It's nice and light now at night it makes quite a difference I just wish I could get out more. Take care darling I love you and think about you always. Your loving wife Lily'.

In October 1996 Lily turned eighty. The love and affection that still existed between her and Randolph, after all that had happened over the years, astonished Brebner and Dorothy. They still liked to hold hands like young lovers and often their behaviour, at times almost childlike, bordered on being comical. For Randolph, Brebner was mentor and protector, more a father figure than a surrogate son.

Randolph, twelve years Lily's junior, remained as strong as an ox. Physically, at least, he possessed those genes that had made warriors of his forebears. He regularly spent his days walking through fields and woodlands on the outskirts of Castle Douglas and sometimes even camped 'among the Galloway hinterland'. Lily drew on Randolph's strength the way he had, for years, drawn on hers. Although in the past she had been intellectually curious about matters of the world, when she was alone her vision was inward looking, dominated by her concerns for her health and for Randolph. In one letter during this period she wrote, 'I've really been terribly ill Randolph and in such awful pain, Dr Watson insisted I must get away to convalesce. I feel so happy today, my dear, with getting your lovely card and letter. When I know you love me Randolph, life takes on a new meaning.' In another, she wrote, 'I am sometimes very lonely my darling since Brebner moved to the borders and I have missed you this summer darling not being able to see you. But this Lady who spoke on the phone today seemed so nice she said she would bring me down, and I thought afterward maybe she could bring you up. I'm so excited my dear.'

Their correspondence was always like this, utterly consumed by their own lives with no consideration given to political or international events going on around them. For example, in the letters sent in the second half of September 1997, Lily made no mention of the fact that Scotland had finally voted for its own Parliament. Ill health would probably have prevented her from voting.

Whenever Lily was ill, Rose would always visit her, despite her loathing of hospitals and the fact that she was unwell herself. A lifetime of smoking had given Rose bronchial asthma and she found it very difficult to breathe. As Rose had started to slow, her daughter Ann had wanted the answer to one question. Why, throughout her life, had Rose never shown affection to her children? 'Because I never received affection myself,' she replied. Rose's atheism bothered Lily, particularly now. Her own faith provided her with such consolation that it upset her to think of Rose alone in her pain. Ann, as devout as ever (sometimes when she and her husband visited Lily in Home Royal House they would all pray together) and sensing that her mother was becoming weaker, went to see her to persuade her to reconsider. She appeared to have been unsuccessful, although Lily was shocked and delighted when Rose confided in her one day that she had prayed and asked Jesus to enter her life. Shortly afterwards, at the beginning of 1998, Lily received news that Rose had died of emphysema.

As much as Lily liked playing the countess for the Boys, and as much as she had always been ambivalent about growing up in Duns, the Borders were her roots – just as the lands of Galloway were Randolph's. The love she felt for her sisters had never diminished, however different (Rose) or disapproving (Etta) they might have been. Rose's death was another link broken. Randolph, in his own way, tried to provide consolation: 'You have been and are in the throes of grief and bereavement . . . I was fond of Rose as I knew that you were yourself. It will leave something of a blank in your family now that she has gone, she had meant a lot to your family and you meant a great deal to her. You have all my love and sympathy.'

A year later, in February 1999, Etta died. 'My dearest,' Randolph soothed again, 'My condolences on the parting of your beloved sister Etta . . . As I remember she was always so youthful and kind. I know you will miss her something awful, but she would be relieved from her suffering. Fondest love my dear in your sadness and bereavement.' Lily responded, 'She had always been so strong, and as you said so kind . . . I'm so very sad – and nervous and lonely. I can't get out, the weather is so cold and I can't go out on my own.'

Lily talked regularly of death. She wanted absolute reassurance from Brebner that her funeral would be a requiem mass, accompanied by members of the St Michael and All Saints' choir. He would try and dispel these maudlin moments by teasing her, saying he would put her in a plain wooden box, but Lily was deadly serious and failed to see the joke. In April, two months after Etta's death, she was admitted to the Royal Infirmary with chest pains. At her request, the priest of St Michael and All Saints' read her the last rites. She was soon discharged. The following month Lily was once again admitted to hospital and then discharged. She continued to write almost daily to Randolph. 'I'm happy you have such a good social life, darling,' she told him at the end of June. 'You don't get the chance to be lonely and I think about you always, and wish things had been different . . . my thoughts are with you always.' In another undated letter to him, in which she mentions Lady Antonia's decision to gift Newhailes to the National Trust for Scotland, provided it bought the contents, Lily goes on to say, 'I remember father [Lord Galloway] telling me that he loved the house very much but I don't think he stayed overnight, he told me he stayed at his club. Those days seem so far away darling but the memory lingers on and how we two, you and I, survived being a couple of castaways.'

By the end of October, Lily was again back in hospital and it was generally assumed she was up to her old tricks. On 4.20 a.m. on the twenty-ninth, however, three days after her eighty-third birthday, she took everybody by surprise and died.

Lily's body could not be released until after a postmortem. By the beginning of November it was established that the official cause of death was a large haematoma found at the back of her abdomen, although her ischeamic heart disease was also listed on the death certificate. On 3 November, Benjamin Budge registered the death under the name of Lily May Stewart (the Countess of Galloway), wife of Randolph Keith Reginald Stewart (the 13th Earl of Galloway), 'landed proprietor', daughter of John Andrew Miller, 'groom and chauffeur'.

A few days later, Lily's wishes were honoured and she was given a requiem mass accompanied by members of St Michael and All Saints' choir. Her coffin was draped with a cloth and covered with scarlet flowers. Randolph sat in Lily's favourite pew wearing an expression of profound bewilderment, surrounded by his three stepsons and the rest of her family. She was cremated privately, and on the first Sunday of advent a burial service was conducted in Christ Church, the Episcopalian church in Duns where she was christened, where she sang in the choir with Papa, and then was disastrously married to Jock Millar. Lily's ashes were buried with those of Sis and Papa, two plots down from Etta. A headstone was later erected bearing the inscription:

Remembering ANDREW MILLER
1890–1971

His wife ANNIE COLVIN
1890–1974

And Their Daughter
LILY MAY
COUNTESS OF GALLOWAY
1916–1999

In the month that followed, obituaries appeared in Scotland and England. In the *Daily Telegraph*, the standfirst under her title read: 'Wife who remained loyal to the heir to the Earl of Galloway's fortune and Scottish estate even after he was disinherited.' The accompanying photograph shows her outside the House of Lords, smiling broadly at the camera in the same way she smiled on the day of the blessing of her marriage to Randolph. On Saturday, 6 November, another appeared in the *Herald*, written by Roddy Martine. It ended, 'Lily Galloway may not have been born into the upper crust, but she certainly showed them how it was done.'

AFTERWORD
The Castaways

This story concerns the living as well as the dead, and so it continues, up to the present day. In time Lily's family applied themselves to the execution of her will, which, true to form, she updated three months before her death. She was, of course, without money when she died. The proceeds of her flat in Home Royal House were given over to the Royal Bank of Scotland to settle the debts she and Randolph had incurred all those years ago, and which interest had increased. The house sale was insufficient to meet the debt, but the bank decided it was time to draw a line under the matter, and the deficit was dismissed.

Lily's belongings were distributed among her family as directed by her will. Brebner Millar was given the portrait. The most important bequest was the Galloway diamonds, which were made over to her teenage granddaughter, Laura Anne Budge, with the following condition:

> My three brilliant cut Diamond ring stamped 'J&M' once she reaches the age of 25 years. It is my wish that this ring should not be sold in any circumstances, but should remain in the family and handed down through the generations, since it was given to me as an engagement ring by my husband, The Right Honourable The Earl of Galloway, the then Lord Garlies.

The ring has since been disbanded. Laura Budge suggested that, in the interests of fairness, each brilliant cut diamond be lifted out of the mount and shared between the three granddaughters.

*   *   *

Randolph Galloway lives in sheltered housing in south-west Scotland. He has a large first-floor self-contained flat, which is bright and clean with two big windows facing onto the street. He scents his bedroom with incense sticks and prepares his own meals in an adjoining kitchen. The walls are covered with his crayon and paint drawings, as childlike as those he sent to Lily and which he has since begun sending to me. On one occasion I accompanied him to an art exhibition held by his mental health recreational club. Locals flocked and fought to buy his work, much of which features his childhood home.

Two of his paintings are framed and hang over his bed. They are, predictably, of Cumloden. The lodge is drawn as an infant child might draw the house of his imagination – two square boxes with four windows and a door and a chimneypot on top. Along the back wall there are three prints of his forebears, dressed for battle. When I asked which forebears, he did not know.

A photograph of Lily is by Randolph's pillow and there are two more over the fireplace. In one she is on a swing, kicking her legs rather coquettishly. The other is a photograph of her portrait. 'Look at her *there*,' he once said to me, a fleeting wry grin passing across his face, 'rather more serious, do you not think?' Beside these two pictures are others of the 12th Countess of Galloway captured at various times of her life, beautiful, smiling and serene in them all. 'Did you love your mother?' I once asked. He nodded.

My friendship with Randolph has grown throughout the research and writing of this book, although it has not been conducted along conventional lines. Often I would make the seven-hour trip from London to Dumfries and then travel on to his small town only for us to lunch and then stroll in utter silence. In the early days of our acquaintance, for that is what it was then, I tried to fill these silences by jollying him up with old photo albums or news of how my research was progressing. But he seemed vague. Occasionally I would detect an expression of loss or pain and, concerned at having pushed him too far into his past, I would announce my departure. Sometimes he welcomed it. Other times he appeared crestfallen and I would stay with him for an afternoon of continuing silence. On one occasion he fell asleep on the old lumpy sofa in the home's smoky communal sitting area, and I did too, waking to find him gently snoring, my head resting on his shoulder.

Randolph is now in his mid-seventies and he retains many of the childhood characteristics that his father and masters tried so hard to knock out of him sixty years ago. Today he invites the same curious looks as he did then. He will often wear a dinner jacket over a charity shop jumper, with a cravat at his neck, and on his head there sometimes sits the kind of black peaked cap seen in Soho nightclubs, except that Randolph pins a daffodil to his. His trousers are usually voluminous and far too long, so that they billow round his ankles, made all the stranger for the pair of white trainers on his huge feet. Sometimes he can be spotted on his bicycle with a brightly coloured Macintosh flapping in the wind. Once, when we were walking through Newton Stewart, the town nearest to Cumloden, he attired adventurously, I asked him what he thought the locals made of him. 'They probably think I'm a yokel,' he replied. I reminded him that indeed he was not a yokel but the 13th Earl of Galloway, at which point he fell silent. When I next turned to address him, he was holding his head higher. He seemed imbued with confidence as he strode forth majestically, his hands clasped behind his back. The transformation did not last long. Soon he became preoccupied once more.

With time I came to realise that his silences were not born out of lack of interest in the story I was trying to tell, so much of it his own, but rather his inability to interact in ways we take for granted. It became obvious to me that he wanted the story of his marriage known, and also the story of his life. Not long after I met him he wrote asking me if I would be interested in seeing the contents of a trunk containing memoirs of his childhood. They are extraordinary books, each one recalling his early life in minute detail. When I asked him if Lily had coaxed him into writing them, he shook his head and then, almost as an afterthought, asked, 'Do you not think it was worth it then?' Of course it was, I replied. There were other occasions when he would become vocal, as if a light had momentarily come back on.

'I think he would have had me living rough like a desert dog,' he commented of his father. He looked pained after he said this, as if he were once again a schoolboy anticipating punishment. 'Maybe I should never have married her,' he added.

'For her sake, or your family's?' I asked, shocked.

'Both . . . we were castaways,' he said, echoing Lily's phrase.

I asked him if he loved her.

'Yes,' he replied, 'she was positive and forward going. My father said to her in the sun porch: "It's pity not love you feel for him. Well, he's your problem now, not mine," but I say pity and love are the same thing.'

When I asked if his thoughts often returned to what had happened to them, he said, 'We lived in different worlds, on different planets. She was more down to earth than me. What would she think of me now, living like I do?'

And then the light flickered off.

I once accompanied Randolph to All Saints', Challoch, Newton Stewart, the church he visited so often with Lily and Duff. Dominating one corner of the graveyard are his family's tombstones, monuments to the achievements of each brave Stewart soldier who lived in the nineteenth and twentieth centuries.

I watched him hover around them: the 11th Earl and Countess, his grandparents; the 12th Earl and Countess, his parents; and Lt. The Hon Keith Anthony Stewart of the Black Watch, Royal Highlanders, his brave uncle whose tombstone reads, 'killed in action at Aubers Ridge in France on May 9th 1915, whilst gallantly leading his platoon . . . Beloved and mourned by his comrades, both officers and men, and by all who knew him, he has left a name for devotion to duty and ability in performance, for kindness of heart and integrity of character, which will never be forgotten.'

'Would you like to be buried here?' I asked Randolph.

After a pause, he replied, 'I don't think it will be allowed.'

'Might you want to be buried with Lily?'

He did not answer.

Much later, quite out of the blue, he said, 'Perhaps I would like one half of me to be buried with my wife and the other half here.'

Randolph stands beside his parents' gravestones in All Saints', Challoch.

SELECT BIBLIOGRAPHY

Alone of All Her Sex, Marina Warner (Vintage, 1983)

Anatomy of Restlessness: Uncollected Writings. Bruce Chatwin. edited by Jan Borm and Matthew Graves (Jonathan Cape, 1996)

A Century of the Scottish People, 1830–1950, T. C. Smout (Collins, 1986)

A Servant's Practical Guide: A Handbook of Duties and Rules, By the author of 'Manners and Tone of Good Society' (Ladies' Sanitary Association, 1880)

An Economic History of Modern Scotland 1660–1976, Bruce Lenman (Batsford Ltd, 1977)

A History of Harrow School 1324–1991, Christopher Tyerman (Oxford University Press, 2000)

A Woman's Place: An Oral History of Working-Class Women 1890–1940, Elizabeth Roberts (Basil Blackwell, 1984)

A Streetcar Named Desire, with Commentary and Notes by Patricia Hern, (Methuen Drama, 1984)

Eccentrics, David Weeks & Jamie James (Phoenix, 1995)

Edinburgh: Portrait of A City, Charles McKean (Century, 1991)

Edinburgh, Allan Massie (Sinclair-Stevenson, 1994)

Falcon: The Autobiography of His Grace James the IV, King of Scots, Presented by A. J. Stewart (William Maclellan, revised edition, 1982)

Great Houses of Scotland, Hugh Montgomery-Massingberd (author) and Christopher Simon Sykes (photographer) (Rizzoli, 1997)

Homing: A memoir, Alistair Moffat (John Murray, 2003)

Life Below Stairs in the 20th Century, Pamela Horn (Sutton Publishing, 2001)

Madness: A Brief History, Roy Porter (Oxford University Press, 2002)

Scottish Voices 1745–1960, T. C. Smout and Sydney Wood (Collins, 1990)

Stone Voices: The Search for Scotland, Neal Ascherson (Granta, 2002)

The Borders: A History of the Borders from the Earliest Times, Alistair
    Moffat (Deerpark Press, 2002)
The Big House, Helen McEwen (Bloomsbury, 2000)
*The First Teenagers: The Lifestyle of Young Wage-earners in Interwar
    Britain,* David Fowler (Woburn Press, 1995)
The Noel Coward Diaries, Edited by Graham Payn and Sheridan
    Morley, (Phoenix, 1998)
The Oxford Companion to Scottish History, Edited by Michael Lynch
    (Oxford Press, 2002)
*Time Exposure, The Life of Brodrick Haldane, Photographer 1912–
    1996,* Broderick Haldane in conversation with Roddy Martine
    (Arcadia, 1999)
The Way The Wind Blows, An Autobiography by Lord Home (Collins,
    1976)
The Prime of Miss Jean Brodie, Muriel Spark (Penguin Books,
    1965)

AUTHOR'S NOTE
Throughout the book I have referred to and quoted from the
following unpublished or self-published memoirs:

No Silver Spoon, The Countess of Galloway
*Monosyllabic Autobiography, A Life Story of Lord Randolph Keith
    Reginald Garlies,* The Earl of Galloway
Ginger for Sport, The Countess of Mayo
Celestial Visions for the New Age, The Countess of Mayo (Cope &
    Fenwick, Edinburgh)

ACKNOWLEDGEMENTS

There are two people on whose help this book depended. My heartfelt thanks to Randolph Galloway and Brebner Millar, for their time, memories, friendship and trust. I would also like to thank all members of the Millar family, particularly Andrew and Linda Millar and Dorothy Millar for four years of hospitality. I am grateful to the many others who have taken the time to advise me, including , including Arthur Allan, Steven and Kathleen Bannister, Joseph Bonnar, Robert Brawley, Cameron Buchanan, Tanya Buchanan, Benjamin Budge, Paul Budge, Nigel Bulmer, Bob Cammiade, Michael Chinnery, Johny Chute, Martin Cornish, Andrew Cubie, Tom Fitzpatrick, Jean François Garrison, Marie-Claude Garrison, Lady Merioth, The Hon. Jonathan Hunt, Martin Hunt, Lady Kinloss, Lord Lauderdale, Stella Laurie, Alice McCormick, Peter McKay, Fiona MacLaren, Marie-Laurence Maitre, Roddy Martine, May Millar, William Mowat Thomson, Christian Orr Ewing, Simon Pollock, Canon Gordon Reid, Mary Rigans, Sheila Romanes, Charles Russell, Lady Saltoun, Michael Sissons, Michael Skelton, Robert Stevenson, A.J Stewart, Sara Stewart, James Stewart Taylor, James Thomson, Michael Thornton, Ann and Geoff Troughton and Roland Wallis.

My thanks also, to Muriel Walker, librarian at The Stewart Society; Jack Utterson and members of the Duns Historical Society; Pam McNichol at the Edinburgh City Archives; Rita Gibbs, archivist of Harrow School and all staff at the Vaughan Library, Harrow School; Michael Osborne, headmaster of Belhaven Hill School; staff at the Edinburgh Room, National Library of Scotland; staff of the London Library and staff of the archive department of Edinburgh University Library; Dr Mike Isaac, consultant psychiatrist and senior lecturer at The Maudsley and Institute of Psychiatry and Dr David Weeks, clinical neuropsychologist and therapist at the Royal Edinburgh Hospital.

I am also indebted to the friends and colleagues who have

provided guidance and patience; Drusilla Beyfus, Catherine Blyth, Mick Brown, Kate Hyde, Pedro Kujawski, Michele Lavery, The Hon. Emma Soames, Kate Summerscale and Catherine Wilson.

I would also like to thank my parents, Pauline and Eric Carpenter; my editor Arabella Pike whose support and subtlety of approach never once compromised her editorial and intellectual rigour; my agent, David Miller, for his humour and for his early and continued delight in Lily Budge; and Susan Boyd, an inspirational mentor and a gloriously funny friend.

Finally I would like to thank Tom Payne for caring about words, for making me happy, often against the odds, while this book came to life, and for our beloved newborn daughter, Dolores.

LOUISE CARPENTER
Bath.
May 2004.

INDEX